The Reminiscences of
Dr. Samuel E. Barnes
Member of the Golden Thirteen

Interviewed by
Paul Stillwell

U.S. Naval Institute
Annapolis, Maryland
Copyright ©1993

Preface

In the first few months of 1944, 16 black enlisted men went through officer training at Great Lakes, Illinois. Of the group, 12 were commissioned as ensigns and one as a warrant officer. They were the Navy's first black officers. Collectively, the group has come to be known as the Golden Thirteen. In the autumn of 1986, the Naval Institute began an oral history project involving the eight surviving members of the group. This volume represents the life story of one of those eight men, Samuel E. Barnes.

Barnes was one of several top-flight athletes in the Golden Thirteen. He particularly excelled in football and track. Except for his stint in the Navy during World War II, he spent nearly all of his professional life in athletics as a college coach or administrator. He coached at small Livingstone College in North Carolina prior to the war and afterward was for many years at Howard University in Washington, D.C. He had a particular knack for picking up the skills involved in a given sport and then imparting those skills to individual athletes. In his postgraduate work, he earned a Ph.D. degree, the only member of the Golden Thirteen to do so. As a result of his sports experiences, he was chosen for the athletic hall of fame at his alma mater, Oberlin College, and also served as the first black member of the executive council of the National Collegiate Athletic Association.

As a naval officer, Samuel Barnes faced the same disappointment as the other members of the Golden Thirteen. They were not given assignments commensurate with their abilities. Rather than being given the opportunity to use his training as a seagoing line officer, he was employed for a while in the recreation program at Great Lakes and later commanded a segregated cargo-handling battalion overseas. In this oral history he talks at considerable length about the training period that the officer candidates went through on their way to becoming the Golden Thirteen. In that regard, it is probably the most detailed of any of the oral histories in recalling the officer candidates' time together at Great Lakes in early 1944. In particular he describes the sense of teamwork that enabled these men to succeed in an atmosphere that placed considerable pressure on them. They had the sense that they were operating not only for themselves but also on behalf of thousands of other black enlisted men in the Navy of that era.

In addition to discussing his naval experiences and professional life, Dr. Barnes spends considerable time on the subject of his family. He tells of the sacrifices that his parents made to see that all their children got college educations. Indeed, stress on the importance of education is a thread that shows up repeatedly in the oral histories of the Golden Thirteen. Dr. Barnes also talks about the contribution his older brother made as a role model and about the values that his parents imparted for achieving success in a society that all too often placed a high degree of importance on the color of a person's skin. Dr. Barnes tells of the strong desire to live a respectable life so that one will be respected--and of the importance of providing assistance and inspiration to those who come along afterward.

In the transcript that follows, both the interviewer and the interviewee have done some editing in the interests of clarity, accuracy, and brevity. Some material has been deleted to avoid redundancy and some has been rearranged for the sake of continuity. The original verbatim transcript is on file with the Naval Institute. The transcription was done by Ms. Deborah Reid and Ms. Joanne Patmore, both formerly of the Naval Institute's oral history staff. Ms. Ann Hassinger has provided valuable assistance in the compilation of the finished volume, particularly through her careful proofreading of the text.

                                          Paul Stillwell
Director, History Division
U.S. Naval Institute
November 1993

SAMUEL EDWARD BARNES

Samuel E. Barnes was born 25 January 1915 in Oberlin, Ohio, the son of James and Margaret Barnes. He attended the Pleasant Street School in Oberlin from 1920 to 1926 and Oberlin High School from 1926 through 1932. In his senior year, 1932, he was elected to the National High School Honor Society. He attended Oberlin College, Oberlin, Ohio from 1932 to 1936, graduating with a bachelor of arts degree and a bachelor of physical education.

From 1936 to 1941 Mr. Barnes was on the staff of Livingstone College in Salisbury, North Carolina. He held a variety of positions, including director of health, physical education, and athletics; head basketball and football coach, director of intramurals, supervisor of the men's dormitory, and assistant to the dean of the college. In 1941-42 Dr. Barnes was boys' work secretary for the Ninth Street Branch of the YMCA in Cincinnati, Ohio.

In September 1942 Mr. Barnes enlisted in the Navy as an apprentice seaman and took recruit training at Great Lakes, Illinois. He was honor man in his company. In December 1942, after being advanced to seaman first class, he was assigned to the "ship's company" at Great Lakes. He worked initially in the physical training department and was later an interviewer to help place graduating recruits in appropriate billets. In January 1944 he was advanced to petty officer first class and went through officer training, leading to his commissioning as an ensign on 17 March 1944.

After being commissioned, Ensign Barnes remained at Great Lakes until the spring of 1945. During that time he served in a variety of capacities, including serving as officer in charge of physical training and recreation for the three camps that trained black sailors, Camp Robert Smalls, Camp Lawrence, and Camp Moffett. In April 1945 he became officer in charge of Logistics Support Company #123, which underwent training at Camp Peary, Williamsburg, Virginia. In May 1945 the company went overseas, first to Eniwetok Atoll in the Marshall Islands and later to Okinawa in the Ryukyus chain. He was promoted to the rank of lieutenant (junior grade) in July 1945, then returned to the United States late in the year and was demobilized at Great Lakes in January 1945.

Mr. Barnes then returned to Oberlin College, where he did graduate work toward his master's degree, which was awarded in 1949. In 1947 he began a long career at Howard University in Washington, D.C., and held a variety of positions. He was assistant football coach, 1947-52 and 1954-58; head boxing coach, 1947-52; head wrestling coach, 1947-49; assistant track coach, 1947-52; head track coach, 1952-60. In 1956 he completed work on a degree of Ph.D. from the Ohio State University, Columbus, Ohio. From 1956 to 1970, Dr. Barnes was director of athletics and head of the men's physical education department at Howard University.

From 1973 to 1975, Dr. Barnes served as interim director of athletics for Federal City College in Washington, D.C. In 1974 he became chairman of the athletic committee and also chairman of the division of health and physical education for the District of Columbia Teachers College in Washington. He remained in that capacity when the University of the District of Columbia was formed by the merger of D.C. Teachers College and two other schools, finally retiring in 1984.

In 1957 Dr. Barnes was sent by the State Department to Iraq as a consultant and clinician in physical education, recreation, health, and physical education. From 1960 to 1964 he was vice president of the northern district of the Central Intercollegiate Athletic Association. He was president of the Central Intercollegiate Athletic Association from 1964 to 1967. He was a member of the executive committee of the National Association of Collegiate Directors of Athletics, 1965-68. Dr. Barnes served as a member of the council of the National Collegiate Athletic Association, 1965-70. From 1970 to 1972 he was on the executive committee of the NCAA, the first black person to achieve that honor.

On 19 December 1943, Mr. Barnes married Miss Olga Lash of Salisbury, North Carolina. They have three children: Olga Michele Barnes, Margaret Nadine "Alexa" Barnes, and Michael David Lash Barnes. Dr. and Mrs. Barnes live in Washington, D.C.

Authorization

The U.S. Naval Institute is hereby authorized to make available to individuals, libraries, and other repositories of its choosing the transcripts of three oral history interviews concerning the life and career of the undersigned. The interviews were recorded on 24 November 1986, 30 January 1989, and 12 May 1989 in collaboration with Paul Stillwell for the U.S. Naval Institute.

The undersigned does hereby release and assign to the U.S. Naval Institute all right, title, restrictions, and interest in the interviews. The copyright in both the oral and transcribed versions shall be the sole property of the U.S. Naval Institute. The tape recordings of the interviews are and will remain the property of the U.S. Naval Institute.

Signed and sealed this 30th day of Nov. 1993.

Samuel E. Barnes
Dr. Samuel E. Barnes

Interview Number 1 with Dr. Samuel E. Barnes
Place: Dr. Barnes's home in Washington, D.C.
Date: Monday, 24 November 1986
Interviewer: Paul Stillwell

Q: Dr. Barnes, it's a real pleasure to be with you here today. Just to begin at the beginning, perhaps you could talk about your parents, your family background, and your early recollections of childhood.

Dr. Barnes: My father, James Barnes, came from Asheville, North Carolina. My mother, Margaret Barnes, was from Kentucky. When they married, one of the things that they decided to do was to raise and educate their family in Oberlin, Ohio, because it was one of the more liberal communities in the United States. My brother and sisters and I were all born in Oberlin. My brother James finished Oberlin College in 1930. My eldest sister, Louise, finished Oberlin College in 1929. Then I finished Oberlin in 1936. My twin sister Becky finished Wilberforce University in 1937. Margaret, another sister, graduated from Howard University in 1947.

We enjoyed rich experiences in Oberlin. My father was a chef at one of the Oberlin College dormitories. My mother owned and operated our family laundry and was also very prominent in politics, in women's work, and in the church. She worked extensively in all three areas. For instance, she was both a trustee and a deaconess in the Baptist Church. She was an alternate delegate in 1936 to the convention that nominated Alf Landon as the presidential candidate for the Republican Party.* She was a prominent member of the party, especially in Ohio. Several women's clubs in the state were named for her. In addition, she was an Eastern Star of the local Masons' organization and a member of the trustee board at Wilberforce University.

My eldest sister, Louise, was the first family member to die. At the time of her death in 1931 she was teaching at a high school in Kings Mountain, North Carolina. My brother died in 1935 while he was the director of athletics and head basketball coach at Virginia State College in Petersburg, Virginia. My mother died in 1947, my father died in 1958, and my twin sister Becky died in 1971.

Q: Did your parents move to Ohio right after they got married?

**Governor Alfred M. Landon of Kansas was soundly defeated by incumbent President Franklin D. Roosevelt in the general election of 1936; he received 523 electoral votes, and Landon received 8. The Republican Party nominee for Vice President was Frank Knox of Illinois; Knox was Secretary of the Navy when the Golden Thirteen were trained as officers.

Dr. Barnes: Very shortly thereafter, yes.

Q: What sort of work had your father done in North Carolina?

Dr. Barnes: He worked in the Biltmore forests and at the Vanderbilt estates in Asheville and Biltmore, North Carolina. He worked with his brother Samuel, after whom I was named. My brother James was named after my father.

After the children were born, the family moved from Vine Street to North Main Street, which was closer to the schools, even though Oberlin wasn't a very large community. There were only 4,500 people in the town at that time.

Q: Had your parents known somebody there? Why did they choose Oberlin particularly?

Dr. Barnes: They didn't know anyone in Oberlin, but they knew about Oberlin. They knew the role it had played in the 19th century underground movement, as a halfway station for slaves escaping to northern U.S. cities and Canada. My parents felt that would be an environment in which they would like to raise their children.

All of us finished college, and this was one of the ambitions of our parents.

Q: Were your parents able to provide any financial support for this?

Dr. Barnes: They did 99% of it. My mother operated a home laundry, because she wanted to be at home when the children came home from school. She did the linen for the Oberlin College dormitories, and she did the laundry for individual students. She employed a student representative in each of the various dormitories. They would collect the laundry, and my brother would pick it up. After she did the washing and ironing, we returned the clean laundry.

The income she received helped pay our tuition. Thus, she was able to see that my brother, my sister, and I were able to finish college at Oberlin. Oberlin didn't give athletic scholarships at that time, though both my brother and I were considered outstanding athletes in high school. I think at the time we were growing up, Dad was making something like $25.00 a week as a chef at Oberlin College. So between my father and mother, we were able to do what they wanted us to do, go to college and finish college.

Q: How hard did the Depression hit the family? It sounds as if you were always able to have some work.

Dr. Barnes: The Depression didn't affect us that much,

because our parents were not working in the kinds of jobs that were cut out. Their jobs were rather steady.

Q: People still have to eat and wear clothes, no matter what.

Dr. Barnes: Well, we were able to do both, because Mom and Dad were good providers. Dad would bring his check home Friday night and give it to her. On Saturday afternoon, I would follow her to the grocery store. Food at that time was much, much cheaper than it is today. When Mom spent $10.00 or $15.00, it would take me a good pull to bring the food she purchased home in my wagon. For instance, eggs were a penny apiece, bread was ten cents a loaf, so she was able to do much with little.

On Saturday, we always had soup. Mom would empty the icebox, and everything edible in that icebox went into the soup. That soup was a meal in itself, because it had everything in it. That's the way she did two things: she emptied the icebox and fed us. So, actually, I don't recall that we were ever destitute. We were not wealthy. We had moderate living conditions. But there was never a time when we had to put cardboard in our shoes or wear patched-up clothes. We had what we needed. It wasn't extravagant, but it was sufficient.

Q: Were you and your siblings expected to pitch in on the family chores?

Dr. Barnes: Oh, yes. We always had a garden. My mother felt that a garden was a necessity, and it was our responsibility, my brother and myself, to plant, to weed, and to harvest the crop. My mother would preserve or use whatever came out of the garden. I remember the vegetables and fruit she put up for the winter. We would also pick and pay for apples, berries, beans, and so forth. Then she would can them and put them on the shelves in the basement. We ate in the winter months. She was very thrifty, as well as a very, very far-seeing person.

Everybody in the family pitched in. The girls cleaned the house. Mom taught my brother and me how to sew, how to iron. From the time I was nine years old, she never did any of those things for us. Dad taught all of us how to cook, because he was a chef. Mom always said, "Well, you'd better learn, because you don't know who you may marry. I don't know whether they can cook or not, or whether they can sew and iron, so you learn to do for yourself." Such advice has been very helpful throughout the years.

Q: Along with these practical sorts of things, did your parents also impart values for life?

Dr. Barnes: Always. I recall one thing that my mother said to all of us, "You're not better than others, but you're as good as others. You have to live the kind of life that will make people respect you, regardless of your color. They don't have to like you, but be sure they respect you. If you do the things that are right, you will be respected."

We'd go to Sunday school in the morning, then after Sunday school would be church. In the evening we would go back to church again for a meeting of the BYPU, the Baptist Young People's Union. So we were in church all day on Sundays, we were involved in clubs, we were involved in church activities, and we sang in the choir. Our values were established at home and reinforced in the church and in the community.

Another thing our parents taught us was, "You must at all times do your best. You must not think in terms of being better than others, but recognize what your potential may be, and you live up to that."

They gave our teachers, both in school and church, the freedom to discipline us. All they had to do was call Mom, because she was always home, and, if necessary, she'd come to the school. It was very embarrassing to look up and see Mom standing in the doorway. She promised us, "If I come and I find that you have been mischievous or not done what you should, I'm going to whip you there." And we knew she would.

The other thing which was good was that adults in town were given the same option. If we were observed or caught doing wrong, they were given permission to whip us, then call home. We could expect to get another whipping when we got home. We knew what discipline was, we knew what being right was, and we knew what our responsibilities were. Not only were we expected to do right, we were required to do right. Such values were embedded in us early and have been very, very supportive throughout our lives.

Q: One of those values, it sounds like, was pride in yourself and your accomplishments.

Dr. Barnes: Pride in one's self and respect for others.

Q: What were the sorts of infractions that might bring these whippings?

Dr. Barnes: Well, we always joked that the only reason we weren't juvenile delinquents was because we didn't get caught doing wrong. We would steal apples, grapes, and other fruits and vegetables. And we would do the mischievous kinds of things which kids do as they're growing up. But there was never anything which was flagrant. We would have fights as kids, especially when we were called "nigger." Now you hear people speak of "blacks." I don't know how many times I fought because I was called that when I was competing on athletic teams away from Oberlin, both on high school and college teams. That wasn't a problem in a small town like Oberlin. We never encountered black on one side, white on other side. We enjoyed genuinely close relationships, and we respected one another. So we didn't have racial problems.

Q: What were some of the places where you encountered the name-calling?

Dr. Barnes: One town was Elyria, Ohio, which is nine miles away, when I was playing football. When we'd play in Elyria, Fremont, Lorain, Norwalk--any school away from Oberlin--we would endure these racial slurs and often were involved in fights. But our teammates were very supportive, so it wasn't a matter where we had to fight by ourselves. If there was a fight, all of us, our teammates and all, were involved in it, because we respected one another. We had practiced together, played together, and we had a very close relationship.

I had more than a couple of fights. For instance, I remember a situation when we went down to play football at Marietta College, which is in Marietta, Ohio, right on the border of West Virginia. I had quite a scuffle there with

S. E. Barnes #1 - 10

one Marietta player. He was a halfback, and I was an end. Whenever I tackled him, he would call me "nigger," which brought on a fight. The officials would put both of us out of the game.

In basketball, this same player was a forward, and I was a guard. When they came to Oberlin and he played, they would take me off the floor. When I was put in the game, he would be taken out. It was a volatile situation that I won't forget, but that's the only time that I remember anything of that sort.

Q: So your parents had truly been successful in finding this hospitable racial climate that they sought.

Dr. Barnes: Yes, and I think it had a lot to do with the attitudes that all of us learned and carried with us. As is said, "As the twig is bent, so the tree climbs." I believe that.

Q: In fostering these opportunities for your education, were your parents seeking to give you opportunities that they themselves had not had? Was that their motivation?

Dr. Barnes: That may have been their intention, but they never said so to us. My mother was a college graduate, but my father wasn't. I don't think he finished more than high school. Where he came from, everybody in the family had to work to help sustain the family. There were times that he might not have been in school because he was working to harvest a crop or whatever it was. But I think he and my mother were very, very well adjusted to one another. They always supported one another. There wasn't a feeling of insecurity on his part because of her attainments.

Q: It's unfortunate she didn't get to use that education in a profession.

Dr. Barnes: My mother was a professional, and the areas in which she worked were as distinctive as any profession. She felt close to her family, and she wanted to be at home and available when we needed her. She was always there for us. No profession could have been more satisfying for her. She dedicated herself to helping us and others.

Q: How good a student were you?

Dr. Barnes: I was just an average student, although I was elected to the high school honor society in my senior year, 1932. I entered Oberlin College, which was, and still is, a very selective institution. It enrolled only those high school graduates who were in the upper 10% from all over the United States. I think one of the reasons why I was admitted was the fact that my family lived in Oberlin and they knew about us. My brother had made a very distinctive contribution to Oberlin as a student and as an athlete.

I was enrolled in Oberlin College and graduated, but it was a struggle. I maintained a C-plus average. During that period, Oberlin had a system whereby one's grades were dependent upon what the grades of the others were. That meant I was constantly competing against excellent students from all over. Oberlin at that time was limited to no more than 800 or 900 students. I did graduate, but I was not a star student.

Q: So your grades were more a reflection of the competition than your actual attainments.

Dr. Barnes: Yes, I would say so.

Q: Did you get involved in positions of leadership there?

Dr. Barnes: Yes, I was a Boy Scout leader, community youth club leader, and church club leader. I formed little clubs of kids all over town and tried to give the participants some basis for developing a steadfast kind of life. This was an offshoot of what we were taught at home, to help where we can, if we can, as long as we can. So I was always involved in volunteer work, which I thoroughly enjoyed. It was a way of giving back something to the community which had given much to me.

Q: What were some of the highlights of your athletic endeavors?

Dr. Barnes: I made all-conference teams in football and basketball in both high school and college. I established a broad jump record at Oberlin which may still stand. My brother had held the record previously; he was really a better athlete than I. What I may have achieved was because I tried to emulate what he had done and what he was. Whatever positions he played, I would play. If he was a sprinter, I was a sprinter. If he was a guard in basketball, I was a guard in basketball. He was an end in football; I was an end in football.

James tried out for the 1928 Olympics. He was beaten out by Eddie Tolan and Ralph Metcalf, so that he was not a part of the Olympic team, but he was a contestant for it. He had broad-jumped at Oberlin, besides running the 100-, 220-, and 440-yard dashes and the 100-yard high hurdles. He had broad-jumped 22 feet, 4 inches, which was the record then. Then later, a teammate broke it, but James told him, "That's all right. I have a kid brother coming along, and he'll get it back."

My brother died in the winter of 1935, and in 1936 I

was a senior at Oberlin. I had never broad-jumped over 21 feet, 10 inches in my life. However, as fate would have it, when I competed in the first spring meet in '36, I broad-jumped 23 feet, 6 inches, and that broke the record of the person who had broken my brother's record, and it came on my first jump. It was fantastic, because I believe subconsciously I was aware of what he had said. That was the best effort I put forward, and fortunately it was successful. If the record is still standing, somebody will break it sooner or later.

Q: Were you involved in the running events as well?

Dr. Barnes: Yes, I ran the 100, the 220, the 440, the mile relay team, and the broad jump.

Q: You were a busy guy on track meet day.

Dr. Barnes: Well, that was a carry-over from high school. Since it was a small high school, one had to compete in more than one event, because we didn't have that many contestants. I recall I once ran against Jesse Owens in the state meet in Columbus, Ohio.* Though Jesse was running in Class A and I was running in Class B, I competed

---

*In the 1936 Olympic Games at Berlin, Germany, Jesse Owens embarrassed Chancellor Adolf Hitler of the host nation with his outstanding performances. He won four gold medals for the United States.

against him that one time. I don't need to tell you what the result was; he ran away from me. But anyway, it was great to be in the same race with him. Jess and I remained friends up until the time he died.

Q: What impressions do you have of him from your personal association?

Dr. Barnes: Jesse, in my judgment, was one of the cleanest-cut persons whom I have ever known, and he was a natural athlete. His style was just picturesque, he ran so effortlessly. He was not boisterous, he was not a showoff, he was not a braggart. He let his accomplishments speak for him, as he did in the 1936 Olympics in Berlin. He, in my judgment, was a very good model for all competitors. I'm sorry now that more of his style is not impressed upon our current youngsters. I just don't really go with much that I see today in athletics. It's unfortunate, because the really essential reason for athletics is participating. Unfortunately, many of our youngsters and coaches don't realize the values that are inherent in athletics and participation.

Q: How would you articulate those values?

Dr. Barnes: Well, number one, I think it's very important that individuals do the best they can, as long as they can, and if you do that, whatever the outcome, you can feel that you don't have to be ashamed. But at no time do less than you're capable of doing, nor do you blame others for your failures. You must remember that in only some sports does the individual himself stand out.

In golf, tennis, bowling, and track and field events where you're competing by yourself, it's as an individual, not a team win or loss. But in the team sports, though individual efforts are important and necessary, the team takes precedence, and everyone works with his teammates. So it's not a matter of one person making 40 points and getting accolades. If the team wins, everyone wins. If the team loses, everyone loses. It's a team effort, and therefore it should be considered that way, and you're a part, a cog, in it, and you do what you can to bring whatever successes you can to the team. That's my philosophy, and that's what I learned at Oberlin High School and Oberlin College.

Q: You must have been in superb condition to do all those events.

Dr. Barnes: Yes, being in top condition was a necessity. I was fortunate to possess some God-given talent and was encouraged by my parents, my brother, and my coaches. To me it was almost a fetish to stay in condition. My brother always told me that conditioning is very important, so I was in good condition. That has followed me even now, because my weight has not varied five pounds since 1932. I weigh the same now as I did then; I wear the same size clothes. What I learned in high school and college still remains with me. I feel that it's better to keep weight off than to take weight off.

Q: What distance did you run against Jesse Owens?

Dr. Barnes: The 100-yard dash. Jesse was much faster than I was. He was stronger, bigger, and definitely more talented. I don't take anything from him. I gave it my best shot, but he still won.

Q: That's the God-given part of it.

Dr. Barnes: I guess you're right. You can only go with what you have.

Q: Graham Martin stressed the value of a coach as someone to inspire the members of his team.* Did you have coaches who served that role?

---

*Graham Edward Martin is a member of the Golden Thirteen. His oral history is in the Naval Institute collection.

Dr. Barnes: Yes, indeed. My high school and college coaches were truly role models. I was impressed with my coaches because they were sincere and honorable men. They were individuals who were concerned more with their players' development than they were in gaining any accolades for themselves. They worked with us and were supportive of us. If we won, fine. If we lost and had done the best we could, that's all that the coaches asked of us. I don't remember any coach ever being abusive or using profanity. They were men whom I respected and fondly remember. Much of what they taught is still a part of me. I tried to teach that when I was coaching. I go back to what I said before: what one is exposed to is what one remains.

Q: Did you have life goals already at that point?

Dr. Barnes: Yes. I knew that when I graduated from college I wanted to be a teacher, and there was nothing else that interested me as much. I could have gone in another direction. When I graduated from college, I was offered a basketball scholarship by the Ohio College of Chiropody. At the same time I received a job offer to teach and coach at a small college in North Carolina. I sat down with Dad, and I said, "Dad, I have two offers here. One is a proposition from the Ohio College of Chiropody to play basketball and go into chiropody as a career.* Then I have this offer from Livingstone College to teach and coach there. What advice can you offer?"

So he said, "Well, son, it's a decision you have to make, but make it in terms of later opportunities and not what it means to you presently. Also, whether or not it's in line with what you would like to do. If I were you, I would talk to my coaches."

So I talked to my coaches, and they gave me the same advice. I talked to the college president, and he told me the same thing: "It's your decision. Whatever you think is better for what you want to do, that's the thing you should do." But one coach said to me, "Well, you have majored in physical education. You have participated in athletics. Why don't you try it for a year? If you find it's what you want to do, you can then continue doing that."

So I called the College of Chiropody, and I told them what the decision was. They accepted the decision but told me they would hold the scholarship for a year. If I changed my mind and wished to enroll, the scholarship would still be available. As it happened, I just stayed in teaching and in coaching. I never did look back, and I've

---
*Chiropody is a medical practice that specializes in the care and treatment of feet.

never had any regrets. Perhaps I'd be better off financially if I had gone into chiropody, but I don't feel that it was a mistake to continue in what I chose.

Q: You never know what might have happened on the road that you didn't take.

Dr. Barnes: That is true. But I was satisfied and happy doing what I was doing, and I never felt that I had made a mistake.

Q: How much of a social life did you have there at Oberlin?

Dr. Barnes: Well, since I was born and raised in Oberlin, I didn't have any problem in making friends. The friends I had in high school were still there, and some of them even went to college with me. There were plenty of opportunities for companionship, but socializing was not that high on my calendar. My brother had told me, "You can't mix athletics and women. You've got to determine your priorities." So I had some dates and went to some dances, but there was never anything serious. I never really got involved in any heavy dating or anything of that sort. Marriage was then far from my mind.

Q: What was the name of the school where you went to coach?

Dr. Barnes: Livingstone College in Salisbury, North Carolina, an A.M.E. Zion-affiliated institution.* My starting salary was $75.00 a month. Since I was hired during the Depression, my classmates were amazed that I had found a job.

When I was at Livingstone, there were between 200 and 250 students in the school. The faculty was made up of 16 people. In most cases each one was a chairman of his department, because he was the only one in it. English and the foreign languages were the only departments with two instructors.

I was the football coach; I had no assistants. On the day of a home game, I would have to get up early to mark the lines on the field. Then I'd come back and tape the players, issue the game equipment, and take the water pail down to the field. I did all of that and still carried out my coaching duties.

In the winter I coached both the men's and women's basketball teams. The girls practiced from 7:00 to 8:00, and then the fellows practiced from 9:00 to 10:30. When we went on a trip, the girls would play in a preliminary game,

---

*A.M.E.--African Methodist Episcopal.

and the men would play the main game. I was also proctor of the men's dormitory. I also taught all of the physical education classes. I was director of intramurals, and I was assistant to the dean of the college. So my time was limited, but I enjoyed every minute of it.

Q: You apparently didn't sleep very much.

Dr. Barnes: Oh, yes. I slept very well because I was tired.

It was a long time before I had any assistance, and then the persons who helped me were friends of mine who would come over in the afternoon and help me with practices. Later on, one of the players whose eligibility had expired came out and was a student assistant coach.

I enjoyed that experience, because the players were very cooperative, both men and women. Finally I asked one of the female teachers on the faculty to help with the women, because there were certain personal things that I could not get involved in. The women discussed their personal problems with her, and that left me free to coach. She also kept me advised when the women players were physically unable to practice or participate in games. But that was a good relationship; it was very helpful to me.

Q: Did you teach any other academic subjects besides

physical education?

Dr. Barnes: On occasion I taught beginning courses in math and biology when a colleague had an overload of classes and asked for help. So I did teach outside of my field, but I preferred not to.

Q: How well did your teams do?

Dr. Barnes: Well, I would say we had average seasons. We won a fair share of our games, so I would say that our seasons were successful. At that time wins and losses were not emphasized as they are now. We didn't have to worry about national championships or conference championships. We didn't have pressure from the alumni or the community; we didn't have that. They came to the games and were very supportive. The wanted us to win, of course, and we tried to win. But whatever the results, there was never any great amount of pressure.

Q: Did you also get involved in recruiting?

Dr. Barnes: Recruiting was not a problem. We couldn't offer any scholarships, but if I could interest a young person who was going to college to come to Livingstone, I would do that. I remember once when there were three young men at Oberlin who were high school football players. When I went home in the summer, I asked what they were going to do. They had no plans, so I asked them if they wanted to go to college. After they agreed, I talked to their parents, and they were happy to have these young men go with me. So I took three of them from Oberlin down to Livingstone with me. One was a quarterback, another one was a halfback, and the other was an end. They made quite a difference in my teams, because they had had good high school training and they were well conditioned.

That was the extent of my recruiting because the only way I could induce athletes to come was to tell them Livingstone was an institution which cared for them and cost less than other institutions. It was also a church-supported institution, so we would get players who were affiliated with the A.M.E.-Zion Church.

Only 12 players appeared for my first practice. Then I had to go around the dormitory and find some people who were available and interested. I put them in uniforms so I would have enough to scrimmage. We finally reached the time when we had 30 players in uniform. Of course, at that time it didn't make that much difference because we didn't have special teams. A person played both offense and defense. I really didn't use as many persons as teams have now.

I was satisfied with the efforts they gave and the

fact that they played as well as they could. That was really the important thing, because one can't carry a football or bounce a basketball the rest of his life. Student athletes must look beyond games and practices; they should prepare for living fruitful lives. Athletics were means, not ends.

I went back to my 50th class anniversary this year at Oberlin College, since I graduated in 1936. The anniversary was when I was inducted into the charter class of the Athletic Hall of Fame at Oberlin. Ten of us were inducted in the first class by the Heisman Club, which is named in honor of John Heisman, who coached at Oberlin earlier in this century.* Our pictures were put up in the gymnasium.

Q: So indeed there can be some honor afterward.

Dr. Barnes: Yes, and I do appreciate being selected. I was both surprised and humbled by the honor that was bestowed on me. It never occurred to me that anything of this sort would happen.

Q: Was that based just on athletic prowess or also on your accomplishments since then?

---
*Also named in his honor is the Heisman Trophy, awarded each year to the top player in collegiate football.

Dr. Barnes: It was based mainly on my contributions while I was a student at Oberlin. The selection was based on athletics primarily and, I hope, on my qualities as a person too.

Q: Were you one of the best players on the team then?

Dr. Barnes: Well, as I said, I participated in all three sports--football, basketball, and track and field--and I was first team in all of them. I was never a substitute on any team on which I ever played, because I was determined not to be.

Q: That sprinter speed would be especially useful as an end in football.

Dr. Barnes: Oh, yes. Yes, it was, at that time. Of course, I would need more than speed to play now, because these guys are so big. I was five feet, ten inches tall and weighed 175 pounds.

Q: Did you have good hands too?

Dr. Barnes: Yes, so I could catch the passes that got to me. I didn't get involved in the line play, because I was always out on the end, on defense and offense. As you say, speed helped. On defense I was able to make tackles that perhaps I wouldn't have made had I not been so fast.

Q: What was your best time in the 100-yard dash?

Dr. Barnes: Nine point nine seconds.

Q: That's certainly respectable.

Dr. Barnes: Yes.

Q: Was football your favorite sport as a coach?

Dr. Barnes: Well, at Livingstone we didn't have a track team. We only had football and basketball at the varsity level. Everything else was intramural, because it was a small school, and it didn't have enough money for a larger athletic program.

Q: Did your teams play against some of the well-known black colleges in the South?

Dr. Barnes: Yes, we played North Carolina A&T. We played South Carolina State. We played what was known at that time as North Carolina College for Negroes, which is now North Carolina Central University. We played Paine

S. E. Barnes #1 - 28

College, Savannah State College, Johnson C. Smith University, Benedict College, Shaw University, and Allen University.

Q: Florida A&M?

Dr. Barnes: No, Florida A&M was too large for us. In addition, we couldn't afford to travel that far.

When we started out, we had to get around town and find people with cars who would help transport the team. So we would leave town with an entourage of maybe ten cars. People would drive and carry the players with them, put the uniforms in the trunk, go play the game, and after the game come back home. Most of the teams were not that far away; we could get back home the same day. If we stayed overnight, it meant that we could get back the next day, so we never played farther than maybe 300 or 400 miles away. Later the college purchased a bus for the away games.

Q: What kinds of adjustments did you as an individual have to make in going to a more hostile racial climate?

Dr. Barnes: It was tolerable since I recognized what it was, and since I really didn't have that much contact with whites anyway. We didn't play against whites. I knew it was a socially segregated situation. In the same town there was a school called Catawba College. Once in a while I went to the Catawba games, and I'd have to sit in the end zone, which was the only place I could sit. So segregation existed, but it never bothered me. Although I was sensitive to the situation, I didn't intend to get involved in anything other than what I was supposed to be doing, which was teaching and coaching and helping our youngsters.

Q: So you avoided situations that could have caused problems.

Dr. Barnes: Yes. When we were traveling on our bus or in the cars, we couldn't stop to eat. If we were on a trip that would take us through the lunch hour, we would have our school dietitian fix box lunches, and we would eat them on the bus. Then we stayed in dormitories at the schools, so there wasn't a problem of hotel accommodations, because there weren't any for blacks anyway. When the game was over, we would get in the bus and come on home. I recognized that racism and discrimination existed and was aware of both, but I avoided contacts with white people unless absolutely necessary.

Q: Some of the other men who eventually got into the Golden Thirteen had a number of unhappy experiences along the way.

Dr. Barnes: I'm not surprised, because several of them were raised in the South and went to school in the South. I guess there were a few who went to desegregated colleges. So their experiences, I'm sure, were very similar to mine. But even when we traveled with the team at Oberlin High School, we couldn't stay with the team. For instance, when we went to the state track and field championships at Columbus, Ohio, which is 120 miles away from Oberlin, we had to stay in segregated dorms or the gymnasium at Ohio State University. So that was an experience. When I was in college, once I had to stay with the coach. We would stop for the team to eat, and when we walked in, someone would say, "We can't wait on them," meaning the black team members.

But there was no argument. The coach merely said, "If you can't serve them, you can't serve any of us." And the entire team would leave. The coaches were very strict in that respect, and I was never embarrassed. I never had to eat across town when the team was eating somewhere else. The team ate together, we played together, we practiced together, because the coach emphasized, "We do all things together."

Q: I can see why you considered your coaches such admirable role models.

S. E. Barnes #1 - 31

Dr. Barnes: They were at all times.

Q: What were their names?

Dr. Barnes: Lyle Butler was the football and basketball coach in college. My track coach was Dan Kinsey. Leo Holden was my high school football coach, and Dan McAfee was my basketball coach.

Q: How long did you stay at Livingstone?

Dr. Barnes: From 1936 to 1941. Reverend Homer Tucker was at the Ninth Street YMCA in Cincinnati, Ohio, as the executive secretary. I had known him at Oberlin because he was our pastor at the Baptist Church there. When he got the job at the YMCA, he called me and said, "I'd like for you to come here as the boys' work secretary." So I went to Cincinnati in 1941 and stayed there until 1942, when I entered the Navy.

While I was boys' work secretary, I was also the director of our summer camp. This new job was similar to what I had been doing--working with young people, especially boys. Some of them couldn't really get to camp, because they didn't have the money. I found out that if they collected sales tax stamps, we could turn them in for financial credit. So I had my YMCA youngsters out collecting these stamps, and the money we received for them was put in the bank for each boy. So when they got ready to go to camp, many of them had already paid their way, even though their parents really didn't have the money to send them. But I felt that this was an experience that each youngster should have. I said to them, "Well, if you really want it, you've got to put some time in it yourself. You've got to really expend the effort. If people give something to you, you won't value it as much as you would if you did it yourself."

Q: Some of the same things you had learned from your parents.

Dr. Barnes: That's right, so actually that experience was very good. Then, of course, I went in the Navy and went to Great Lakes.

Q: Why did you pick the Navy?

Dr. Barnes: Partly because of its stress on cleanliness. And I chose the Navy because it was in the North. If I'd gone in the Army, I don't know where I might have been sent. It was likely to be in the South, and I didn't want that. My future wife was very disappointed with my choice, because the Navy had limited opportunities for advancement by blacks. She said, "You'll be a sailor all your life."

My twin sister Becky was still in Oberlin, and she knew the lady at the local draft board who was responsible for the number of persons who would have to be inducted regularly and so forth and so on. One day my sister called and said, "Hilda says that your name will be in the next draft."

So I said, "Thank you," and the day before I would have been drafted, I went and joined the Navy as a volunteer. I almost chose the Marine Corps.

Q: What was the appeal of the Marine Corps?

Dr. Barnes: A very close friend of mine in Cincinnati joined the Marines and talked me into it too. So I went down to the Marines to join, but I got there late. So I was told, "It's too late today, but you come back tomorrow." But then after I got back home and thought about it a while, I decided the Navy was best for me and eliminated the idea of joining the Marines.

Q: When did you enlist?

Dr. Barnes: I enlisted in September 1942. I went to boot

camp at Great Lakes, Illinois.* One thing that I recall quite vividly was the first night that we were in boot camp. You know, at that time we slept in bays. We slept in hammocks, and these hammocks were slung between posts. All night long, it sounded like a drum. People were falling out of those things all night long, because you didn't know exactly how to get in them and stay in them. If you'd roll one way or the other, it would just tip you.

The other thing I liked about the Navy was that it's a clean service. We had to wash our uniforms daily and hang them up, and the next day everything was fresh. You'd keep your uniforms rolled and in your seabag, ready to go at a moment's notice. So there was never anything dirty in your ditty bag or in your seabag.

Q: Your mother's training came in very handy there.

Dr. Barnes: Well, it helped. It certainly did. As I said, the Navy is a clean service, and they would respect it. When we had inspection, the inspecting officer would come around with white gloves. He'd run his hands under the tables, places like that. If he got them dirty, then you got a bad mark. So that meant that you had to be thoroughly clean--spic and span. He'd look at your shoes;

---

*Great Lakes, Illinois, a town on the shore of Lake Michigan, north of Chicago, was the site of a large naval training station that included recruit training and a number of other schools. It is now known as Great Lakes Naval Training Center.

he'd look at your uniform; he would check. You couldn't have any mustaches; you couldn't have any beards; your hair had to be cut. You had to be ready at all times. That was good discipline, good discipline.

After I finished boot camp, I stayed there in ship's company as a third class petty officer.* When we were in ship's company, we had to go through short-arm inspections.** If we'd go out to Chicago on liberty, we had to be checked in when we came back. This was a check for venereal disease. If they found any evidence that you contacted anything, they wanted to find out where you got it and the name of the person so it wouldn't spread. Available to you going out the gate, they had machines in which people could buy protectives for a very small sum of money. So those inspections were routine kind of things that happened regularly, and they were sometimes unannounced. Of course, in boot camp we didn't have that problem, because the recruits never left the base. But those in ship's company were inspected.

Q: I presume this was both blacks and whites.

---
*The term "ship's company" does not here refer literally to those serving in a ship. Rather, it describes those who were on the staff of the Great Lakes Naval Training Station, as opposed to those who were being trained. Interview three of this oral history goes into detail on Dr. Barnes's experiences in boot camp and ship's company.
**This is a euphemism for the examination of a man's penis.

Dr. Barnes: Oh, everybody on the base. Because, you see, with the men being as close as they were, you'd have an epidemic on your hands before too long.

Q: How did your officer training come about?

Dr. Barnes: One day when I was sitting in the interviewing office, the commanding officer came in and said, "Barnes, you are relieved. You must report to the main side." Naturally I was concerned, because the only time blacks were summoned to the main side was for something unusual. The main side was strictly whites only.

Q: Who was the commanding officer who did that?

Dr. Barnes: Commander Armstrong.* He was in charge of Camp Robert Smalls.** Two other men in the interviewing office were told at the same time to go to the main side, Goodwin and Williams.*** So the three of us went, not

---
*Commander Daniel W. Armstrong, USNR, was officer in charge of Camp Robert Smalls. He was a 1915 Naval Academy graduate who resigned his regular commission after World War I and was recalled to active duty for World War II.
**Within the Great Lakes Naval Training Station, Camp Robert Smalls was the site of training for black recruits. It was named for an escaped slave who captured the Confederate steamer Planter during the Civil War and turned her over to the U.S. Navy. He served as pilot of the Planter and later of the gunboat Keokuk.
***Reginald Ernest Goodwin was a member of the Golden Thirteen. He died before he could be interviewed by the Naval Institute's oral history program. Lewis Reginald Williams was one of the black enlisted men who took officer training in early 1944, but he was not commissioned.

knowing why. When we reported to the commanding officer's office, we walked in and saw several other blacks there. We didn't know any of them.

Q: Did you have any idea at that point why you were being called over?

Dr. Barnes: No.

Q: Was it explained to you when you got there?

Dr. Barnes: Not at the moment we reported. Finally, the aide to the commanding officer came to the area where we were waiting and called, "Attention." We stood up when the commanding officer came in. He said, "At ease," and then asked, "Do you know why you're here?"

We said, "No, sir."

Then he said, "Well, the Navy has decided to commission Negroes as officers in the United States Navy, and you have been selected to attend an officer indoctrination school." The announcement surprised all of us. Then he said, "Today you take your physical examinations and report back here. But before you go, in order to be considered for officer candidate, you must be at least a chief petty officer or a first class petty officer. So all of those who are neither, as of this moment, are first class." I had been a third class petty officer almost a year, and in less than a minute I was promoted to first class.

Q: That was a nice boost.

Dr. Barnes: Now, isn't that the truth? The commander instructed us, "Go to ship's store and get your new stripes, have them put on, and then report back to take your physicals."

Q: Were you told why you were included in the group?

Dr. Barnes: I never did know, and the question's been asked me many times, "Why were you selected?" I'm sure there were other sailors that were qualified, some better than I was. I don't know why I was selected or by whom.

Later the facts came out. The Navy had decided to commission black officers as a result of Mary McLeod Bethune's efforts.* She was very close to Mrs. Roosevelt.** Mrs. Bethune was instrumental in getting a

---
*Mary McLeod Bethune (1875-1955) was a black educator who in 1904 opened at Daytona Beach, Florida, a small school called Daytona Normal and Industrial Institute. It merged in 1923 with Cookman Institute to form Bethune-Cookman College, with Mrs. Bethune as president.
**Eleanor Roosevelt (1884-1962) was the socially conscious wife of President Franklin D. Roosevelt.

S. E. Barnes #1 - 39

change of attitude. Then the Navy contacted the naval districts and told the commandants, "We're looking for qualified Negroes to be considered for officer candidate school. So you submit your names." I heard later--and this may or may not be true--that the first list included 500 names. After that they did a very thorough job in investigating us--going to our homes and checking our backgrounds.

Q: Did you know that you, in fact, were checked on?

Dr. Barnes: Not until I went home after I was married. Olga and I were married in North Carolina in December 1943.* Then we went to Oberlin for a reception with my family. My friends wanted to meet my bride. It was there that I was asked why strangers were in town asking different people questions about me. I couldn't answer because I knew nothing about it at that time.

Q: How did you and your future wife get together? You said that marrying was not something on your mind when you left Oberlin.

Dr. Barnes: Oh, that's true, very true. When I first went to Salisbury, North Carolina, to teach at Livingstone

---
*His wife's maiden name was Olga Lash.

College, I had not met her, even though she came from there and her younger brother was a member of the college football team. At that time she was teaching at Morristown College in Tennessee. Therefore, I didn't meet her the first year I was there. But I met her the second year, because her sister-in-law became pregnant. At that time the rule in the school system was that a job would not remain open for a woman who was pregnant. If she had to take a leave of absence, then the job would not be available to her when she returned. So Olga Lash, the young lady who later became my wife, came back to Salisbury to hold the job for her sister-in-law. That was the first time I met her. I knew her brothers. He younger brother John was in the Alpha fraternity, but her brothers Wiley and Traugott were members of the Omega fraternity. Since I was Omega too, I got to meet them. One day a friend of mine, who was teaching in one of the high schools, and who knew her sister Nadine, said to me, "What are you doing tonight?"

I said, "Well, I'm not busy."

He said, "Why don't you come and go with me? I want you to meet somebody."

I said, "Okay." I had nothing else to do. So I went with him to visit Nadine, and I was introduced to her sister Olga. Several weeks later I called her and asked her if she would like to go to the movies. She said she would like to. Interestingly enough, at the time we met, she was engaged and I was engaged. We had no idea that this relationship would go beyond a friendly level. We would go to the movies or take a drive in my car, sometimes sit on her porch and talk. But it wasn't serious on the part of either of us.

Then later on, we found that our feelings were a little bit stronger than just a friendly relationship. So when she left later that year to work on her master's degree at the University of Chicago, we corresponded back and forth. Eventually, the feeling grew stronger, and we decided to become engaged, which we did.

Then later we discussed marriage. After she had successfully completed her master's degree at Chicago University, she accepted a job at a high school in Trenton, New Jersey. However, a rule existed in Trenton that prevented a woman from marriage until she had been on the faculty for three years. So that meant that we had to wait for three years before we could get married. The end of the third year came in June, and we got married in December of the same year, 1943.

During most of our engagement I was a seaman first class, not even a petty officer yet. By the time we were ready to get married, I had been promoted to third class petty officer. Than I looked at my monetary resources, and I didn't have enough for us to get married. Johns Manville

S. E. Barnes #1 - 42

asbestos had a plant right next to the base, and they were hiring people part time, so I went over and got a job with them. After I completed my duties on the base and had dinner, then I went to Waukegan and worked in the plant until midnight. I did that five nights a week. On Saturdays and Sundays, when Johns Manville wasn't open, I'd go to Chicago and work in the Campbell Soup factory. I got off at the naval base at noon, so I could work all Saturday afternoon and evening. Later I'd go to the USO to sleep for a few hours. Then I'd go back and work Sunday and get off at 6:30 on Monday morning. I would then catch the 7:00 A.M. Skokie Valley railroad back to the base and report at 8:00 A.M.

I followed this schedule for three months so I could get enough money to travel to North Carolina, where the wedding was held, and enough money for our honeymoon after the wedding. We left North Carolina and went for a few days to my home in Oberlin, Ohio. From there we went to Chicago. She stayed there for a week and then went back to her job in Trenton, New Jersey. When I returned to Camp Robert Smalls after my leave, that's when I found out what I had been chosen for this officer training program. Out of about 100,000 blacks in the Navy, 500 were selected. The list went down to 225, to 100, to 50, and then finally to 25.

S. E. Barnes #1 - 43

We were housed in a separate barracks. We had a separate commanding officer, separate executive officer, and separate instructors. We were separated from everybody else. We went to classes from 8:00 in the morning until noon. We would then go to chow, return, and go to class from 1:00 to 5:00. We had no contact with any other personnel at Camp Robert Smalls. We were isolated completely.

Q: Did that bother you?

Dr. Barnes: Well, at first we were really concerned, because we didn't understand what was going on. But we were told, "You are here for a specific purpose. We want to see what the situation is, so we don't want any distractions."

Q: The ultimate group that went through the training course was 16. At what point did it get whittled down from 25 to 16?

Dr. Barnes: Somewhere in there they disappeared. We don't know why. Then actually only 13 were commissioned.

Q: There's a new book out called <u>Strength for the Fight</u>. It indicates that the Navy arbitrarily decided to start

S. E. Barnes #1 - 44

with only 12 black officers, and they later added a 13th as a warrant officer. So the others, I presume, didn't necessarily fail, but for whatever reason the Navy had just picked that number.*

Dr. Barnes: Well, I don't know if it was an arbitrary number. All I know is that in the final analysis, there were only 13 men commissioned.

I do know one thing, and perhaps the other fellows have told you this. After we were sent back to the barracks, we had a meeting that first night, and we said, "This is an experiment, and we know it. We're determined that it's not going to fail." So it was then that we vowed to follow the motto of the Three Musketeers: "All for one and one for all." We decided then that what any one of us knew, all of us would know. So we studied together and prepared together. We were determined to succeed in spite of the burden that was being placed on our shoulders. We knew that we were being showcased. We believed there were people who hoped we'd fail, but we were going to fool all of them. Because we were the foot in the door for other

---

*Bernard C. Nalty, Strength for the Fight (New York: The Free Press, 1986), makes the following statement on page 192: ". . . on January 1, 1944, sixteen black enlisted men entered a segregated officer candidate school at the Great Lakes Naval Training Station. Although all of them successfully completed the course, only twelve received commissions, a purely arbitrary number adopted by the Bureau of Personnel for reasons never explained. Of the remaining four, one became a warrant officer, and the others reverted to enlisted status."

blacks, and we were determined not to be the ones responsible for having the foot removed.

So each night we'd study together. Everybody studied, and we would grill one another. The lights were supposed to be out at 10:00 o'clock. We'd go into the head, cover the windows and doors with blankets, and study in there. We didn't care about any one person excelling; we decided to excel as a class. We didn't intend to compete with one another. What one of us knew, he would teach the rest. So when we went to class, we were all prepared. Any questions that were asked in any of the classes, we all were prepared to answer. What we had in class any day, we would go back over. Because of our dedication and determination, our class average when we completed our courses was the highest average of any officer candidate school up to that point. It was around 3.7 for the class, not any individual.

Q: Did you find that these sessions with each other in the head and so forth were more useful than the classes themselves?

Dr. Barnes: No, because the classes themselves gave us an idea of what we needed to study. We knew that we were being given a very intensive course.

S. E. Barnes #1 - 46

Q: Who were the instructors?

Dr. Barnes: Those I don't recall. They were all white, with one exception. The person who was teaching us mathematics was a black chief petty officer named Noble Payton, but he was the only one. In fact, when the course was over, one officer admitted to us that he had been sent there, not because he wanted to be, but because he was assigned there. He said that he deliberately put pressure on us, hoping that we would not be successful.* But when the course was over, he congratulated us. He said, "You were given, in these two months, training equivalent to a semester at the Naval Academy." And he said, "I did this deliberately. I want to congratulate you for the way you handled the pressure and the fact that you did it well." So that helped us to realize that what we had done went beyond the expectations of many people.

We did have some very unhappy moments. When we were first commissioned as naval officers, the white officers would deliberately cross the street to avoid saluting. These kinds of things disgusted us, but they didn't discourage us, because we knew that we were in the spotlight. Everybody was watching to see what we were

---

*This officer was Lieutenant (junior grade) Paul D. Richmond, USNR. In his Naval Institute oral history he also recalled that the course was demanding. He said, however, that it was made difficult so that the officer candidates would be well trained, not so they would fail.

S. E. Barnes #1 - 47

going to do. So when we were commissioned and we took the oath, we were told to go to ship's stores and get our uniforms, because we were given an allowance to cover the cost. Instead, we went to Chicago and had our uniforms individually tailored. Of course, it cost us a little more, but when we came out, our uniforms fit and were spic-and-span. They were first class.

Q: One man said he did get his out of the ship's store, and that was George Cooper.* He said that made him the first black officer to wear a uniform.

Dr. Barnes: A Navy uniform out of the ship's store? Probably true, though this is the first time I heard that story. I'm sure it did not matter who was the first black officer to wear a Navy uniform since we were all officers.

Q: What were the subjects that were covered in these lectures morning and afternoon?

Dr. Barnes: They were the same as those taught at other officer candidate schools, as well as at the Naval Academy. I do remember some of the courses: navigation, gunnery, aircraft recognition, naval history, Navy regulations, signaling by both flags and Morse code, seamanship,

---
*George Clinton Cooper is a member of the Golden Thirteen. His oral history is in the Naval Institute collection.

survival techniques.

Q: Did you have opportunities for practical applications?

Dr. Barnes: No, we didn't. The only applications we had were right there in the barracks. For instance, when we were taught navigation we worked out the problems on the blackboard and with pictures. We rarely left the barracks and never went aboard ship. We did receive rifle range practice and duties with assigned recruit companies. For the most part, we had to learn vicariously rather than through actual experience.

Q: What was John Dille's role in all this?

Dr. Barnes: John Dille was a battalion commander, and he really took a liking to us for some reason.* He was one person who was sincere in his efforts to help us. He was what I call the person who really kept us from becoming discouraged, and he was interested in us, sincerely interested. It was a great boost to us, and we still have the greatest respect and admiration for him. In fact, Dalton Baugh had some stationery made up that showed the

---

*Lieutenant (junior grade) John F. Dille, Jr., USNR, was part of the officer organization that ran Camp Robert Smalls. He described his experiences there in his Naval Institute oral history.

S. E. Barnes #1 - 49

"Golden Thirteen Plus One."* The "plus one" is Jack Dille, who is and always has been our greatest supporter.

Q: I've seen that stationery.

Dr. Barnes: He has been a benefactor; he's been a friend; he's been a confidant. He's really been, I think, one of the greatest influences we've had, and he still is. We have the greatest respect for him.

Q: You wouldn't go so far, though, I take it, to say that he was the difference between your making it and not making it, would you?

Dr. Barnes: No, I wouldn't say that, but I'm saying that he certainly gave us encouragement when we needed it. His support gave us more incentive to succeed.

Q: Did you have any contact with Commander Armstrong?

Dr. Barnes: Well, interestingly enough, I did, and it was in an athletic situation. I was on duty in the drill hall one day when I was a petty officer, before the officer

---

*Dalton Louis Baugh was a member of the Golden Thirteen. He died before his oral history could be included in the Naval Institute collection. The stationery has a picture of the Golden Thirteen, a listing of their names, and a design printed faintly in the center of the sheet: "13+1".

training. Commander Armstrong came in and asked me, "What's your name, sailor?" I told him. He said, "Do you play badminton?"

I said, "Yes, sir," though I never played badminton in my life.

He said, "Well, I want you to have the nets up tomorrow, and I'll be in here at 12:00 o'clock, because I want to play badminton.

I said, "Yes, sir." Immediately I went and found a book on badminton. I read it and practiced what I read. He was a good player. I tried to make the games interesting and competitive but not beat him often, because he was a person who enjoyed winning. I would allow the games to be close, and sometimes I would beat him just to keep it honest. He would come in every day at 12:00 o'clock, and we would play badminton for an hour. I would have the court prepared when he got there. The rackets were out, the birds were out, the net was up, and everything was in order for the game. So that's how my contact with him was established.

Q: That says something for your skills, that you could pick it up that quickly and be competitive.

Dr. Barnes: Well, coordination had a lot to do with it. In addition, I was younger and had been involved in athletics for a number of years. It was just a matter of knowing the rules and then using the skills that I had. He was a good player, very competitive, very intense, and really battled every point. For instance, if we played four games, he'd win three, I'd win one. If we played six, I would win two, he would win four. He always came out on top in the number of games won.

Q: How well do you think you would have done had you given your maximum effort?

Dr. Barnes: Well, I really think I could have won the majority of the games played. He had more knowledge of the game and experience. I just knew the bare fundamentals, but I had the advantages of youth, speed, and coordination.

Q: Did you have the feeling that you would be made to suffer if you would beat him?

Dr. Barnes: I didn't want to take that chance, to tell you the truth. I made it competitive so that he would get a good workout, but I would not do it in such a way that it would embarrass him. I wasn't going to embarrass him under any circumstances. I made it so that it didn't appear that I was giving into him. You know, it would be a match point or something like that. I'd volley with him and then I would make a serious error. I'd miss the bird, or I would drive it back too far. So he would win the game. But he never knew that I was deliberately doing this, so we made it competitive. I did know that he was not a kind of person you crossed, especially as an enlisted man way down the line. In fact, I was only a seaman first class. So no, there was no way he was going to lose.

Q: I think that takes a great deal of skill to make it competitive but not to win.

Dr. Barnes: Well, that was not too difficult, because, as I say, he was an older person than I was. He couldn't get to certain shots that I could make. But I would never drive him into a position where it didn't make him exert some effort, but I would not smash it. I might flutter, so he would be able to get over to it and he could return it. But instead of taking advantage of a situation which I could have taken, because he's over here and I'm ready to smash, and it's over here, I would always in some way or another make it something besides a smash. The bird would stay in the air long enough for him to get over there and return it. Or if I did smash it, I would hit the net instead of smashing it across. So it was competitive, and he had to exercise. But he didn't ever know what the true intent was. Like you say, it's difficult to do that, especially when you see openings that you know you should take advantage of, but you never did. This is the commander. No way. We don't want to do that. I made sure that he would win, but I wasn't going to be embarrassed.

Q: Could you have beaten him, had you gone all out?

Dr. Barnes: Yes, I think so. I may not have won that many games, but I would have won more games than he did because it was just a matter of wearing him out. He had a terrific smash shot, and I knew that I could not permit him to get that shot, because he always, always returned it with gusto. So I had to learn about moving him around. That's what I did, mostly because I said, "Well, I know he's older than I am, and he cannot move a lot without getting tired, so I'm going to have to move him around. I'm not going to put anything up there that he can see." But I was using drop shots, and I was using smashes over in the corners. He kept me moving too. I'm telling you, it took all that I had to keep with him or ahead of him. He was a great competitor. I enjoyed working against him.

Q: Did he cheat in his efforts to win?

Dr. Barnes: Never. But you can't cheat much in badminton, anyway. The only way you could have cheated was if the bird appeared to be out of bounds and it was in, or vice-versa. But those kind of things, I never debated with him. If he said it was in, hell, it was in. Didn't make a bit of difference to me. But if it came close, I knew what the verdict would be.

Q: His verdict.

Dr. Barnes: Better believe it. If he said it was in, it was in. But if there was the slightest doubt, I'd give him the benefit of the doubt. Of course, if it was way outside, he couldn't pull any tricks and say, "Well, that was in."

"Commander, you sure that was in? It looked out to me."

He would say, "Yes, it was in."

"It certainly was, now that you call it to my attention."

Q: Did your officer training include marching and drilling, as boot camp had?

Dr. Barnes: No. We had little time for anything but classes and study. We did march to chow and back three times a day, but that was the extent of anything resembling marching or drilling. At least we were not subjected to marching to the sick bay for short-arm inspections.

Q: What sort of living accommodations did you have as officer candidates?

Dr. Barnes: We were housed in separate rooms with two in each room.

Q: Were you inspected in that environment?

Dr. Barnes: Oh, yes. We had daily inspections. Sometimes we were there. Sometimes the quarters were inspected when we weren't present.

Q: How much opportunity, if any, did you have for liberty while you were undergoing officer training?

Dr. Barnes: None. We never left the base after we went into this barracks. We didn't leave Camp Robert Smalls until we went over to the main side to be commissioned.

Q: It was almost like being prisoners.

Dr. Barnes: Not really, because we were in training. And being the first blacks to be given an opportunity to become commissioned officers, our interests were limited to succeeding and not going on liberty. We felt that had we not succeeded, it would have been more difficult for later commissionings of blacks. We were the trial horses. Fortunately, we recognized that. We were a nice congenial group of fellows and had much in common.

Q: I would just like to run through the names of your fellow classmates and get your impressions of them as individuals. Also, you've mentioned the cooperative nature of the venture. I'd appreciate it if you could talk about what each one contributed to that group effort.

Dr. Barnes: I don't think anyone stood out particularly in any category. Nelson, of course, was more gregarious.* Arbor was more loquacious.** But all of us, I think, did a job of putting our resources together. Nelson was very aggressive and very pompous. George Cooper was a chief petty officer, but nobody took any precedence over anybody else. It was a very well amalgamated group.

Q: But each has an individual personality, and that's what I'd like to get at, if I may. For example, you've talked

---

*Dennis Denmark Nelson II is a member of the Golden Thirteen who eventually retired from the Navy as a lieutenant commander. He died before he could be interviewed as part of the Naval Institute's oral history program.
**Jesse Walter Arbor is a member of the Golden Thirteen. His oral history is in the Naval Institute collection.

about Arbor as being loquacious. I've gathered he is also very enthusiastic and a spirit lifter.

Dr. Barnes: Yes, Arbor was a jokester. He kept things lively. Nelson was very efficient. Cooper was more sedate and more mature. Hair was quiet; he didn't have much to say.* White was a very intellectual person and was not what you'd call a person seeking to be identified.** He was a person who thought through things very well. He was withdrawn but very intelligent.

Q: Very analytical.

Dr. Barnes: Yes, very analytical. Baugh was very industrious, and Baugh had, in my judgment, a great deal of mechanical ability. When the war was over, Baugh formed his own engineering company in Boston, which was very successful.

Q: Charles Lear.

Dr. Barnes: Lear was quiet, effective, efficient, but not a showoff.*** In fact, there were no blatant showoffs.
_____
*James Edward Hair is a member of the Golden Thirteen. His oral history is in the Naval Institute collection.
**William Sylvester White is a member of the Golden Thirteen. His oral history is in the Naval Institute collection.
***Charles Byrd Lear was a member of the Golden Thirteen. He died before he could be interviewed as part of the Naval Institute's oral history program.

Nelson might have seemed to be a showoff, but he did it unconsciously. I don't think he was conceited, but he was just aggressive. The way I remember the fellows is that no one stood out as being this or that. We were a group of individuals meshed together to do a job, and no one was going to be outlandish. We were all going to be outstanding, not one of us. Nelson was the only one who stayed in and on active duty until he retired. The rest of us returned to civilian life.

Q: One man who was different was Goodwin, in that he was sort of a liaison man over to the main side.*

Dr. Barnes: Yes, and he was quite a mature person. He was the person we looked up to, not because he was older but because he was one of the first blacks to receive a ranking grade at Great Lakes. He was a third class petty officer who was very much respected. He would be one person I would recall as being astute, and he didn't involve himself in any kind of frivolity.

Q: Very businesslike.

Dr. Barnes: Yes, very businesslike.

---

*Reginald Ernest Goodwin was a member of the Golden Thirteen. He died before he could be interviewed by the Naval Institute's oral history program.

Q: I've gathered that was a useful role, also, that he played.

Dr. Barnes: Oh, yes. As I recall, Goodwin might have been older than the others of us and probably had been involved in many more activities in civilian life than we were. I got to know him a little better than the others. When we were commissioned, we got this statement that there were no quarters available to blacks on the base. Therefore, he and I lived in a house in Lake Forest with a man and his wife. Goodwin and I went together to the base each morning in his car. So he was a roommate, and I got to know him better than I knew the others because of that. Nelson stayed somewhere near the base, since he was in charge of the remedial reading program. Lear was a company commander, and White was attached to the public information office after we were commissioned. Only four of us stayed on at Great Lakes.

Q: Were you related to the other Barnes at all?

Dr. Barnes: No, we weren't related. Phil was a very quiet and inconspicuous person.* Barnes had very little to

---

*Phillip George Barnes was a member of the Golden Thirteen. He died before he could be interviewed as part of the Naval Institute oral history program.

say, but Barnes was a person who could be depended upon. He was never a person that you could walk into a room and immediately identify as being an outstanding figure. Goodwin, on the other hand, did make an instant impression, because he was a nice-looking guy and carried himself with a great deal of pride.

Q: I've gathered that Phillip Barnes was self-conscious about his weight.

Dr. Barnes: Yes, he was. He was chubby, and I think he felt a bit sensitive about it. He was the chubbiest one in the group.

White is small in stature, but he has a tremendous ability when it comes to analysis. I don't know whether he told you or not, but he's recently been asked by Secretary of the Navy Lehman to be a member of one of his task forces, which is quite an honor.* White is the kind of person who is a very deliberate thinker. He is not flashy, but you can see him thinking, and whenever he speaks, he has something to say, something to add.

Q: Profound.

---

*John Lehman served as Secretary of the Navy from 1981 to 1987.

Dr. Barnes: I'd say that's a good description. He is a profound person.

Q: And also a witty man.

Dr. Barnes: Yes, he has a very subtle wit. I think that if you were to get the group together, it wouldn't be too long before Arbor would be the one to start off the conversation. He would probably be involved in much of the conversation. Cooper is what I call the statesman. Martin is quiet and one who doesn't make snap judgments. He is a very quiet, very attentive person and knows what is going on. But he is not a person who would thrust himself into the foreground. The persons who would do that, for whatever reason, would be Goodwin, Arbor, Nelson, Cooper, and Baugh. Those were the conspicuous ones, because they would be the ones who would do the majority of the talking and the presentations.

Q: Nelson was an exception, wasn't he, in being so flamboyant?

Dr. Barnes: Yes, he was, for Nelson was a very, very precise person. One of the things that I recall about Nelson is that he never carried anything but new money. When he was paid, he would take his dollars to the bank and get brand-new dollars. Call it an idiosyncrasy if you wish, but that was the way he was.

Q: How would you explain that?

Dr. Barnes: It was part of his appearance. He was very neat, almost to the point of being obnoxious. This attitude included his car. He and Goodwin, I think, were the only ones of our group who had cars. Nelson washed his car every day. When it rained, as soon as it stopped, he wiped the car off. That demonstrated the kind of meticulous person he was. He was meticulous almost to the point of being absurd, but we respected him for doing that. His uniforms were always cleaned and pressed. He was the only member in the group who had every conceivable type of uniform, formal and informal, that any naval officer could have. Of course, being in the Navy and staying in, he would naturally need all types of uniforms. But Nelson never had anything less than what was necessary, and he carried himself thus. Very suave.

Q: What do you recall about Frank Sublett?

Dr. Barnes: Frank was quiet.* Frank is still quiet, but

---
*Frank Ellis Sublett, Jr., is a member of the Golden Thirteen. His oral history is in the Naval Institute collection.

Frank is aware of what's going on. When he speaks, he has something to say. Johnny Reagan's the same way.* Johnny is not loquacious. Johnny is quiet, but Johnny is also aware of what's going on, and he will contribute to whatever's going on. His contributions, as are Frank's, are very, very intellectually arrived at. In fact, there are no scatterbrains among these guys. They, I think, were good for one another. You know, if one got out of line, then the others would put him in line, not in terms of squelching what he had to say, but, by the same token, letting him know that each person has a contribution to make. The contribution made by each person was respected, and no one dominated to the exclusion of the others.

Q: Reagan and Sublett were the two youngest members of the group, which may be why they were the quiet ones.

Dr. Barnes: Could be, but I think that by nature they were that way. Because over the years, since we've been meeting regularly, my impression of them has not changed.

Q: And yet Sublett is very congenial.

Dr. Barnes: He has always been that way. This was true of the entire group, but Sublett especially was. I don't

―――――――――
*John Walter Reagan is a member of the Golden Thirteen. His oral history is in the Naval Institute collection.

think there was one person who attempted to outshine anyone else. We never paraded before the others whatever our accomplishments were. I mean, even at these ages we still have great respect for one another.

Q: And a sense of pride runs through all of you.

Dr. Barnes: This has always been true. The pride we have is because we know what we went through, and we know the contributions that each one made to the total effort. When we meet, there's a very close relationship that exists even now between us.

I went overseas during the war, and you'll get from the others what their duties were. There were only four or five in the group who actually were on ships.

Q: Was that a disappointment to you?

Dr. Barnes: Yes, but we at the time said, "Whatever duties we are requested to perform, we will perform to the best of our abilities." Hair was on board a ship; Reagan was on board a ship; Sublett was on board; Martin was on board; and Baugh. I think that they're the only ones.

I was sent with a logistic company to Okinawa, where I had command of 120 men. I stayed on Okinawa until the war

S. E. Barnes #1 - 65

ended with the Nagasaki and Hiroshima incidents in Japan.*

Q: Most of the men who did get seagoing assignments really were in small craft. Hair going to the USS Mason was the only bona fide ship.**

Dr. Barnes: We won't be able to talk to Baugh, but Baugh was aboard a ship. He was the engineering officer aboard a large ship.

Q: I didn't know that.

Dr. Barnes: I think you'll find that Baugh was on duty on a ship up in the North Sea. I don't recall the name of the ship.

Q: I'd also like to cover the three men in the group of 16 who didn't go all the way: Pinkney, Alves, and Mummy Williams. What do you remember about those three?

Dr. Barnes: Well, you see, I continue to say that there

---
*B-29 bombers of the U.S. Army Air Forces dropped atomic bombs on Hiroshima, Japan, on 6 August 1945 and on Nagasaki, Japan, on 9 August 1945. The Japanese surrendered shortly afterward.
**In 1945 Hair became the first black officer in the destroyer escort Mason (DE-529), a ship with an all-black enlisted crew.

S. E. Barnes #1 - 66

was nobody who was a pusher or who tried to be above anybody else. It was a very closely knit group. I think Mummy's nickname itself indicates the kind of person he was.* He was very quiet and didn't have a whole lot to say, but what he did have to say was respected. Pinkney was more flamboyant but very intelligent.** I don't know the reason for his disappearance. I think he was not too outgoing, perhaps, in the sense that he preferred to be a loner.

Q: What do you recall of Alves?

Dr. Barnes: Alves had previous seagoing experience, because he had been in the merchant marine, I believe, before he entered the Navy.*** I think he had previously identified himself as being of a nationality other than what he was, and finally he was found out. At that time, of course, if you could pass, all right; it was to your advantage to do so. I think that had a lot to do with his disqualification.

Q: So are you saying that in the black culture, if a person could pass for white, you'd say more power to him?

---
*Lewis Reginald Williams.
**J. B. Pinkney
***A. Alves.

Dr. Barnes: That's right. I haven't kept up with it for many years, but statistically it shows that X number of people disappear from the black race, and it's a crossover. If they were lighter, then they were never questioned. They were acceptable, so skin color determined what you were. Many of them took advantage of that because they said, "Why should I suffer this when I can move here and get some of the advantages which color seems to give?"

Q: What else do you remember about Alves?

Dr. Barnes: He was a quiet person and very efficient. He helped us a great deal, because he had had actual experience in some of the things that we were going through, such as navigation, while our experience was vicarious. By putting what he knew with what the fellows themselves were trying to learn, it gave us an edge.

Now, we got into the legal aspects during training. White helped us a great deal with Navy Regs, as did Goodwin. They took over when we got to that part of it. Arbor was a quartermaster, so Arbor was able to help us with navigation. The experiences that they had prior to that were helpful to us, because they gave us the real feel for it, you see.

Q: So you believe Alves represented himself as being

S. E. Barnes #1 - 68

foreign born, or something of that sort?

Dr. Barnes: That's the impression we finally got.

As I said, we were never given any knowledge of why people disappeared. I know Mummy Williams was very, very disappointed, very disappointed, and I think it still affects him even today. Since he and the others did not remain throughout the training, we were never as close to them as we were with those who went through the total training period and were commissioned.

Q: Justice White said that he felt particularly bad, because Williams is the one who brought him into the Navy. White made it and his friend didn't.

Dr. Barnes: I can appreciate that. Mummy and Goodwin and Bill Thomas were the three fellows who were top blacks at Camp Robert Smalls, because they had enlisted early and come in with some of the first companies. They were the three who had third class petty officer ratings when I entered the Navy. They were looked up to, because at that time seeing a black petty officer was like seeing a commander today. They were petty officers, and we had a lot of respect for that. At that time, we saw nothing that would even indicate that there was going to be any change in attitudes toward blacks as far as the Navy was concerned. That's why it came as a complete surprise to us when we were called to the main side and told we would be going to officer school.

Q: In this very cloistered existence that you had, did you get a chance to get out and exercise and have sports?

Dr. Barnes: Certainly very little in an organized way. What we did was done individually. We didn't go out as a group and exercise. We didn't go out and play touch football or have a softball game or any of that. We did exercises, but it was more individual than as a group.

Q: Could you correspond with your friends and family?

Dr. Barnes: Yes, indeed. We did write letters and receive letters. These helped to keep up our spirits, as well as to know what our families and friends were doing. We didn't have the time to do other things, and I don't think at that time that any of us were particularly interested in going on liberty anyway, because every moment we had, we needed for study or classes.

Q: I wouldn't think it was lack of interest. You, as a newlywed, would certainly have some interest.

Dr. Barnes: Well, yes, I will agree. I don't recall making a telephone call or receiving a telephone call, but I was receiving letters regularly. But so far as recreation was concerned, it just was low on the list of things that we were permitted to do.

Q: What were the emotional feelings when you did get the commissions and became officers?

Dr. Barnes: Well, first of all, it was a relief, especially after what we'd been through. Then there was a determination that we would, as I said before, be an image for others to follow. No one could say that because we failed, that other blacks were not capable of being commissioned.

Of course, the honest-to-goodness reality didn't set in until we put our uniforms on. Then we were, in many instances, embarrassed and made to feel that we weren't really bona fide officers. We were denied privileges to the officers' club on the main side, and we were also denied the opportunity to become officers of the day. In our first assignments, we were junior officers of the day, and the officer of the day was white. We would wear a web belt; the white officer would have a web belt, a gun, and the authority. We just trailed around behind him on duty. We felt that we were certainly capable of handling more, so

S. E. Barnes #1 - 71

we pressed for recognition and insisted that we were mature enough to recognize the responsibilities involved. We felt that our initial roles were demeaning. We didn't feel it was necessary for us to be junior officers to a white officer. So it was finally decided, okay. So then, finally, we became full-fledged officers of the day, with total authority when we were on duty.

Q: How long did that take?

Dr. Barnes: It must have taken several months. The change came just before some of the black officers were reassigned to different places. I recall that not many of us actually had the experience of being officers of the day at Great Lakes. I remember the first time that I went on duty as junior officer of the day. I felt quite deflated, because I certainly felt capable of handling whatever situation might arise. Moreover, the black sailors were unhappy to see black naval officers not being treated with the respect shown white officers. Once we got the opportunity, we didn't in any way discredit the duty or responsibilities placed upon us.

Q: Were there other embarrassments besides not being able to get housing and go to the officers' club?

Dr. Barnes: Well, of course, not at Camp Smalls, which was segregated anyway. The recruits at Smalls were very proud of the fact that there were black officers, and they really respected us. At no time did they ever show disappointment, disdain, or antagonism. That's another reason why we were determined that we would not in any way be other than first class.

Q: Did you have any unpleasant experiences out in the civilian community?

Dr. Barnes: No, not much. Black civilians were proud, in Chicago and Milwaukee, because of these first black officers. We were given a great deal of recognition because of that. I was happy to say that no one showed disrespect. We were humbled by the fact that we had been selected and the fact that we had achieved. Instead of making us arrogant, we were more determined to be respected and respectable.

Q: With that very detailed screening process, I think the Navy was probably looking for people who would not be arrogant as a result of getting that opportunity.

Dr. Barnes: Well, they did a thorough job if that was their intent. When I went back to my hometown, my friends asked, "Why were all these people around asking questions about you?"

I said, "What do you mean? What kind? Who were they?"

They said, "We don't know, but these people came and asked many questions." They asked people in the community: the ministers, my high school teachers, the college people, and townspeople. They did a thorough job of finding out all they could about me. In fact, I'm sure they knew more about me than I knew about myself. I was surprised, because that's the first time that I had been investigated by anyone, and I wondered, "Why would they be investigating me?" I couldn't imagine what I'd done to bring this about. It was later that I found out why.

Q: Jesse Arbor said that he was tailed, even after he was commissioned.

Dr. Barnes: He told us that story.

Q: Did you have any comparable experience?

Dr. Barnes: No, I don't recall ever having that kind of experience.

Q: Were there cases when you weren't treated with the

respect due an officer?

Dr. Barnes: Yes. Some of the enlisted sailors refused to salute when I was personnel officer of our battalion on Okinawa. One day I went to a Marine installation, because I found out a friend of mine, whom I had known from Cincinnati, was stationed at a place called Naha. My commanding officer gave me the day off to go see him. So I took leave in a jeep and went over there to the Marine barracks where he was. My friend, who was a noncom, didn't know I was coming.* He didn't know what to do when he saw me—whether to salute me or what. So I laughed at him and told him, "This is between us. You don't have to do all that." But he was very happy, very proud, because the Marines had never seen a black officer. There weren't any black Marine officers. So I said, "Well, let's take a ride."

We took the jeep, and I was going through the post gate. I got to a particular exit, and there was a third class petty officer on duty. When I pulled up, he didn't salute—no respect at all. So I called him over and said, "Sailor. Did you forget something?"

He said, "No."

I said, "No, what?"

He immediately replied, "No, sir."

---
*Noncom—non-commissioned officer, the Marine equivalent of a Navy petty officer.

Then I said, "Let me remind you of something you already know. You see this eagle on my cap? You see this bar on my jacket?"

He said, "Yes, sir."

"You're not saluting me. You're saluting that emblem of rank. Hereafter, you forget the color and you remember the rank. You forget everything except that in the future. And whenever you see one, you salute this. You don't have to salute me as a person, but you salute that insignia as long as I have it on. I'm going to put you on report."

"Oh, don't do that."

"I certainly am." This is not Navy Regulations, and you know it, and I know it. You're not saluting me because I'm colored, but that has nothing to do with Navy Regulations. Maybe you out to go back and read your Bluejackets' Manual."*

That incident was one that I recall very vividly. Of course, then the sailor was very, very apologetic, and then he saluted. My friend, the Marine, was quite happy about the fact that I didn't ignore the incident.

Q: Did you, in fact, put this sailor on report?

---

*The Bluejackets' Manual, which has been published by the U.S. Naval Institute in various editions over the years, has long been considered the "bible" for Navy enlisted men. It is a basic textbook and reference volume on a wide variety of naval subjects.

S. E. Barnes #1 - 76

Dr. Barnes: I did.

Q: What came of that?

Dr. Barnes: I was told that he was promptly disciplined. I was notified that the report had been received and that action had been taken. Now, what the action was, I don't know, but I was satisfied with that.

Q: I daresay you didn't have that problem after that.

Dr. Barnes: No, I didn't. The thing that irritated me was the fact that he would not have done that to a white officer. Maybe the fact that I was a black officer made him think that I didn't require a salute. So I just wanted him to recognize that Navy Regulations were the same all over, for everybody; it didn't just mean for some.

Q: At the time you were commissioned, you got a letter from Frank Knox on your new status as an ensign, which was ironic since he had been dragging his feet on getting blacks commissioned.*

---

*Frank Knox (1874-1944) ran unsuccessfully for Vice President of the United States in 1936. He was publisher of the <u>Chicago Daily News</u> when made Secretary of the Navy in 1940. Knox died in office 28 April 1944, just over a month after the Golden 13 were commissioned.

Dr. Barnes: We had a little laughter about that. We weren't laughing because of the fact that he had perished, but a little joke among us was that once the Navy commissioned blacks, it was just too much for him to accept, and that was what killed him. He died very soon thereafter. It was an unkind thought, but we were not serious. But at the time that it happened, that was the first thing we said, "Do you think our being commissioned had anything to do with his death?"

Somebody said, "Well, maybe it sort of expedited it." So we laughed about that. But he really did drag his feet for a long time, he really did, and very reluctantly gave his approval to it. We do know that was true.

Q: I think it was given to him as a fait accompli, really. He had to do it.

Dr. Barnes: I think he had no alternative, because the order came from President Roosevelt. He did it, but he did it reluctantly.

Q: One of the interesting things you told me when the tape recorder wasn't running was the fact that your sister Margaret was also an officer in the armed forces during the war.

S. E. Barnes #1 - 78

Dr. Barnes: Yes, she was a lieutenant in the Army, and I was commissioned in the Navy. We were the only brother-sister officers in the service at that time, both in different branches. A great deal was made of this fact. It was a unique situation, as far as the blacks were concerned. She enlisted first, and actually she tried her best to get me to enlist in the Army, because she was already in the Army. I elected the Navy, however, because of the reasons which I gave you. She stayed in the service after World War II and retired as a major. Her husband also retired as a major. She advised me to stay in after the war, but I elected to come out because the opportunities at that time didn't appear to me to be worth remaining in the Navy.

Q: She must have been one of the very first black women officers in the Army.

Dr. Barnes: At the time that she enlisted, the WACs had already been open to black women.* She didn't enter in the earlier classes, but she came in shortly thereafter. In fact, she was a student at Howard University in Washington, D.C., when she enlisted in the Army.

Q: What sorts of assignments did you have during that period at Great Lakes after commissioning, in addition to

───────────
*WAC--Women's Army Corps.

your duty assignments?

Dr. Barnes: Well, I was in charge of the recreation and athletic program for three camps: Camp Robert Smalls, Camp Moffett, and Camp Lawrence. For instance, Lena Horne came out once to entertain, and I was responsible for setting up her visit, acting as her escort, and seeing that she was given all of the VIP treatment.*

I had to arrange all the recreational activities, such as company competition in terms of softball and basketball. I arranged the schedules every day so that the drill hall would be available for certain activities. I set up schedules of activities in all three camps.

Q: That was a natural for you.

Dr. Barnes: I enjoyed it because I had had some previous experience with that. We had plenty of equipment, and I had many assistants from ship's company. Then in terms of the drills and so forth, I was responsible for these. I have a picture which I value very much because it shows me and a whole drill field full of cadets going through their exercises and so forth.**

I remained in this job until I received orders that I

---
*Lena Horne (1917-   ) is a long-time black singer. She still appears in advertisements because she looks younger than her calendar years.
**The photo appears on pages 60-61 of <u>The Golden Thirteen: Recollections of the First Black Naval Officers</u> (Annapolis: Naval Institute Press, 1993).

S. E. Barnes #1 - 80

was to report to Williamsburg, Virginia, for reassignment.

Q: There were some very good athletic teams fielded by this training station as a whole. Were you involved in that?

Dr. Barnes: No, I wasn't.

Q: There were the four of you who stayed there--you and Goodwin and White and Nelson. Did you tend to get together and compare notes from time to time?

Dr. Barnes: We would see one another from time to time, but we were going our different ways by that time. Nelson had a car, and he had contacts in Chicago. Goodwin, the same way. So I was more of less base-bound because I didn't have a vehicle. The only way I could travel would be to Chicago on the Skokie Valley or the Lake Shore railroad, which I did. Many of my recreational activities were with families in those two cities. So we really, I think, individually made our own recreational activities. We didn't often get together to compare notes, because we were in different places.

Q: Did you initiate the reassignment that eventually took you to Okinawa?

S. E. Barnes #1 - 81

Dr. Barnes: No. One day I was in the drill hall, and I was told to report to the main side. At the commander's office there I was notified that I was to be reassigned. Within a week I was detached and sent to Williamsburg. At Williamsburg I was given training as a logistic support commander of a group of men, including administrative duties. That's when I went to a firing range for practice. That's where we had to get our equipment, and we were assigned to a company. After several months at Williamsburg, then I was sent to San Francisco. That's where my company and I boarded a ship bound for overseas duty.

Q: Were these all-black outfits?

Dr. Barnes: Yes. There was still no integration. When I was sent to San Francisco, I got aboard the transport ship, and we got our equipment all aboard. We were fully equipped at Williamsburg. The officers were given .45-caliber pistols, web belts, and machetes. When we were getting ready to go, I happened to look across the deck, and I saw this oil tanker come alongside. I looked down, and there, to my surprise, were Martin and Sublett. I hadn't seen them since they left the base at Great Lakes.

S. E. Barnes #1 - 82

I was permitted to leave the ship for a very joyous reunion. I mean, we had a great time together.

After that, our ship put to sea.

Q: Was this a Navy ship you were on?

Dr. Barnes: It was a troop transport. I don't remember whether or not it was a Navy ship.

Q: Do you remember the name?

Dr. Barnes: Not offhand. I don't remember the name, but I know we were at sea for a while, constantly zigzagging to avoid submarines. We left San Francisco and went to the Marshall Islands. We were there for a week or more, and going ashore was great. Then we went to Eniwetok, and you talk about a barren island! When I saw that, I was very happy that I wasn't a Marine because of what these men had to endure to take this island. There were no trees, there were no bunkers, nothing to hide behind.

After three weeks we left Eniwetok and proceeded to Okinawa, and that's where I was finally based. I was the only black officer from the time I arrived until the time I left. One of the white officers was Steve Belichick, who is now an assistant football coach at the Naval Academy.*

------
*Lieutenant (junior grade) Stephen N. Belichick, USNR. He later spent many years on the football coaching staff of the Naval Academy. In 1991 his son Bill became head coach of the Cleveland Browns in the National Football League.

Steve was from Youngstown, Ohio, and I had known him because he played football in Cleveland at Western Reserve. He became a very close friend of mine. The first time I walked into the officers' club in Okinawa, almost all the other officers walked out. The only officers left in there were Steve and I. So I said, "Well, Steve."

Q: How well had you known him before?

Dr. Barnes: We had met earlier in Ohio, but I got to know him better after we got to Okinawa since we were both officers in the same regiment. Steve was one of the most unprejudiced persons I'd ever seen. So he said, "Hell, Sam, don't even worry about it. Let's enjoy having the club to ourselves."

After several similar incidents, I guess the white officers got tired of leaving when I came in. It got to be ridiculous, so after a while they would remain when I appeared. It hadn't really bothered me that much, because I wasn't any more anxious to meet them than they were to meet me. But after a while I guess they realized I didn't have a tail, I wasn't going to bite them, and I wasn't going to disappear. Then they decided to stay around even if I did show up. So that's the way it worked out. I will always remember that first night I walked into the officers' club, and all the white officers got up and walked out.

Q: George Cooper said he had a deliberate program to cultivate people and to show them just the things that you've said. Did you ever try any missionary work like that?

Dr. Barnes: No. As I was saying earlier, you lead by example. I tried not to be auspicious or conspicuous. I didn't seek out people as though I desperately needed their companionship. It didn't matter to me, because I felt that I didn't need them any more than they felt they needed me. I felt that after they saw the kind of person I was, and that I wasn't going to stop going to the club, then I think that they decided that, "He's not as bad as we thought he might be."

I didn't go into a deliberate program of education, because I felt that it was unnecessary. I had been taught that people couldn't be forced to accept someone, so I didn't try to cultivate them. I believed, "If you accept me, you accept me as I am." After a while they began to see that I wasn't going to let their attitudes affect me, and I wasn't trying to force them to accept me. If they wished to be friendly, fine. If they didn't, that was their prerogative. I lost no sleep over it.

Q: For your own morale and sense of well-being, Belichick did you a tremendous service.

Dr. Barnes: Well, the commanding officer of our unit was a nice person too. He was from Arlington, Texas, where he had been a civilian lawyer. He was very, very nice. He and the other white officers in our command were congenial. Even though I was the only black officer with the command, they were very supportive, and I had no problem with them. We ate together, slept together, and there was never any differentiation. I never had a feeling of uneasiness. We accepted one another, and nobody even considered color, maybe because ours was an all-black outfit.

Q: What kind of quarters were you in?

Dr. Barnes: We lived in tents on Okinawa, because it was not a permanent base at that time. When we first moved in, we slept in pup tents until we were able to erect platforms to make living in tents more pleasant. I stayed in tents the whole time I was on Okinawa. I never lived in any building.

Q: Where was the location on the island?

Dr. Barnes: The island was small by dimensions. I think it was something like 70 miles long and maybe 20 miles wide. It was a beautiful island, the closest U.S. base to Japan. In our outfit each officer was given responsibilities once our company was established. Lieutenant Musick was the commanding officer, and he decided officer duties.*

Q: He's listed on this roster as a troop commander, and altogether there are about ten officers. What was the nature of your work?

Dr. Barnes: Okinawa was to be a supply base if the U.S. decided to launch an attack on Japan. My company of 120 men was assigned to unload ships.

We would leave the base at 10:00 o'clock at night and work until 7:00 o'clock the next morning, when we were relieved by another shift. Each night I would assemble my 120 men, and we would go to the spot where we were to work. There I would assign persons to duties such as driving trucks and unloading trucks. I'd assign other people to go on board the anchored ships and bring the materials out of the holds. Others would load supplies onto landing craft, and others would bring the supplies back to shore. Other

---
*Lieutenant L. W. Musick, USNR.

people on shore would unload the supplies and put them on trucks. The trucks would drive them to another supply base on the island, where other men would unload them.

I had to make those assignments every night, and I had to know where everyone was and what his duties were. I drove a jeep, making the rounds to be sure that everything was working well. I didn't need to go out to the ships, because the ships' officers handled that area. But on shore we were responsible for getting supplies to the proper bases.

When my unit was relieved, I would return to the base and have breakfast, then try to sleep. As hot as it was out there, that was not the most pleasant kind of experience. After working all night and after eating, you really weren't sleepy. Then when we did go to sleep, it was so hot that one really didn't sleep that well. You'd probably get most of your sleep after dinner, when you'd probably catch about two hours, two and a half, three hours, before going back on duty. So I'd have to hold muster every night and muster every morning when we got back to the base. My troops got a citation for effectiveness.

One thing I recall very vividly about Okinawa was that two typhoons hit over there.

Q: Those were in the fall of 1945.

Dr. Barnes: I will never forget them.

Q: You had gotten there when--about June?

Dr. Barnes: Yes.

Q: This duty list from Musick is dated the seventh of June.

Dr. Barnes: That's right, and this happened in September. We had been in there a while when this first typhoon hit.

Q: I think one was in late September and one in October.

Dr. Barnes: Probably true.

Q: Both after the end of hostilities.

Dr. Barnes: That's true. We were still based on Okinawa. I've never seen such devastation in my life. The velocity of the wind was at least 150 miles and hour; that's where the needle dropped off. It swept across that island just like you'd take your hand and just wipe off the top of the table. Many tents were blown away. The wind shuffled the tin off the Quonset huts in which some persons lived. It was dangerous to venture out of whatever shelter was available.

Okinawans had a tradition. It's a very beautiful hilled country, and the natives would dig out the inside of a hill and establish a crypt. When a person died, he was fully clothed and placed in a box inside the crypt. At the end of seven years, a maiden who was a virgin would come and then scrape the bones off and put them in vases. Those remains were placed on shelves inside of these hillsides. When the Japanese arrived, they blasted open the entrances to the burial crypts. Since the caves were open and safe, that's where I spent at least 18 hours during the typhoons. I sat inside among these vases placed in tiers.

The way things were flying through the air, that was the safest place to be. You wouldn't walk around, because 2-by-4s and other materials were flying through the air like toothpicks. It was just an unbelievable scene. After the typhoon had passed, the devastation was overwhelming. It was hard to calculate the damage because bodies were being washed up on shore everywhere. I felt sorry for the Marines, because they lacked the shelters we had access to. They came to our base to eat, because the Navy, even under those circumstances, had daily hot meals. These poor Marines were eating K rations and C rations and anything else.

Q: Did the cargo stop flowing in when the war ended?

Dr. Barnes: No, but it slowed down.

After that I found I had the 52 points necessary for an honorable discharge.* I decided that I would leave. I made the decision to be discharged, even though a naval regulation was distributed which promised a promotion to the next rank for anyone who would reenlist for a minimum of six months. That would have meant the lieutenant rank for me, but I'd had enough of Okinawa by that time.

Q: What was your reaction when the surrender did come?

Dr. Barnes: Well, I think it was the same as everybody's: relief and exultation. It was unfortunate that the war ended the way it did, but it would have been a very, very bloody and extended war if we had tried to invade Japan. I don't know how much longer it would have taken. But it was a relief when Japanese surrendered. Of course, there was a lot of shouting and happiness when it happened.

After my discharge at Great Lakes in March of 1946, I went back to Oberlin, Ohio. My mother wasn't feeling well,

---

*For the demobilization of the U.S. armed forces after World War II, the services had a point system to determine individual priorities for leaving the service. Points were awarded for length of service, overseas service, battle stars, decorations, and dependent children. Those with the highest number of points were the earliest discharged.

and she still had the home laundry business, so I went back to Oberlin to help her and dad. While I was at home, I decided, "I might as well get my master's degree." Oberlin then offered me a position in two areas: as a trainer and a supply person. Those jobs would pay my living expense. Of course, I didn't need the assistance for tuition, because I had the GI Bill.* But I decided the working experience would be advantageous. So I was the athletic trainer and the supply manager in the athletic department at Oberlin College the year that I was there working on my master's degree.

After I got my degree, a friend of mine, who was the athletic director at Howard, came to Oberlin and asked me if I would join him as a coach and a teacher at Howard.**

Q: Did you get your master's in physical education also?

Dr. Barnes: I got it in both physical education and administration. I came to Howard after that. After seven years in both areas at Howard, as a coach and a physical education instructor, I was eligible to apply for sabbatical leave. That meant I could get a half year at full pay, or a full year at half pay, so I decided to go

---
*The GI Bill, officially the Servicemen's Readjustment Act of 1944, provided educational assistance and other benefits to all veterans honorably discharged with six or more months of active service after 16 September 1940.
**Howard University, Washington, D.C.

get my doctorate. Even before then, I was taking extension courses in the Washington, D.C., area from New York University and also Columbia University. I also had some doctoral courses from Howard. My request for a sabbatical was granted, so I decided to look into NYU and Columbia.

Q: This was in the early 1950s?

Dr. Barnes: Yes. I was accepted, but when I went to New York to visit both institutions, I found out that the person who was in charge of the physical education program at Columbia had made a declaration to the effect that no black would get a doctorate degree in that department while he was there. So then I went over to NYU. After interviews at both schools, I just decided not to remain in New York. I had already made application to Ohio State University, which was in my home state anyway, and had been accepted. So then I called my father in Oberlin and told him, "Dad, I'll catch an early train, and I'll be in Oberlin as soon as possible. Then I'm going to drive to Columbus and enroll at Ohio State and work toward a doctorate degree." I stayed at OSU for one year while I was still on leave from Howard.

I returned after that year to my positions at Howard and continued to work on my degree during the summer sessions at Ohio State. Finally, I took another leave of absence from Howard without pay and completed my degree requirements. During the period while I was still doing research on my dissertation, I lived at home in Oberlin, 120 miles from Columbus. I had to meet with my committee members, for everyone who is studying for a doctorate degree has an appointed committee. I would write daily at home, and then I would drive periodically to Columbus to show them my progress. After their critiques, I would carry their suggestions back to Oberlin. My twin sister Becky would type up the changes for me, and I'd take the revised material back to the committee members at an early date. I followed this round-trip travel for several months since every member of my committee would have to go over the dissertation and make necessary corrections or suggestions. This regular routine took me a whole summer.

Finally, my dissertation was completed and accepted. The doctorate degree was conferred in 1956. Though my mother had died, my father, fortunately, was still living. Both he and my wife were present at the time I received my doctorate degree. It had been definitely a very interesting experience, for while at Ohio State I was employed to teach as a graduate assistant. For every type of experience which I had, I do believe that experience played an important part in my life.

S. E. Barnes #1 - 94

Q: How do you think that the Navy experience helped?

Dr. Barnes: Well, the Navy experience did help me personally, because it reinforced discipline, teamwork, and a constant work ethic. But one of the things that I didn't appreciate about the Navy was the fact that many times the Navy, which is a microcosm of society, too often judged persons for promotion not on the basis of qualifications and performances but politically on the basis of whatever certain persons thought of one. That's not something that one could do much about. Notwithstanding that, one should always strive to do his job, be on the job, and do more than necessary--not because you expected accolades, not because you expected a pat on the back, but because you wanted to do it for your feeling of well-being and satisfaction.

Q: A sense of self-worth.

Dr. Barnes: That's right. And I think that this may have been an incentive for me to achieve. Another thing I did learn from the Navy was the value of daily inspections. They were so thorough that the slightest deviation from orderliness would result in a reprimand. I learned much in the Navy, and I will accept the fact that the Navy reinforced what I had already known. But I became more conscious of the implications and the value of always being true to oneself.

Q: Meeting high standards?

Dr. Barnes: Yes, meeting high and higher standards. Such advice has been helpful, and I certainly appreciate the parts that were strengthened in the Navy. Also not to be overlooked are the contacts which I made and the people whom I met. Many of those whom I met became friends for life. I have tried to live as though there was no one to judge me, except myself, because one must set and abide by the highest standards.

I say the same thing about our home. We are not going to clean up the house because guests are coming. The house will be clean because we want it clean. Friends are always welcome, but accept us as we are. Whatever we're eating, you're welcome to eat. We are not going to overdo just to make an impression. We don't believe in that. I don't believe that I have to strive to impress people. Accept me for what I am. I try to be honest, sincere, and to do what I'm required to do, in the very best way possible. That's the philosophy that was passed to me from my family and through the Navy.

Q: What discipline was your doctorate in?

Dr. Barnes: It was in administration.

Q: What was your dissertation on?

Dr. Barnes: My study was an attempt to ascertain the role of intercollegiate athletics within the total program of higher education. That included its influences in and on student life, its educational values, its effects on institutional morale, its public relations, and its relationships with secondary schools. The study hoped to direct attention to an area of higher education which demanded astute and careful appraisal of athletics within institutional educational philosophies, which do contribute to the aims and objectives of higher education.

Q: This is the title of your master's thesis: "Optimum Running for the Middle and Long Distance Races." That sounds more like athletics than administration.

Dr. Barnes: What we have here is administering a program within athletics. This is a very interesting thesis. What I did was take the running split-times of champion runners for middle and long distance races. In other words, my study was an attempt to show the recorded times of all these great runners. I researched all of their races I could locate, and I tabulated their individual times for the 880-yard run, the mile run, and the two-mile run.

The study was an attempt to devise a means of determining whether or not middle and long distance runners were being trained to attain the maximum of their efficiency as runners. The study was developed to evaluate the running patterns of champion runners, which indicated that these runners have a tendency to run closer to even times than "average" runners. A chart for the most favorable conditions of the optimum distribution of times based on the champions' patterns was established. It is believed that if the optimum chart is followed, champions will run more wisely, and average runners will run more evenly distributed races.

Q: And this was before a four-minute mile had ever been run.

Dr. Barnes: Yes. But I took championship times, and I checked the split times of champion runners and then calculated the possibilities necessary to run a four-minute mile. Since the completion of this study, the four-minute mile has been run many times. It would be interesting to follow the running patterns of those who broke the four-minute mile as compared to the patterns set up in the study. I started at one time to publish it, but I never did.

Q: The title of your doctoral dissertation was "Criteria for Evaluating the Administration of Intercollegiate Athletics." This indeed is administration. It's Ohio State University, 1956. What was the overall thrust of this one?

Dr. Barnes: Well, what I was trying to find out was the role of athletics in institutions of higher learning, and perhaps ascertain whether establishing standards for athletics in the country was necessary and imperative. What we were trying to determine was whether standards could be established whereby an individual school could evaluate its program. This we did, but it involved a whole lot of calculations.

Q: Is this in terms of academics?

Dr. Barnes: Yes.

Q: It would be interesting if you did the same study today. I would say that conditions have deteriorated.

Dr. Barnes: If I could follow the same criteria which I used then and have access to the same resources, it would be interesting to attempt a followup, just to see if a school would evaluate its program in terms of the level that they wished to maintain with integrity. It's gotten to the point now that the role of athletics and the use of athletics are ludicrous. Coaches, boosters, and alumni have assumed roles which are detrimental to the image of intercollegiate athletics. Too often we see evidences of where the tail--athletics--is wagging the dog--collegiate institutions. This is not only unconscionable but unforgivable.

Q: The almighty dollar has become the main criterion now.

Dr. Barnes: The colleges have seemingly lost control. One should not forget the academic reasons for being in colleges and universities. This is best stated philosophically by the president of Oberlin College, Ohio, S. Frederick Starr, who said, "Winning is not something that you should be ashamed of, but winning in the context of the philosophy of the institution is important." It's not a matter of whether one wins but rather how one wins. It's also what one learns. If you were to ask me, "What was the score of the Oberlin-Wooster game in 1936?" I would not remember. But I do remember something that I learned from that game, which I can certainly say helped me in later life, and I think that's what athletics should emphasize. We've lost the values inherent in athletics.

As we go back through the history of athletics, one will find that the historical rationale for athletics was to be a recreational outlet for students, especially for those who had the skills to participate at higher levels with others who had the same skills. However, athletics still remained part of and not apart from the stated educational philosophy of an institution. I mean, one wouldn't be playing if he weren't in college, and one went to college to obtain an education. However, that doesn't seem to be the case today. One has only to check the number of athletes who complete their eligibility without completing enough credits to graduate.

It's going to take time and effort to correct this imbalance, but somebody has to take the initiative. I recently read an article in <u>Sports Illustrated</u> about a booster at the University of Texas who favored firing the present coach and told the athletic director that the coach had to be fired. The article went on to insist that it is time that boosters not be given so much authority that they can dictate who is to be hired and fired. Darrell Royal was the coach then. He had done well during the time he was the head coach. He had won 78% of the games. That's apparently not enough. Coaches are expected to win all the games. They must always contend for the national championship. One has to be the national champion yearly. If not, one is a failure, no matter how much he contributes to the total development of his players.

Q: Only one school can win it each year.

Dr. Barnes: That's true but seemingly not believed.

Q: I would appreciate it if you would cover more about what you did at Howard. You said you went there right after you left the Navy and got your master's degree.

Dr. Barnes: Yes. When I went to Howard I was an assistant football coach. I coached the ends. I was also the boxing coach, the wrestling coach, and the assistant track coach. My boxing team was quite successful. In fact, I had an Olympic champion. In 1952 Norvel Lee won the light heavyweight championship in the Olympics over in Helsinki, Finland.

Q: Where did you learn to coach boxing?

Dr. Barnes: Same way I learned badminton. When I was told that I was to be the boxing coach, immediately I got a boxing book, read the book, and stood in front of a mirror. As I'd read the book, I'd take the various stances, and I would follow what it said. No one ever suspected that I didn't know boxing, because I would go to all the boxing matches, talk to boxers, read everything I could find. I even went to Jersey Joe Walcott's camp.* He was a friend of mine. I had three championship boxing teams for our conference. We went to the national collegiate boxing championship at Wisconsin University in Madison, Wisconsin, and I took four boxers to this tournament. We didn't win any championships, but our boxers did well. I was wrestling coach for only one year, because it was too difficult to coach two sports simultaneously. Being assistant track coach was something that I knew something about. Football was something I knew something about. These were the athletic activities that I was involved in besides teaching.

Q: What kind of a place was Washington to live in in those years, in the late Forties and early Fifties?

Dr. Barnes: There were few places one could go in Washington, definitely none of the hotels downtown. One couldn't eat in most of the places downtown. I understand from some women that if they went into Garfinckel's and wished to try on a hat, they were required to put a shield on their heads. It was very embarrassing, and it was

---
*Joe Walcott was world heavyweight boxing champion in 1951-52.

difficult to accept. One had to ride in the back of the buses and accept all types of discrimination. The same kinds of things that were happening in the South happened in Washington.

I can remember driving east from Washington and not being able to stop anywhere en route to go to a restroom between here and New York. Of course, this treatment was both embarrassing and frustrating, which was just a continuation of the same kinds of obnoxious treatment that occurred in too many places during that time span.

Eddie Jackson asked me to go to Howard as a coach and teacher. I stayed at Howard for 24 years, then left in 1971 to go to the District of Columbia Teachers College. While at Howard I was selected to be both the athletic director and chairman of the physical education department, positions I held until the year before I left Howard to accept a professorship at D.C. Teachers College.

After I'd been at D.C. Teachers College a year, I was asked if I would become the athletic director and chairman of the department of physical education and recreation. Later, Federal City College was just forming, and the people there asked me if I'd be the interim athletic director. President Cooke of D.C. Teachers College permitted me to accept the position temporarily.* So I

---

*Dr. Paul Cooke, president of the District of Columbia Teachers College.

went over and helped out for one year.

There were some other things that I am really proud of. It's unfortunate that you have to say "first," because there are times when it should have happened before, but it didn't. Anyway, I was the first black to be an officer of the National Collegiate Athletic Association. I served as secretary-treasurer from '71 to '73. I was a member of the NCAA Council for ten years. Then the other honor was that I was selected as a charter member of the Athletic Directors' Hall of Fame. Then, being commissioned by the Navy. This year, 1986, I was elected as a charter member of the Heisman Athletic Hall of Fame at Oberlin College. These are things that I'm proud of.

Then the Naval Recruiting District, Washington, has given me plaques for my contributions to their recruiting efforts. In addition, I was an elected member of the United States Olympic Committee for six years. I was selected as a member of the official U.S. delegation to the Pan American Games in Cali, Colombia, South America, in 1971 and a member of the official delegation to the Olympic Games in Munich, Germany, in 1972. I feel that the experiences I've had have been very helpful in whatever else I may have been involved in. I don't feel puffed up about any of these exposures, but I'm happy about them, proud of them, for it makes me feel like perhaps, after all, that I might have made some contributions somewhere.

That, to me, is very important. I accept the recognitions with humility, and I accept them happily.

Q: This is the thing that Graham Martin feels a great deal of satisfaction about--being able to influence a great many lives for the better.

Dr. Barnes: Graham did influence many lives as a coach, as a teacher, as a citizen. He was involved not only in athletics at the high school, Crispus Attucks, but also in community activities in Indianapolis. As I said before, Graham was a very soft-spoken, inauspicious person, but he was very unselfish. As I recall "our" guys, there wasn't one that I feel wasn't sincere in what he was doing and what he had done, and that all efforts were made to help in any way possible, whomever possible, whenever possible. I think that's the one thing that I really admire about the guys who were the Golden Thirteen.

I guess you know that at one time there was some thought given to try and get a ship named after the Golden Thirteen, but, of course, the traditions of the Navy would not permit that. But I understand now that they're thinking very seriously of naming a dormitory at the Officer Candidate School up in Newport, Rhode Island, after the Golden Thirteen.* I don't know too much about it. This is what I hear. I got a letter from Jack Dille, who again has pushed this project all the way up to the Secretary of the Navy, through Senator Lugar, who is a friend of his from Indiana.** Jack has really been in our corner every step of the way.

So these kinds of efforts are very, very humbling, but by the same token very, very satisfying.

Q: Could you address some of the differences in roles between being a coach and the athletic director. This really called upon your skills as an administrator.

Dr. Barnes: Yes. Actually, it's much more difficult than people think, to be an athletic director, because the athletic director is responsible for the total athletic operation. Whatever's right, you get credit. If it's wrong, you also accept that. One has to actually and constantly deal with different personalities in different sports. Each person thinks his program is the most important. The football coach wants a whole lot, as do the basketball coach, the track coach, the golf coach, and the

---
*Instead, a recruit in-processing facility at the Great Lakes Naval Training Center was named in honor of the Golden Thirteen in 1987, the year after this interview. For details, see pages 260-263 of The Golden Thirteen: Recollections of the First Black Naval Officers (Annapolis: Naval Institute Press, 1993).
**Senator Richard G. Lugar (Republican--Indiana).

wrestling coach--all of them constantly looking for more and more. Well, there's only so many pieces one can get out of a pie. The athletic director is not only responsible to the administration, but he's responsible to the coaches. He must be responsive to all. He doesn't get the accolades, he doesn't get the notoriety, he doesn't get the recognition the coaches get, but he has to carry the burden, and he's the one who must accept responsibility. Even though he may not have been the one who did a particular thing, he still has the responsibility of it.

Coaching, I think, provides a personal kind of satisfaction, because one can see individual development. When you're the athletic director and in charge of the entire program, there are no identifiable individuals, because all of them are part of the wheel. But as a boxing coach, I could see a person developing. It was a one-on-one kind of a relationship, and I could help each one individually. So, actually, as a coach you're not only the coach, but you're also a father figure, you're also a pal, you are the confidant. It's a very, very responsible position.

Those coaches who take the total welfare of their players seriously may not be successful in terms of wins and losses, but the contributions they make to the lives of these young men are incalculable. For that reason, I would say that I got more satisfaction from coaching than I ever got from administration. As I said, it was because of the one-on-one relationship that I had with the players, and to see them developing, you feel a part of their lives. Though very understanding, I had to know when to apply the whip and when not to apply it. With some people you've got to be more harsh than with others. Some you've got to sympathize with; others you've got to figuratively kick in the hind parts. So one is a psychologist dealing with different personalities with whom you're involved, to mold them into one cohesive unit where everybody is working toward the same objective, without any one person feeling superior to any other person. They're all part of the whole. To answer your question, yes, I got more satisfaction out of coaching than I ever got out of administration.

Q: You're the guy who had to pick the coaches too. What criteria did you use?

Dr. Barnes: The criteria I used were the same criteria that I learned earlier. First of all, I wanted an individual who was sincere and who really was less concerned about himself and who was concerned with the development of his players. Wins and losses, of course, are important, but I wanted to see somebody who was involved in the development of young men, not only physically but also emotionally, socially, and, if necessary, psychologically. A coach has to be available at all times to his players when they need him, because he is the person to whom the individual is responsible. He actually has more practical involvement than even the person's parents, because he's with them every day.

I would look for a coach, then, who really considered the welfare of his players above whatever ambitions he might have had personally. So I selected on that basis. And, of course, you can't ignore what kind of experiences he has had. The record is important, yes, but more important is the relationship he had with his players, with the administration, with the student body, the faculty, and the alumni.

The coach is really a sort of a public relations person. He is the one who has to set the tone, and he's the one who must maintain the image. Sometimes he must do it at a cost to himself, because he has to say no sometimes when it's practical and plausible to do so. There's only so much money; therefore, it has to be spread out with everyone given a fair share of it. But some coaches are more ambitious than others and expect more and demand more, and so it's a constant psychological thing.

Then the athletic director is working when everybody else is asleep. He's got a budget to prepare. He has to present the budget, justify the budget to the administration. If more is needed, justification must be made for it. At the end of each year, the athletic director must show how and where the budget was spent. He must remind the coaches sometimes that there are certain things which can't be done, not only because there is no available money, but because it's impractical. I liked coaches who are impartial--I mean, coaches who apply the same pressures to the whole team, not picking out any one individual and treating him one way and another player another way. He applies the rules equally to everybody. I think fairness is the word that I want to use--fair and equitable in his disciplining.

Q: And also being with the NCAA, you have a special consciousness of meeting standards very scrupulously.

Dr. Barnes: The NCAA, I think, does a good job, in spite of the fact that there has been a lot of criticism placed on it, especially on executive director Walt Byers, whom I admire very much.* I know what Walt has been through, because I was on the council for ten years. Walt did a lot to stabilize the collegiate athletic situation, in spite of the fact that he was not popular in many instances because he was so stringent in his disciplining. He said, "You just can't do this."

---
*Walter Byers, executive director of the National Collegiate Athletic Association, 1952-87.

There were ambitious people in the NCAA institutions. When I first went on the council in 1950, the NCAA guide was very thin. Now it's almost like a Bible. The number of rules and regulations contained in that book are just unbelievable. There are set rules for every exigency that has arisen or will arise. There are individuals who can find ways and means to get around anything. Then a rule must be established, and the rule must be applied. Then resolutions are added constantly. The NCAA manual is thick and getting thicker each year. So I don't know whether that answers your question or not, but that's my attitude and feeling about it.

Q: A good many of the rules, I'm sure, came about because somebody else found a loophole, and you had to close it.

Dr. Barnes: When you close one hole, it opens another one. You know, it's just gotten to the point now where one really needs the athletic director, especially, to be conversant with all of the rules. The one thing that I used to do when I was an athletic director was sit down with each coach and explain what the purpose of the institution is, what the philosophy of the institution is, and that we don't deviate from that position. If one does, then, of course, he doesn't fit into what is considered a vital part of the institution. The tail doesn't wag the dog. In many instances, I found that the coaches were very amenable; some were not.

I also know that it's very difficult to be democratic in a non-democratic situation. I had people--if you treat them fairly, were all right, but others would take advantage of that attitude and would deliberately put one in a position where you're going to be embarrassed when it wasn't necessary. But sometimes coaches are self-seeking, self-serving, and sometimes place their own ambitions above the philosophy, the ideals, and the aims and objectives of the institution and the department.

I tried to arrive at all decisions with everyone involved. I didn't make decisions which everybody didn't know had been made and had been agreed to. But once a position has been agreed to by the majority, it became a policy. I accepted that. And I don't believe in digging holes just because it's my prerogative to do so. However, if that is what the majority feels is right to do, then, of course, it's the thing to do. But I don't think I was very successful at that, because I think I was too democratic in an undemocratic situation.

One of the things I learned--too late--was that you can't be loved and respected at the same time. You have to make the decisions. You just have to take a position. As long as the position is right, then you stand on it.

Popularity is not anything that an athletic director or any administrator should be concerned with. One can't be popular and efficient, and I believe that.

Q: It's nice if you can have that, but that shouldn't he the determining factor.

Dr. Barnes: But very often it is. I know it was in my case. As I look back upon it, I know it was a mistake. If I had it to do over, there would be a difference in the handling of problems altogether, because one can't be kind to the exclusion of being effective. You just can't do that. These are the feelings I know. It's just something you have to ignore, how you feel about a person and so forth. "This is how we're approaching it, this is how it is. Do you or don't you agree? If you don't agree, then let's part company. If you do agree, then you've agreed that we're going to do it this way. I'm not going to interfere with your practices; I'm not going to say to you what play you should run or anything of that sort. That's your business. But as long as it stays within the philosophy of athletics, I have no problem with it. If the money's there, use it. If it's not there, then don't try to use it."

Q: During that long tenure at Howard, you, of course,

observed a lot of changes in American society. What changes in your program came about as a result of a much more integrated society?

Dr. Barnes: Well, actually, I don't think that affected us that much. We had a few white players while I was there. We didn't have that many, so it really was incidental. We played and scheduled white schools. At that time, desegregation had begun to set in, so it really wasn't what it was when I was at Livingstone. At Livingstone you didn't even consider playing against a white team. It was always against the institutions who were black. But at Howard, because of the Howard name, and because of its recognition and location, it was not difficult to schedule other schools. I always left it to the coaches to determine at what level and what schools we would schedule. "We're not going out here, for instance, and schedule Notre Dame. We're not going to schedule Ohio State. But who do you feel that you have an equitable chance against? Thinking of the resources and all the other things to take into consideration, what do you think?" After such discussions, we would set up schedules.

But in the area of segregation, I never ran into that at Howard. The schools that we wanted to play, who would play us, a lot of it was because of the relationship that I had established with them in the NCAA. We set up what we called the Athletic Directors' Association here in the District, and I knew the athletic directors at Catholic, at American, George Washington, Georgetown, Maryland. There were six of us, and we would meet once a month over lunch. Each month one of us would host the meeting. We always met at Bish Thompson's restaurant on Wisconsin Avenue. Only one of those people still active now is the athletic director at American U., Bob Frailey.* But we met regularly and exchanged ideas. As a result of that relationship, I was able to schedule Maryland, which wouldn't play us in soccer before. We had good soccer teams, so I said to the athletic director over there, "Why don't we play each other?" We would laugh and joke, and I'd say, "You don't want to play us because I'm black."

"Oh, Barnes, you know that's not so. We'll play you."

"Fine, let's set up a schedule." So we not only played Maryland, but also American, Catholic, and Georgetown. It was on that type of mutual respect that we competed against schools we had not been able to schedule before. So to answer your question, I didn't run into any problems with scheduling white schools, although the majority of our program involved games against black institutions.

---

*Robert Frailey was athletic director of American University from 1964 to 1987. Altogether he was part of the university's sports program for 39 years, including his service as an athlete and coach.

Q: I've heard one ironic twist on all this, that Jake Gaither at Florida A&M, for example, lamented the fact that he was not getting as many good football prospects as before integration set in.*

Dr. Barnes: True. You see, the reason for that is that Jake had a "lock" on Florida. Many of the coaches in the black high schools were his former players; therefore, the majority of their players were funneled to Jake at Florida A&M. But when desegregation set in, and coaches at other Florida institutions began to recruit the outstanding black ball players, Jake wasn't getting the cream of the crop anymore. He was still getting good ball players, but he was now being challenged for the cream of the crop. He no longer enjoyed carte blanche in Florida, and it certainly affected the program at Florida A&M. However, Jake's presence was still respected, and he set a standard at Florida A&M that's been very difficult for succeeding coaches to match. It's unfair too, because they were always working in Jake's shadow. Jake was an extraordinary person, well respected.

He was respected always in the coaching circles

---

*Alonzo S. Gaither joined the football coaching staff at Florida A&M in Tallahassee in 1937 and became head coach in 1945. At the time of his retirement in 1969, his record as head coach was 203-36-4.

nationally, just like Eddie Robinson is at Grambling.*
Eddie was a president of the National Football Coaches'
Association. He was president of the NAIA.** He was
respected on the basis of his ability and successes.
Although there are persons who resent the fact that he
surpassed Bear Bryant's record for collegiate football
wins, they still respect the fact the Eddie conducted
himself in a manner which was beyond reproach.***

I think that has a lot to do with bettering
relationships between coaches of different races. I don't
like having anyone say to me, "You know, you're different."
I'm not different because I don't believe there's any color
on sincerity, honesty, dedication, commitment; I don't
think there's any particular coloration on these
attributes. However I act, it's not because I'm trying to
ape anyone or because I'm trying to impress. This is me.
And that's the way I look at it. I think people are more
apt to respect you if you respect yourself and are
respectable. I really believe this. It might take time
for some people to respond positively, but as I said, just
like on Okinawa, it did not matter to me how those white

---

*Eddie G. Robinson, head coach at Grambling University, Grambling, Louisiana. In 1985 he won his 324th game as head coach, setting a new record for college football.
**NAIA--National Association of Intercollegiate Athletics, an association for small schools; it is comparable to the NCAA, which is a federation of larger institutions.
***Paul W. Bryant is best known for his tenure as head coach at the University of Alabama from 1958 to 1983. His record as college coach included 323 game victories.

officers reacted to me. I knew who I was, I knew where I was going, and I didn't feel that I had to do certain things or act in certain ways in order to impress people. I didn't then and I don't now.

There are two things I don't practice; one of them is that I wear no man's hat. By that I mean I want to live in such a way that at no time can anyone say to me, "You owe me one." I don't owe anyone anything. So I may not be popular, and I may not be in the inner workings of an organization, or whatever else. I'm not going to be in high society; I'm not going to be a visible person. I'm not going to be that recognizable. But I have to live with myself by being myself. This is what we try to get across to our youngsters, that when you live a respectable life, be respected, you have one thing going for you, and that is you have the satisfaction of knowing you've done the best you can do, and you're tried to hurt no one. So I feel that, regardless, I have done more good than I've done harm. The harm that I've done was not done deliberately, but if it was accepted that way, there's nothing I can do or say about it.

Q: You've talked about the value of setting an example. I think one very vivid case there is that your son Michael has gone into the Navy. Perhaps you could talk about that, please.*

Dr. Barnes: My son got the same advice and opportunity when he came along as our parents gave us: "You can go as far as you want to go. We'll help you." He went to Howard University for a while, and he wasn't happy with that experience. So then he dropped out and took a job in the government, and he remained there for a while, but he wasn't happy there either. The next thing I knew, he had joined the Coast Guard, mainly because his aunt and uncle told him it was a very selective service, and they felt he would probably do better there than he would in another branch of the services. So he went into the Coast Guard, where he stayed for four years.

Those years made quite a difference in him. We noted the difference, and it was not, we thought, one that we were particularly proud of. After that tour, he decided he would go back to college. So when he came home, he enrolled at the University of the District of Columbia. He remained for one year. So then we sat down, and we talked. I said, "You know, Mike, you're going to have to make a choice what you want to do, and you don't seem to have a marketable skill. Why don't you give the Navy a chance? It has much to offer."

---
*During a break in one interview, Mrs. Barnes made the point that Michael Barnes is the only son of a member of the Golden Thirteen now on active duty in the Navy.

He thought about it, and the next thing I knew, he said, "Dad, I think I'll go into the Navy." So he joined the Navy. He did, from time to time, threaten to get out of the Navy, for whatever reasons he had.

So I said, "Well, that's your decision to make, but I would think very closely about certain things. Number one, what marketable skill do you have? If you come out, what are you coming out to? And what are you coming out with? Because I hear that times have changed, and jobs are not out here beckoning and waiting for you. People are losing jobs who have been on those jobs for years and years and years." I also said, "Not only that, but it's gotten to the place now where the competition is very stiff. Unless you have an extraordinary skill at something marketable, you're not going to find it easy out here."

His two sisters have both been very successful. One of the daughters, Michele, who is the eldest, lives in Knoxville, Tennessee, and is an associate professor at the University of Tennessee in special education. She's thought of very highly there and is now on tenure. She didn't cost us anything in college. She graduated from Howard University as a Phi Beta Kappa.

The other daughter, Alexa, is an architect. She attended Howard University in the school of engineering and architecture. Upon graduation she received her master's degree in architecture from Harvard. Now she is a partner in an architectural firm in Westchester, New York, and she's doing very well. Her picture appeared recently in Ebony magazine as one of the foremost female black architects in the country. She's very talented. She's what I call a perfectionist. When she was a youngster, she would draw pictures and then she'd tear them up. When we would ask, "Why did you do that, Alexa?" she would reply immediately, "It ain't right. It's not the way I want it."

We would say, "Well, honey, you know you have to build on each of these kinds of things, and everything isn't perfect every time. So don't be so critical of yourself." Well, she's that way now, and the jobs that she completes are extraordinary. Her partners have great respect for her work. In fact, when her present partners opened their firm, one of the first recommendations they got was about her from her employers at the time. She was interviewed, was hired, and today she's a partner and is doing very well.

She also liked art. Now, that picture you see next to the steps leading upstairs. That's what she calls a conglomeration. What she did was to try and picture what she called the "typical black." So she researched magazines, journals, and newspapers. Out of one source, she would find the eyes that she wanted; in another one she'd find a nose; in another one she'd find a chin; in another one she'd find the hair; in another one she'd find the lips; and so on. Then she put her choices together, and she came up with what she said was "typical." At first she was going to be an artist, and we said, "Well, honey, that's a fine field, but it's not very lucrative unless you become well known. There are many fine artists who are living under barren circumstances which I'm sure you might not particularly like. You have to remain low-keyed until you're discovered or you find yourself. So why don't you try something that's a little more practical? So she agreed, and therefore she chose architecture. It has turned out to be an excellent choice.

But I have to say that we have never compared Michael's choices with his sisters. We've never expected him to be anything other than whatever it is he sees for himself, but to be the best of whatever it is he chooses.

Q: What job does he have in the Navy?

Dr. Barnes: He's a photographer. He has 12 years of service, lately aboard the USS Eisenhower.* Michael is a third class petty officer. When I was on the Eisenhower, I talked to officers aboard the Eisenhower, and they all respected him and said he's a fine person, but "We just can't get him to push, and we know he's capable."

---

*USS Dwight D. Eisenhower (CVN-69), an aircraft carrier.

I asked him, "Michael, why would you be satisfied to be third class when you ought to set your goals higher?" Remember the old saying, "You shoot for the stars and you may hit the treetops." I told him, "You know, whatever decision you make, you have to live with it. You're 32 years old, but you've got a future to think about. You'll be surprised how soon you'll be older. You look at yourself now, you're 32, and you've got the vitality and so forth, you think you'll never grow older. But one day you'll look up, and you're 40. The next thing you know, you're 50. And before you know it, what have you got? You ought to prepare for that now, because it's like money in the bank. If you don't put any in, you won't have any to take out." But, like I say, that's a decision he has to make. He's responsible for his own future.

Q: To bring your story with the Navy up to date, it was in 1977 when the Golden Thirteen got together again. It was like you'd been rediscovered after all these years. Could you hit the highlights on your reunions?

Dr. Barnes: We met again at the first reunion in Berkeley, California. Nelson was responsible for that reunion. I'm sure the other fellows would agree to that. Nelson remained in the Navy, and while on active duty wrote a book.* Thus he was responsible for keeping the pressure on to bring us back together again. So in '77 we received word that the Navy was inviting us to our first reunion since we were commissioned. With the exception of Nelson, I had not seen any of the others since we'd left Great Lakes 33 years earlier. To see those fellows again for the first time made that reunion one of the most heart-rending experiences you can imagine. We hadn't seen one another for years, yet we retained the same close feelings about one another. When we met in Berkeley, our wives were also invited.

We decided then that we had a responsibility to assist the Navy whenever and however we could. We would decide how and in what ways we could be of assistance to the Navy in their recruiting program. So we committed ourselves and dedicated ourselves to that program. Since that time we have made contributions. We formed assistance committees within our individual communities of persons whom the Navy would perhaps never meet. They are influential people, and we made these contacts available to the Navy recruiters. We developed meetings in Boston, in Dayton, and in Washington, D.C., and we're continuing in other communities too. Baugh was very active in Boston. Cooper was elected president of the Navy League in Dayton. I try to be active in Washington, D.C. I received an invitation to join the

---
*Dennis D. Nelson, The Integration of the Negro into the U.S. Navy (New York: Farrar, Strauss and Young, 1951).

local Navy League.

The reunion in Berkeley brought back all the things that had happened when we first met in the commanding officer's office in 1944. I didn't know the fellows then, for we were strangers to one another. But being thrown together in this situation drew us very close to one another. We shared one another's ambitions, one another's hurts, and one another's anguishes during our experiences as officer candidates. When we saw these guys out there in Berkeley after all those years, it was just unbelievable.

Since that first reunion, the Navy has given us a reunion every year. The second year was in New Orleans; the third year was in Orlando, Florida; the fourth year was in Washington, D.C.; the fifth year was in Boston; the sixth year was in Dayton, Ohio; the seventh year was in Indianapolis; the eighth year was in Memphis, Tennessee; the ninth year was in Philadelphia; the tenth year was in Oakland. The 11th year, if the Navy still wishes, will be in Chicago.

We have lost five of our classmates since 1944, and I'm sure the fellows have told you the order in which our shipmates passed.

Q: Lear, I guess, was the first.

S. E. Barnes #1 - 126

Dr. Barnes: Lear was the first, then Phillip Barnes, then Reginald Goodwin, then Dennis Nelson; the last one to pass was Dalton Baugh. But the rest of us always look forward to getting together, for it's an opportunity to compare what we've done and to keep alive the class feeling that we have always had for one another. It has been and still is very close, very close.

Q: Lear's death was a very sad thing. What are your perceptions of how that came about?

Dr. Barnes: Well, I really don't know, even though in 1944 Lear and his wife Blanche lived at the same private home where Reginald Goodwin and I stayed in Lake Forest, Illinois, since we were not permitted to live at the BOQ.* After I had come out of the service, my wife and I remained in touch with Mr. and Mrs. Alphonso Williams, with whom I lived, and where my wife Olga stayed when she came out to visit me. When we were informed that Lear had died, we were shocked, and asked her what had happened. The way we understand it, and the way the information was given to us, was that Lear was very despondent because he really wanted to stay in the service. When he applied, his application was not accepted. The way it was told to us, he went to his wife's bedroom and was at the foot of her

_____
*BOQ--Bachelor Officers' Quarters.

bed, where he shot himself. That's the only information I have. I do know what I was told, which was that he took his own life.

Q: I've heard several different versions. One is that he was a very devoted husband and maybe found out that she was seeing someone else, and that would contribute to his feeling of unhappiness.

Dr. Barnes: Well, that's a possibility, but I really don't believe it. I think that Lear and Blanche were a devoted couple, and even if this rumor was true, Lear was not a person who would have killed himself, even if there were domestic problems. Knowing Blanche as we did, and knowing Lear for what he was, we can't believe infidelity was the issue. I'm not saying it wasn't, but I don't believe that he killed himself because Blanche was unfaithful. Now, there may be other stories out. There may have been certain possibilities that existed with which we were unfamiliar, but the story we received was that he took his own life because he was refused retention in the Navy at his present rank.

Q: If that's true, it's most unfortunate that it may have been a by-product of his commissioning. Had he just stayed in an as an enlisted man, maybe he could have made a career after all.

Dr. Barnes: Yes, I think the main factor there, perhaps, was the fact that he was despondent, because he wanted to stay in and would have, I think, stayed in. Now, what the circumstances were that negated that possibility, I still am not knowledgeable of that. I guess the only one who could answer that is the one who can't answer it, Lear himself. But living there with them, and from our impressions and their outward appearances, he was a devoted husband, and he and Blanche were a very happy couple. That's the reason why we were so surprised when we got the news.

Q: Going back to your experience on board the USS Kidd, I've gathered that was a real highlight for all of you.*

Dr. Barnes: Oh, that reunion was beautiful. We saw things that were just unimaginable. When we were in the service, these kinds of things were not available. But to see the technology which is involved now in the Navy is just unbelievable. We were aboard this ship for one week. The USS Kidd was one of the ships that had been ordered

---

*From 13 to 15 April 1982, the nine surviving members of the Golden Thirteen held a reunion on board the guided missile destroyer Kidd (DDG-993) at sea in the Atlantic. See PH2 Drake White, "Golden 13 Together Again," All Hands, August 1982, pages 8-11.

originally by the Shah of Iran. Then when he was ousted, the ordered ships were kept by the United States. So I said to the captain, "This ship, with all the sophisticated offensive and defensive capabilities it has, it has the firepower to combat threats coming from either the air, the surface, or beneath the surface. It has great maneuverability, capable of making complete turns in a minimal amount of distance, with superb speed. It is a self-sufficient ship."

The commander answered by saying, "We couldn't afford them."*

I asked, "What do you mean?"

He said, "I mean the United States could not afford these ships if they were building them for our own Navy."

It is a beautiful ship. Beautiful. Everything is done electronically. On many ships the captain remains on the bridge. On the Kidd, everything is done below decks. When we were in school, we learned how once given the longitude and latitude of a ship, the speed in knots that it was traveling, and in which direction it was traveling, we were then shown how to map out our firing strategy. We were taught that the first shot goes over the bow, the second shot falls astern. The third shot is supposed to hit amidships. We learned to calculate the above manually.

---

*The commanding officer of the USS Kidd (DDG-993) in 1982 was Commander William J. Flanagan, Jr., USN. In 1992, as a vice admiral, Flanagan became Commander U.S. Second Fleet.

S. E. Barnes #1 - 130

But that <u>Kidd</u> experience was really one that I shall never forget. It was a beautiful revelation. It was aboard the <u>Kidd</u> that Hair reappeared. Did Hair tell you that?

Q: Yes, he told me a cute story. He said when he came aboard, he asked for the captain so he could request permission to come aboard, and somebody said, "Well, the captain's not here."

He said, "Why not?"

He said, "Well, he got sick, because he thought you were the reincarnation of the Shah.

Dr. Barnes: Seeing Hair came as a big surprise but one of the most pleasant surprises, because we didn't know where Hair was. Nobody knew where he was. He explained it by saying it was the spelling of his name. Everybody spelled his name H-A-R-E, but actually his name is spelled H-A-I-R. We kidded him once he came aboard and we had our reunion, which was exciting after so many years. Then we kidded him, saying, "Hair, if you hadn't read that paper, you wouldn't be here now."

He asked, "What do you mean?"

"Because we know you passed [for white]. You decided it was better to be over there than over here, and your skin was light, and your hair was flaking. So all these years, you just passed. Maybe now you figured you were missing something, and when you read about us being aboard the USS Kidd in the paper, you decided to re-enter our race." He laughed, as we did. But that was our way of greeting him. We were truly elated to see him again. But it was really heart-rending. It was a joyous reunion. I wish that we could show you the pictures of his coming aboard and our greetings.*

Q: I've seen those pictures.

Dr. Barnes: Yes. Perhaps you could see how happy we were to see him again. That was just something great, great. It's been that way ever since then. Now, last year, when we went to Oakland, Cooper didn't join us, because his wife was ill. I guess he told you that she was bitten by his guard dog. That's the first one he's missed. Hair continues to remind us, "You owe me four trips."

We answered, "Well, if you hadn't been so damn ambitious and gone over the line, you would have been with us. But, you see, it's your fault. We owe you nothing, because it was all your fault."

He insisted, "You owe me some trips. I missed Berkeley, and I missed New Orleans." He also missed Orlando and Washington. He actually missed five meetings.

---

*One such photo, showing Barnes hugging Hair, is on the back of the dust jacket of the book The Golden Thirteen.

So we told him again, "That's the price you pay. No better for you."

But the experiences we have had, though, have been very satisfying. We look forward to these meetings, because it's the only chance we get to see each other. Sublett, Arbor, and White, who live in Chicago, have the opportunity to see one another more often, although I understand they don't see one another that often.

Q: That's what I understand also.

Dr. Barnes: No, they don't get together as often we imagined they would. We are pretty well spread apart. Cooper is in Dayton, Ohio; Martin is in Indianapolis; and I'm here in Washington. Reagan is really the farthest from all of us, for he lives near San Diego. So like I said, we always look forward to our meetings and get-togethers, for we remember what we went through together. Our closeness is something that will never change--never change. It will always be like that while any of us is alive.

Q: We've reviewed your entire life here this afternoon. To go back to your earlier years as a boy and young man, I'm wondering who your heroes were.

Dr. Barnes: My brother James was the only hero I ever had. People think that's funny. Some people say Joe Louis, some say Hank Aaron, Willie Mays, Jack Dempsey, and others whom I admire, but my brother was the only idol I ever had.* He was always my idol, has been, and will ever be. He was the only one who ever really made an impact on me, who made me try to do more than I knew that I was capable of doing. Because of my admiration and respect for him, I think I exceeded what I would have done or been had it not been for him, because whatever he did, I tried to do. What he said to me was gospel. He had a lot of influence on me, and still does today. The straight line which I try to walk is because of the emphasis that he put on excellence. He was my model. He didn't expect me to do what he didn't do.

One of my greatest disappointments came when he died. He was selected to be athletic director and basketball coach at Virginia State College. He said, "Well, kid, as soon as you come out of college [he always called me "Kid"] and when you get your degree, I'm going to hire you, and you're coming down here with me." And I looked forward to that. I was just one year away from that, because he died in 1935, and I finished college in 1936. I doubt that he would have hired me right out of college, but he might have. I did look forward to working with him on a more

---

*Joe Louis and Jack Dempsey were world heavyweight champion boxers; Hank Aaron and Willie Mays are in baseball's hall of fame.

adult level, but it never happened. But as I answer your question, he's the only idol I ever had. I never idolized anybody else--man, woman, or child. Outside of the Heavenly Father, he has been my only model.

Q: Now we come to the interesting point in which you and the other members of the Golden Thirteen can serve as heroes and role models. I think you have a useful role in that regard.

Dr. Barnes: Well, we try. We try to do that without being haughty or feeling that we are the selected few. The questions which have been asked us, "Why were you selected?" Well, as I told you earlier, I don't know. I have no idea. Because I'm sure there were others who were as qualified, and many others who were more qualified. But we have a responsibility. We made that pact together back there in 1944, which has been our guiding light; wherever we can be of assistance, we are willing to do what we can wherever we can. When we're introduced as the first black naval officers, you know, it's a real honor. But by the same token, we wonder why it took so long, because there were others, many others, who were deserving and had acquitted themselves admirably under adverse circumstances. It makes me feel that, yes, it was nice, but we aren't the only ones who should have been commissioned officers.

So what we do when we speak to groups or to individuals, and we hear, "Well, he's one of the first black naval officers," we realize that it means a lot to some people and we hope that it does. But we regard ourselves only as stepping-stones, upon which will be built a significant structure. Whatever we did, no matter wherever it was, or whatever it was, we did it sincerely. And we strived, as did the old man who crossed over a chasm and looked back. When asked why he, after he had crossed, had begun to build a bridge, answered, "Because behind is a young man who must cross this chasm tomorrow, and this bridge is being built for him." That's what we have tried to do, just build a bridge, because behind us we knew others would be following. We want the crossing to be easier for them than it was for us. So we accepted the challenge that--as the first black naval officers--we had an obligation to think of others.

Q: I think an important point to be made is not just that it happened to be you 13 or 16 that got the chance, but that you made the most of it, and thereby helped so many others get the chance later.

Dr. Barnes: That's what we hoped for. We see things now that we never imagined we'd see. First of all, we never imagined we'd ever see a black officer, and now we look up and we see black admirals. We didn't even consider that, because all we saw were enlisted personnel, and we respected these people who had petty officer stripes. We looked up to these petty officers, because all we saw were cooks, bakers, and steward's mates. Now and then we might see a boatswain's mate, but that was all. But once we were commissioned, our attitude was that the higher up one moves, the greater his responsibility. You have to remember, number one, from whence you came, and, number two, the responsibility you have for those behind you, so you've got to reach down and pull these people up. If we can do this by being a worthy image, by what we say or whatever influence we might have, we can be proud of our efforts on behalf of blacks and the Navy.

Q: Yes.

Dr. Barnes: In Washington we had one Naval Junior Officer Training Corps at Woodson High School. Jeff Pollard, who used to be here as a minority recruiting officer, and I were talking one day, and I said, "Jeff, it seems to me like more black youngsters should have the additional opportunities to see firsthand what a naval career has to offer."

He asked, "What do you mean?"

I said, "Well, you've got one NJROTC unit; it's way

out in northeast. So why can't there be another unit in another section of Washington?"*

He answered, "Well, first of all, it has been stated that there are no other possibilities for additional units, for the maximum has been reached, and there can't be any other program in Washington."

I said, "Well, Jeff, let's talk about the possibilities of having a consortium. There is a unit now at Woodson. Why can't students from other D.C. schools go there for their training?" So we discussed this possibility but finally decided against this option, because such an alternative could negate the possibility of getting an NJROTC unit at McKinley Tech.

So we continued to work, even though we got the same answer: "There are no openings." Captain Fitch from Norfolk visited McKinley Tech. At that time, however, the principal of the school didn't make a very good impression on him.

Later, Mrs. Topps came in as the principal. We talked to her, and she was very interested. We asked her if she would support our efforts to obtain a unit. She replied, "Of course. What is it we can do to assist you?"

---

*NJROTC--Naval Junior Reserve Officer Training Corps.

We explained why we felt that an NJROTC unit would benefit both the school and the students. Eventually, we persuaded Captain Fitch to return, and she really impressed him. She told him, "Whatever is necessary, we're willing to provide: space, personnel, whatever." Such a cooperative attitude quite impressed Captain Fitch.

After his visit, we talked with Colonel Raymond Smith, who was the officer in charge of all the high school military units in Washington. He was receptive and offered his support, but we still got the same reply: "No, there's no space." However, we continued working, because one never knows who's talking to whom at what levels. I talked with members of the Recruiting District Advisory Committee of Navy Recruiting District Washington, with which I was affiliated. The next thing we heard, out of the clear blue, was that McKinley had been approved for an NJROTC unit. An NJROTC unit was established, and it has been a positive influence at the school. The training has given interested and qualified youngsters an additional opportunity to see other career options which are available to them.

When I talk to groups or individuals, it's always Navy. But I don't, however, rule out their consideration of the other services. I do stress the waste of talent when one is unemployed, uninspired, and uninterested. One can walk the streets and get involved in a number of dead-end activities. So we're saying to them, "Look, here is an option. This is an opportunity, and it's available to you. Think about it. I prefer you consider the Navy, but if it's not this branch, the Air Force, Marines, Coast Guard, Army, and merchant marine are also available. Whatever you do, don't be inactive, because the devil finds things for idle hands to do." So I formed a minority committee of interested citizens in the community, with whom I talked and who know what the situation is, especially for the black kids. They are wiling to lend support whenever or wherever they can. This group has been a positive influence in the recruiting process.

Q: Before we turned the tape machine on, you showed me a picture of the ceremony at Robert F. Kennedy Stadium with the Redskins. Maybe you could cover that too, please.

Dr. Barnes: Naval recruiters had tried on several occasions to form a Redskins recruit company, but they hadn't been successful. So about four years ago I talked to Bobby Mitchell, special assistant to Mr. Jack Kent Cooke, owner of the Redskins.* Bobby is a friend of mine, and I told him what the situation was and asked him if there would be a possibility of a Redskin company. He

―――――――――
*Robert Mitchell had previously been a running back for the Cleveland Browns, 1958-61, and Washington Redskins, 1962-68, before joining the Redskins' front office.

said, "Let me talk it over with Mr. Cooke." As a result of his intercession, Mr. Cooke approved the idea of a Navy recruit company named for the Redskins. So I called the Navy and told them about it. I met with a chief petty officer, a lieutenant, and the commanding officer, and we went out to Redskin Park and had a conference with Redskins officials.*

We asked them if the Redskins would be willing to adopt a Navy recruit company and call it the Redskin Company. There would be no cost to the Redskins. They would lend only their name to the group, and the company would be inducted between halves of a football games when the Redskins would be playing. The Redskins officials would determine which game it would be. The first Redskin Company was formed about four years ago, and this company was inducted during halftime of an exhibition game. It was a very renowned group. During their boot training, they won 15 honors, which was the most for any recruit company during that period.

In one RDAC meeting last year, the idea of another Redskin company came up.** I was asked to pursue the possibility. So I called Bobby Mitchell again. I went out to Redskin Park and talked with him. Later, I contacted Captain Zuberbuhler, who was in command of Navy Recruiting

---
*Redskin Park in northern Virginia is the training facility for the Washington Redskins team of the National Football League.
**RDAC--Recruiting District Advisory Committee.

District Washington, and Lieutenant Commander Petty, who was the XO.* The enthusiasm began to build. During the meeting Bobby asked whether the Redskins would consider induction of another company during the halftime of one of the team's scheduled games for the season. Well, the way it worked out was unbelievable.

They decided on the Dallas-Redskin game, which was a long-standing rivalry. The Air Force had originally planned to participate, but later, for some reason, it decided to drop out. They were originally going to have an airplane fly over, but this event was also eliminated. So I talked to Jack Fauntleroy, who is a judge in the Superior Court of the District of Columbia and also a member of the minority committee. Jack was a Blue and Gold officer; he contacted the Naval Academy and requested the Navy band. So not only did the band perform, but also the Naval Academy drum and bugle corps.

This was a big induction ceremony. The Secretary of the Navy swore in the recruit company. Mr. Cooke was present. The Navy drill team also put on an exhibition. As a result of what I was able to do, I was honored with pictures of the ceremony. When the company graduated, the Navy sent Bobby Mitchell and me down to Orlando, Florida, for their graduation. Bobby presented the outstanding recruit of the company with an autographed football from

---

*Captain William Zuberbuhler. XO--executive officer.

the Redskins players, as he had promised them earlier.

Now, in that company was a recruit named Stethem. His brother was the one who was murdered and thrown out of the airplane in Lebanon.* The Navy received national publicity as a result of this Redskin company. I feel that we can make a contribution, and any time we can do something like this, we do it.

But, as I said, I have a fond feeling for the Navy, and I still feel that it's the premier service branch. But if I had a second choice, that choice would be the Air Force. The next choice would be the Army, then the Marines, and finally the Coast Guard. But I prefer the Navy, because I think it's a first-class operation, especially after the Navy officials got over their first shock of recognizing blacks other than as stevedores and cooks and bakers. There's still prejudice, and there are still some people who continue to hang onto their racist attitudes. But I recognize that the Navy is merely a microcosm of society, and the same kinds of feelings that are in society are also in the Navy. But generally speaking, I think there are genuine efforts to be fair--I really do. I think there are attempts to do what is right, both in words and, I believe, in actions.

---

*In June 1985, terrorists hijacked a TWA aircraft at Beirut, Lebanon, and killed Navy Seaman Robert D. Stethem, USN, one of the passengers on the plane. The recruits joined as part of the Redskins-Cowboys game on 10 November 1985.

Of course, actions always speak louder than words. If the Navy believes this, then let's see the results of it. But then I hold our people responsible too. I say to black officers and enlisted personnel, "I don't mind fighting, I don't mind pushing your case. So if you come to me with something, if you're genuine, then I'll pursue it as far as I can. But I'm not going to pursue anything which is going to embarrass both of us when we get an audience and find out what you've told me is not true. If you've done all you can and you still feel that you've been discriminated against, then in my judgment that's a fair case to follow up on and see what can be done about it. I know that I'm not influential enough to change any decisions, but I can certainly enlighten people as to what's going on." So this is my posture and will continue to be.

Q: You've made a great many contributions over your lifetime, and you've made another today by putting this on the record. I'm very grateful to you for that.

Dr. Barnes: Well, I'm sorry to hold you for such a long period.

Q: You need not apologize at all. I enjoy it.

Dr. Barnes: I'm glad, and I appreciate your interest. I

talked to George Cooper recently, and he said that he had received a transcript from you of his interview.

Q: Yes.

Dr. Barnes: I told him that you were going to be talking with me, but don't you disclose how long we talked, because the first thing George and I were saying was, "What the hell did Arbor have to talk about for four and a half hours?" [Laughter]

We said, "Well, hell, that's Arbor." Arbor, I'm sure, told you about the World War II Navy Veterans, because he's definitely involved with this organization. He's been wearing two hats. He's trying to get all of us interested and active as World War II veterans.* I haven't made a meeting so far, although I do contribute financially and will continue to do so, and look forward to attending future meetings.

Q: Any final thoughts?

Dr. Barnes: Nothing except I am very proud to be affiliated and associated with the Golden Thirteen, because they are, in my judgment, a group of fine persons. Over

---
*The black Navy veterans trained at Great Lakes in World War II have an ongoing organization that holds periodic reunions and publicizes the contributions the group made to the war effort.

the years my attitude towards them has not changed. I have and do feel very close to them and have the greatest admiration and respect for each of them. They're a really class group, and it's a pleasure to be one of them.

Q: Thank you very much.

Dr. Barnes: Thank you, sir.

S. E. Barnes #2 - 146

Interview Number 2 with Dr. Samuel E. Barnes
Place: Dr. Barnes's home in Washington, D. C.
Date: Monday, 30 January 1989
Interviewer: Paul Stillwell

Q: This is version two, Dr. Barnes, to fill in some of the things we didn't talk about before. We talked briefly about your parents' relative educational backgrounds. Could you go into more detail on that subject, please.

Dr. Barnes: Well, as we said before, my mother was a college graduate but my father wasn't. In fact, I don't think he finished more than high school. There were times when he might not have been in school, because he was working to harvest a particular crop to help sustain the family. Outside of that, we really had no discussion of schooling, because we accepted them as they were; we were very proud of them. My mother and my father were very, very well adjusted to one another, and whatever either one was interested in doing, the other was very supportive. There wasn't a feeling of insecurity on either part as far as the other was concerned.

Q: What were the types of things that your mother majored in when she went to college?

Dr. Barnes: She went to a small school, and even though she eventually taught for a while before being married, I don't believe she really went to college to make a profession of teaching. At that time, you remember, there weren't very many professional opportunities for blacks. One was either a preacher, a teacher, a porter, or in some other capacity of that nature. There were no persons in the banks and this sort of thing. So she did a lot at home. Finally, after she went away from home, she met Dad, and then they decided to get married.

Q: Did they really stress to you as children the value and importance of education?

Dr. Barnes: Oh, yes. In fact, they had made their decision that we would not only attend school and graduate and go to college, but they intended that we should all graduate, which we did. They had five children, and all of us had college educations. We were at different institutions; my brother, my elder sister, and I finished Oberlin. My twin sister finished Wilberforce, and my middle sister finished Howard University.

Q: So college was just taken for granted.

S. E. Barnes #2 - 148

Dr. Barnes: Oh, yes. They said, "You're going to school." There was never any question about that.

Dad was making at that time $25.00 a week as a chef in one of the dormitories at Oberlin College. He would go to work at 6:00 in the morning and wouldn't get home until 7:00, 7:30 at night. He always turned his check over every Friday to my mother, and that was added to what she was making from the laundry. She ran a bill at the college, and at that time, rather than to accept a full payment, she would only accept part. Then she would be on a sort of an ongoing thing for our college tuition, because at that time we didn't have any football scholarships, or basketball, so my brother and I couldn't use that as a means of helping out.

Q: Your parents had deliberately taken you to Oberlin because of its liberal approach on race questions. How much awareness did you have of the racial situation in the rest of the country--in the South, let's say?

Dr. Barnes: Oh, yes, we knew about the South from reading the newspapers. We knew that there were separate fountains, and there were separate toilets. One couldn't eat in the restaurants; you had to go around the back to get food, and so forth and so on. I knew about it; our parents didn't insulate us from it. They told us to recognize that it existed and that you make the best of the situation, so I never felt threatened.

I didn't like it, but I could live with it. When I went to teach at Livingstone College, I said, in effect, "Well, I'm no more interested in socializing with you than you are with me. I don't need to." Therefore, I didn't.

Within the confines of segregation, the white persons whom I met in the South were very, very nice. But there was something interesting, too, and that's the reason I use my initials, "S. E." You notice I never use my full name, because in the South people were always on a first-name basis. If they'd known my name was Sam, that's all I'd have been called. So when they asked me what my name was, I said "S. E. Barnes." When they asked me what the S stood for, I said, "It doesn't stand for anything."

"What does the E stand for?"

I said "Just E. My parents named me S. E. Barnes. That's what I am." So they never got to call me Sam. They would rather call someone "Professor" or "Reverend" before they'll call him "Mister." So I said, "Well, that's all right," but I never had that many real opportunities for socializing. I would meet white people and speak with them, but that was the extent of it.

Q: What do you remember about travel conditions?

Dr. Barnes: One of the things that I really and truly recall vividly is that from Oberlin we went to Wellington, a little town about nine miles away, where we would catch the train. Now, I rode wherever I wanted on the train from Wellington to Columbus. In Columbus, I had to change trains to get on the Southern, going down to North Carolina. As long as I was in Ohio, I had no problem. But once I started south, then I had to leave the coach I was in and go to the segregated coach, which was right behind the coal car. That was the closest thing.

It was just interesting, because up to now I sat where I wanted and I didn't see anybody who felt uncomfortable. I was never able to fully accept it, but there was nothing to be said or done about it because doing so would have brought a very, very unhappy circumstance.

Q: So you'd deliberately avoid the situations where you perceived you could get some unpleasantness.

Dr. Barnes: That's right. You could sense it, and so there was no point in trying to battle it except maybe in subtle ways. But nothing ostentatious, because you know there's only one end to that problem. You had no opportunities for redress, so you just didn't get involved.

Q: How much enjoyment did you derive in the Twenties and

Thirties from the black culture: athletes, entertainers, literature, and so forth?

Dr. Barnes: Well, they were always role models. I didn't appreciate it then as much as I do now, what they endured and the kind of circumstances that they went through. But they maintained a dignity, which is the one thing that I really and truly remember about it. Whatever they did, it was done with dignity, and it was done without confrontation. But it was a situation in which the individual proved, by virtue of the type of person he or she was, that, "You don't have to like me, but you have to respect me."

I still have that same attitude, and I tell the kids the same way. I said, "One thing that you must accept, you were born black. Nothing will change that. So what you have to do now is to take that where you are and move out to where you can go, and stop talking about, 'Well, I can't get this because I'm black.' You knew that when you were born. You had nothing to do with it, any more than whites had anything to do with how they were raised and from whence they came."

That's what I learned from it. This was fostered by my parents, and certainly the coaches that I had in high school and in college were very instrumental in giving substance to the fact that the important thing is know who you are, what you're capable of doing. And regardless of what you meet, never forget that. You don't have to be confrontational in order to show that you are a person of dignity. The churches did that, too, which was all we really had.

Q: Did your parents talk to you specifically on the question of race?

Dr. Barnes: They didn't have to so much while we were in Oberlin because we never encountered it. But they made us aware of the fact that, "What exists here, you will not find everywhere, so you might learn to adjust to wherever you are. But never lose your dignity." They preached this all the time.

Q: Of course, it's kind of hard to respect somebody else's dignity when he's not respecting yours.

Dr. Barnes: That's the sort of thing you must adjust to. There's no win, so if you can avoid confrontation, you do so. You go about quietly making the kinds of adjustments which are necessary to exist. This is what we did.

Q: What was the role of religion in your family's life when you were growing up?

Dr. Barnes: Our parents insisted that we attend church. My father was a deacon; my mother was a trustee. And, of course, there were the church clubs.

On Sundays first we'd go to Sunday school, which was at 9:00 o'clock. After Sunday school we would join the church--except for my father, who couldn't come because he was cooking. We always sat in the same pew. After church was over, we'd go home and we'd have dinner. Then we'd go back to the church at 6:00 for a young people's meeting, which was called the BYPU, the Baptist Young People's Union. We sang in the choir; we were ushers. Whatever duties there were in the church, we did.

So the church played a very important role, and it substantiated what our parents had said to us time and time again. So the church was very, very strong in our backgrounds. There was no question about you attending whatever was necessary on Sunday. Sunday was a day given over to service in the church and the choir. So it was an all-day affair then, and the church has been very influential, because it was something our parents believed in, and they inculcated that in us.

Q: Well, much more so than today, the idea then was that Sunday was just an off day from what you did the whole rest of the week.

Dr. Barnes: Well, the Bible says, "Six days thou labor and the seventh shall rest." We believed that. We didn't work on Sunday; we were in the church all day Sunday. It was a central focal point of our lives, and our parents insisted that we attend church and be very involved in church activities.

Q: It sounds as if it was a social center also.

Dr. Barnes: It was. That's where you knew you would meet. Of course, in Oberlin, there wasn't a day go by that you didn't see most everybody you knew because the town was that small. Outside of that, the church was the center of our activities, except while we were in school, playing basketball or taking part in some school activity.

Q: Did you get from church, from your school, from your parents examples of achievements by black people that you could take pride from?

Dr. Barnes: Well, they made us aware of the struggles that had been going on from slavery times. At that time, you know, there weren't any books or any magazines especially for blacks. It really was not structured for anything, but you'd get bits and pieces, and, therefore, you would know that efforts were being made by individuals such as Du Bois and some of the others who were writers.* So we knew about the achievements of blacks. We knew that it was a struggle, but it was a worthwhile struggle. Therefore, whatever time, effort, and energy--and even blood, sweat, and tears--given to it were for a better world, a better life, if not for me but for those who might follow.

So those were the kinds of people who, in their ways, made contributions upon which were built the achievements and accomplishments of blacks that followed them.

Q: How much awareness did you have in those years of the role of the NAACP?**

Dr. Barnes: At that time it wasn't that strong, nor was the Pullman porters' union. I was out teaching when I first heard about the NAACP, the Urban League, and the Pullman porters' association, and so forth. They were rather late, see, because I'm talking about the Thirties. Very little done at that time.

Q: I know that Randolph was organizing the Pullman porters.***

---

*W. E. B. Du Bois (1868-1963) was an American editor, educator, and author.
**NAACP--National Association for the Advancement of Colored People.
***A. Philip Randolph organized the Brotherhood of Sleeping Car Porters in 1925.

Dr. Barnes: That's right. At that time, the persons who were the Pullman porters were all black. There were no white Pullman porters. So it was he who decided we ought to organize, and this way as a unified organization we would get more attention than we would if we tried to do it individually. That was one of the first efforts made at organizing a particular group of people to stand together, work together, and show how important their efforts and contributions were to the total picture.

It's interesting, because skin color seems to dictate many things, which to me are insignificant, because you had nothing to do with who you are. But what you do is the thing that we have always stressed. Who you are, you had nothing to do with. You couldn't select your parents, so you didn't have the same opportunity your father and mother had where they could, if they loved one another, selected one another. This is what they wanted. This is a different situation altogether. You had no power over that. They married, you come out as a whatever nationality and race. That shouldn't be the reason you are accepted and others aren't. It's too bad.

Some time ago someone said, "If suddenly we went to bed one night and the next day we woke up and everybody was the same color, we wouldn't have any more problems." So the problem is color, and that's true. If everybody became white, you'd have no problems. If everybody was black, you wouldn't have the problem of feeling more superior than somebody else because of the fact that you were one color, as opposed to their color.

Q: Did it bother you growing up, this notion that blacks are inherently inferior? How did you deal with that?

Dr. Barnes: Well, to tell you the truth, I was fortunate to grow up in a town like Oberlin. Actually we never encountered it, because it was a small town. Everybody knew everybody, and we all went to school together; we went to class together, and we never thought anything about it. It was never really stressed until I went south; that's when I saw the difference.

I never encountered it at Oberlin, except when we would go away to play high school teams in other cities, and we were called "niggers," and so forth and so on. We always had our teammates to support us, and we were not that far from home, so it really didn't make that much of a difference. It was like dropping water on us; it would flush off. You would just never let it touch you. Just play that much harder. So if somebody called me that, I would pay him back if he came around. I would see that he was tackled very hard, and I wanted him to know that I was there. But I never made an issue; I never pointed at him or stamped at him, or anything. You know, I just let him know that it's a game, and everybody in it is even. So that's the way we played.

Q: It gave you a little extra motivation.

Dr. Barnes: Oh, yes, oh, yes.

When I was in college, there were only two of us on the football team. We'd go to a place like Marietta, which is the southern part of Ohio, right across the river from West Virginia. You got a whole crowd, and there weren't any black spectators. You were there by yourself. Without the support of your teammates, anything could have happened. I never permitted that to influence what I did, but I was always prepared to take care of myself in case something like this arose.

Q: Did you ever have a sense of fear in those situations?

Dr. Barnes: No, I didn't because I was still from Oberlin. I was with Oberlin friends. We didn't have to live in Marietta; we didn't have to stay there. We'd play the game and go home. So at that time, I didn't have to worry that somebody would run down and lynch me or hang me from a tree or anything of that sort. I never worried about that. It never occurred to me.

Q: What was your view of, perhaps, the popular stereotype of the black in the media--the minstrel, the Amos and Andy type of thing?* How did you view that in those years?

Dr. Barnes: Well, actually, it was entertaining, and we always knew that this was not an example of what blacks really were.

But the black actors had to eat, and this was the only type of role that was available to them. Even now the stereotype sometimes exists. What they were doing was actually all that blacks were doing. You know, they were Pullman porters, they were house servants. And they were limited in what they could do, so that when they went in, that's what they had to do, because that's what they were known to be doing. We were not particularly proud of it, but we felt that if the only way they can get in there through the media, that's what they have to do.

Q: Even if the rules are rigged, you still have to play by those rules.

Dr. Barnes: That's true. You play by the rules. That's what it's all about. People will not have the same motives for stigmatizing you if you are not what they say they expect you to be. For people like Stepin Fetchit, that

---

*"Amos and Andy" was a popular radio comedy show in which white actors portrayed the principal black characters.

type of role wasn't anything they wanted to do, but it was all they could do.* There was no other roles available to them, so they did what they could where they were at the time. And even though they didn't reach the heights that they expected to reach, they made it better for the ones who followed, because they played their roles very well.

Q: It's truly ironic that the actors who played Amos and Andy were not black.

Dr. Barnes: That's right. They certainly weren't. Now, that sort of piqued us, because we felt that this was an imposition. Why would you paint white faces to play blacks when you had blacks who could play the part? But at that time blacks were not permitted, so they just used other people. But they characterized blacks in the roles that they had.

It's interesting, Paul, that some of these things we look back upon now are beginning to appear again. One thing was respectability. I don't have to accept you because you're white. I accept you because you're respectable and respected. That's all color means to me and always has meant that. But that's not true with many other people. For example, on the Geraldo show, we saw the

---

*Stepin Fetchit was the stage name of a black Vaudeville performer who performed in the minstrel tradition. He perpetuated the stereotype of the black caricature: grinning, shuffling, eye-rolling, and subservient.

skinheads and they had that fight.* See, we thought this sort of thing was dead. It stopped in the Fifties, but now it's beginning to rear its ugly head again. We're beginning to see a tearing apart of the respect, the respect that others had.

I think it's all exemplified in one thing which I remember, "You go to your church and I'll go to mine, and we'll walk along together." That says to me, "I will not attempt to change you. If that's what you want, fine." Just like drinking. I wouldn't tell you to stop drinking. If that's what you want, that's your business--as long as you don't impose that on me. Then you be whatever you want to be, go wherever you want to go, but just don't impose what you believe on me. Because I think that's unfair, and I think it's taking advantage.

If I know that a person is a racist, I'm not going to get into a discussion with him. Definitely not a confrontation, because when it's all over, who's gained what? You still feel the same way you do; I feel the same way I did, so what was gained from this? I can't make you respect me, but what I can do is to so conduct myself that in spite of yourself, you have to say, "Well, he's not the worst person in the world."

Q: So what you're saying is that you earn respect, even
___
*Geraldo Rivera has a sensationalizing television program that sometimes exploits the negative aspects of society.

though it may be grudging.

Dr. Barnes: I think that you command respect; you don't demand respect. I think when you demand it, it's something that is, in my judgment, demeaning. You should get it because you've earned it. But you don't go out and tell people that, "You have to respect me." I don't have to respect you. I will because of the way you carry yourself and the way that you do things.

This is what I've always believed, and this was part of our training at Oberlin. As I look back upon it, I can't think of any place that I'd rather grow up. If I had my druthers and had to go back over it again, knowing what I know now, that's where I'd go. That's where I'd want to be raised. That environment was just the type of thing that helped give substance to whatever or whomever I encountered later on.

I don't feel inferior to anybody, because our parents always told us that, "You're not any better than anybody else, but you're no worse than anybody else." So you live that way. You see, we're not in a situation where the king is automatically up here, you have to respect him because of his position. You respect people because of who they are and what they do, not as something you have to do because they happen to be such-and-such.

So that was good training. And now that I look back on them, I'm so glad that it happened when it did to me where it did.

Q: There are so many people who live with regrets about this, that, or the other. It's interesting that you feel so much satisfaction about the way things have gone in your life.

Dr. Barnes: Oberlin was the ideal place to be. It really was, and it still is. Of course, I don't know that many anymore because the persons in Oberlin now are the grandchildren of the persons with whom I grew up. So I don't know anyone. And the town has changed, as naturally it would. I don't have the same landmarks I used to have when I was in Oberlin.

The only ways we had for getting around were walking and riding bicycles. Students couldn't have cars at Oberlin College. Everybody had a bicycle. I could walk from my home on Main Street, which was going up town. I could go at noon, high noon, and never meet a soul, neither walking nor riding. It was just the truth. There just weren't that many people. Saturday night you could find everybody, because they had the band concert down in the middle of town. If you'd been a thief, you'd have had a gala time, couldn't you? People weren't home; they were all down there listening to the band. Kids were playing around; they had ice cream. It was an evening downtown every Saturday night. We would all go down there, and the kids would be running around, laughing and talking, sitting around drinking Cokes, or whatever. It was a very wholesome atmosphere--very wholesome and very friendly.

Q: Were the entertainment and the social environment essentially integrated?

Dr. Barnes: Yes. That was the kind of environment which was there. You'd see kids playing together. Parents were not scolding them and telling them, "Now you come away. Don't you talk to him." We never had that. The parents would be talking; the kids would be playing; the band would be playing and we just enjoyed it. There was never any racial tension that I can recall in Oberlin the whole time I was growing up. You'd get these epithets every now and then. Somebody might get mad at you and call you a nigger, or something like that, but it wasn't difficult to handle that situation because it was one on one. When it was over with, you put your arms around him and walk down the street, both of you bloody but undaunted.

Q: Were there any restrictions on where you could sit in movies or buses?

Dr. Barnes: No indeed, never a thought of it. You could get on the bus, wherever it was, and go where you were going. It was in Ohio. And we went to Cleveland, which is 35 miles away. Going to Cleveland then, when we were growing up, was like now if you go to New York or California. That was a big trip then. You'd run into some of it there, but we never had any problem.

Now, when I went to Cincinnati in 1941 to work in the YMCA, there was plenty of segregation. You couldn't even eat downtown, couldn't sleep downtown. If you ate, you'd have to go around the back and get it. You couldn't come in the front door. Cincinnati is just across the river from Kentucky, so it was around you all the time. They kept you informed and advised you of the fact that, "This is the way it is, and you're not going to change it. Take it or leave it."

Q: Ohio is such a big state. It's interesting there were that many differences.

Dr. Barnes: Yes. When you start going south in Ohio, you begin to run into problems. And Columbus and Cincinnati were really as southern a town as you could find anywhere. It wasn't as intense, but it was there. When we went to Columbus for the state tournament at Ohio State University, we had to sleep in the gymnasium or else in a house in a colored neighborhood. That was it. But I don't recall a situation where we had an all-out black-white fight. Never. We had individual battles, but never on a constructed basis, you know, where it was known, and that's the way it is and if you come here, that's the way you'll be accepted, because it's not going to change.

Q: As you were growing up there, going to grade school and high school, were there teachers who inspired in you a love of learning?

Dr. Barnes: I never had anything but white teachers in school while I was at Oberlin: in grade school, in junior high school, and in high school. But I never saw any differences from the teachers to their students. If you needed whipping, you got it, whether you were black, white, green, yellow, or gray. They didn't discriminate on color. If you did wrong, then you were chastised. If you did right, then you were given the respect. But they were very close.

Q: I don't know what percentage of people in our society have Ph.D.s; I suspect it's very small. Somebody must have really given you a boost or several somebodies to get you to go that whole road.

Dr. Barnes: It started with my parents and was supported by my teachers and my coaches. When I went down to Livingstone at that time, you could count the number of black Ph.D.s on your hand and have fingers left over. But it was always there, and that's what you aspired to be. If I stayed in teaching, I knew I would have to have advanced degrees in order to do it. Plus I'd be better prepared to teach. I knew that when I went to Howard that I would have to have a doctor's degree if I was to stay in teaching at Howard. That was a way of ensuring that I would have a job which would make it possible for me to support my family.

But you always had that desire, that inspiration to continue, go as far as you can, as long as you can, when you can. So it was never a thing where you say, "You can't do this, you can't do that because of this or because of that. You never accept less than your potential and your ability. If you have it, you'll be remiss not to profit from it."

So, yes, I was given that in Oberlin at all times. My best friend in Oberlin was a youngster named Everett Lampson whose mother taught at the college. He and I were close all the time. He was a quarterback on the football team; I was an end on the football team. I'd go to his house; he'd come to my house. We never felt uneasy about visiting our friends in their homes; and they never felt bad about our blackness. And their parents treated us like anybody else. It wasn't a matter of, "What are you doing bringing him home?" Never that. And my mother never questioned why was Everett coming over to the house. He came over to the house because we were friends, and that's the way it was. I believe that I came up in an exceptional situation. I really and truly did.

The older I get, the more I respect that, because this was unusual. This society wasn't that way for many others. But it was the thing that gave me the motivation and sustained me at times when I really and truly needed it. And I always look back on that. It's sort of like closing your eyes and imagining where you are or where you would like to be, and open your eyes and you're there. And that's the way it was. I'll never forget it as long as I live.

Q: Did you enjoy reading and learning for their own sake?

Dr. Barnes: Well, in Oberlin, you see, in high school everyone was on what they call a college track. It was known that when you got through, you were going to college. Now, later they had what is known as the industrial arts, which was for those students who were not interested in going to college. They preferred to get into an occupation which they knew they could capitalize on immediately. So I didn't go. But as I look back now, I wish I had gone, because some things now that I could do if I had learned, like brick work, masonry, auto repairs, carpentry, whatever--those kids had it. I think it's good to have a mixture of both, and I'm sorry that I didn't.

In the black community, people always felt that you should not be less than you're capable of being. So they pushed; even the older persons who didn't have an education themselves were educationally conscious. They'd always say, "Well we didn't have it, so we want you to have it. So what we didn't have, we expect you to have. What we can do, we will do."

It was just a part of our training. I mean, it wasn't something that they took you aside and sat you down and talked to you about. But it was always present, it was always present. The atmosphere actually inspired you and encouraged you to do this. Because if you weren't, somebody would mention to you, "What are you doing? Why aren't you doing so-and-so?" They did not accept less than what you were capable of doing.

My parents never accepted poor grades. They said, "You can do better than this." They would place certain restrictions on us if we didn't, because they said, "Education is free. You're stupid if you don't take advantage of it."

Q: What kinds of restrictions?

Dr. Barnes: Well, for instance, you'd have to stay home. You couldn't go to a party. In our family we always had to be in the house. When we were in grade school and after, we had to <u>be</u> in the house by dark. When I was in college, my father and my mother had a restriction that, "You must be in this house by 10:00. If you're not here, you'd better call us and tell us where you are and why it is you're not here." Because I've seen my father go to a dance and bring my sister and me home. We'd look up, and there's Dad standing in the doorway, or Mom. And we'd go home.

Q: That doesn't happen very many times.

Dr. Barnes: It did to us. I'm telling you, they did not permit us to come in the house later than dark when we were in high school and no later than 10:00 o'clock when we were in college. You were in the house. You weren't in the streets. For parties we had chaperons. There was no question. Nobody rebelled. If your parents sent you home, you went home. There was no question about it. Nobody chastised you or laughed at you because you left, because they were leaving too. I look at some of these high school kids now, and they have these parties and rent rooms out here when they graduate. No parents, nothing. Cars, the whole nine yards. That was out of the question. We never even thought of stuff like that. Of course, we didn't have any cars either. But you wouldn't think about going to a dance without a chaperon. No. But these kids now, they just have freedom galore.

Q: Sometimes too much.

Dr. Barnes: Much more than they should have, and I think it has a lot to do with the kinds of things that we're seeing here and now that are just unbelievable. I saw a youngster the other day who was maybe one or two years old. His mother was trying to shop, and he hit her and screamed at her. I just had to turn away. I walked the other way. I said, "If that had been my mother, I would still be there." She would take care of me then, not when I got home--then. All she had to do was look at you after that. You knew what that meant, so you straightened up.

I think my mother had the longest arm in our church. As I said, Dad was working, but Mom was sitting in the pew, then was my eldest sister, then was my brother, then my other sister, then my twin sister, and I was on the end. She would look at the minister up there, and if she looked and saw me do something, she could hit me across my sister, my brother, my other sister, and my twin sister, and never take her eyes off the minister. All she had to do was peek like that and you straightened up, because you knew that she would whip you in church. Or she would take you out of the church and whip you outside, and bring you back and sit you in the church. You knew she would do it, so you straightened up. You never questioned the authority of your parents, but these kids now. I said, "This is a shame. It's too bad. I guess I came along too early."

Q: I have a feeling your brother and sisters were ducking down to enable that long arm to get to you.

Dr. Barnes: They didn't want it to hit them. Even if they were sitting there, they were all straightened up looking at the minister. I was playing down at the end and she never took her eyes off the minister. She would hit me way down at the other end. I said, "How the hell did she do that?" Later on, as I thought about it, I said, "That was a long arm." If they were singing a song, she kept on singing; if he was preaching, she kept on looking. And I was sitting down with my ears buzzing. But I straightened up. You'd better believe I straightened up.

Q: Are you saying that your father essentially worked all the time?

S. E. Barnes #2 - 173

Dr. Barnes: Remember, he was a chef at the dormitory, so they had three meals a day, seven days a week. So he had to have breakfast, because those students with 8:00 o'clock classes had to have breakfast before they left. So he had to be in the kitchen no later than 6:00 o'clock, because he had to serve breakfast by 7:00. Then he had to get ready for lunch, and then after lunch, he had to get ready for dinner. Then he couldn't go home until the kitchen and all was straightened up. So he worked at least 12, 14 hours every day, seven days a week. Whenever he could, he took part in the activities, which we were interested in, but he always supported us. He couldn't go, but he would always support us.

Q: Were you able to spend much time with him as you grew up?

Dr. Barnes: No, but as I got older, I was able to, because I used to go pick him up after I learned to drive. I never took him to work because he went so early. So he always walked to work, but we'd go pick him up at night and bring him home. So that was a chance to talk with him. Then, again, we didn't get it much because he was tired. He was so tired, and he would go to bed early, but he would always let us know that he was there for us if we needed him. Mom took over the prominent role, because she was always present, and, in fact, started the laundry because she wanted to be home. When we came from school, she wanted to be there. So she had an extension put on the house which is where the laundry was located. She had the machines out there; she had the mangle out there; she had the irons out there. That's where I learned how to iron clothes--tablecloths, sheets, pillow slips, and so forth.

Q: It's unfortunate that you weren't able to have some of the types of father-and-son experiences that are so enjoyable.

Dr. Barnes: They are, and then some kids don't have it even with a father who isn't working. Maybe some of it is due to the fact that they didn't learn respect for their parents when they were growing up. But that was one thing we had, and they required us to have. And they always carried themselves in such a way that you did admire and respect them. They didn't have to demand it; they commanded it. So we always tried to do what they would want us to do and wherever they could support us, they did.

Q: Did they have a chance to come out and see your ball games and track meets?

Dr. Barnes: Mom did at times, but she couldn't come so

often because she was running a laundry. So we rarely saw them. She would come when she could, which wasn't very often. Dad, never because he was always busy. He never had a day off. So I don't think Dad saw Jim or me participate. I don't remember seeing Dad at any activity that I engaged in.

Q: Perhaps your brother was something of a surrogate father in that regard.

Dr. Barnes: When they decided to have an athletic hall of fame at Oberlin a few years ago, I was inducted in the charter class. Last year I went to Oberlin because they inducted my brother. So it was really an experience that was gratifying and was extensive because everybody was interested in what you were doing and inspired you to do better.

Q: We talked about this reading you did. What sorts of things did you read for pleasure?

Dr. Barnes: My father and mother saw that we had magazines. The college had one of the most extensive libraries in the country, because Oberlin was a wealthy school, very wealthy, small and wealthy. They had a library downstairs for youngsters. Of course, upstairs the college students were studying, the high school students. It was available to the whole town. I mean, it wasn't a case of saying, "If you don't go to college, you can't come in here." No. So my parents saw that we read. They got books for us to read. We had magazines; we had newspapers. There was always reading material in our house. It wasn't unusual at all that we'd all be sitting reading something all the time. Reading was something that was required of us. But we never had a chance to really sit down and discuss with them. Well, we might talk to Mom in the laundry while she was working. Dad sometimes whenever we could catch him. We actually were introduced to reading early. And reading was something we just automatically did because it was there for us to do.

Q: Did you enjoy fiction, classics, history--what sorts of things?

Dr. Barnes: Well, actually, we read a lot about blacks in history. Much of it was history, and, of course, current affairs. Then, you see, it was substantiated in the schools. Because in classes, you know, you'd discuss what was in the newspapers or you'd ask your question, and so forth. You were really always involved in some aspect of reading. So, yes, we were taught to read early, and we were expected to read. And we still do it now. When our children were growing up, we always got magazines for them. When they were old enough to read themselves, we always had books that they could use. If they ran into a problem, we tried to help. My situation was different from my father's because I did have time off and my wife did too. But we did read, and we read very extensively.

Q: I see a difference between the way I came up and my children, because TV is such an influence now.

Dr. Barnes: We didn't have it. Can you recall when radio was so important? We would sit down and listen to the radio for hours. TV we didn't have, which was very good, as I look back on it now, because sometimes you are actually and truly indoctrinated without realizing it. You don't read the newspapers, because all you have to do is turn on the evening news, and everything is there.

So I really don't envy the present crop because I think they're missing something, which they'll find out later on is very important.

Q: Well, I've got a son, for example, who if he reads for 15 or 20 minutes, he gets uncomfortable. He wants that stimulation that comes from TV.

Dr. Barnes: Yes, that's it. They were saying that the

average family looks at about six or seven hours of TV a day.

Q: I wouldn't be surprised.

Dr. Barnes: I would not be either. Because I look at my granddaughters, and they look at television all the time. But their mother monitors the programs that they can see, their programs on their level. But I see these kids now, and they can quote the soap operas verbatim. Now they can watch at night and they see this pornographic stuff. How are you going to prevent them from seeing it?

Now they've got these telephone numbers you can call and get these sexually oriented conversations. I said, "I don't know where we're bound for." I really don't. You can't really stop it because the only way you can do it is to take the television out of your house. Then they use the telephone, so you take the telephone out. But that wouldn't stop them because they run into it everywhere. You go in the stores, and here are the magazines there for them. They don't actually do anything about monitoring who buys them.

Same thing we've got in Washington now about these guns. I don't know where the hell they get them. I don't know how they have the money to get them, but somehow or another, they get them. I think that part of that is due to the fact that too often there is only one adult in the household. Really and truly, it reminds me about when I was reading about Rome. Nero fiddled while Rome burned. That was the same kind of thing that was happening then. It became a moral degradation, and then it became physical, and the whole place went up in smoke. I think we're heading in that direction. It bothers me, but you can't talk to these young people now.

They listen to the music. I listen to beautiful waltz music and I say, "How in the world can they compare that to the modern stuff?" To me the older music is not only good, but it's also soothing. But now it's bumpity, bumpity, bump, bump, bump. That's all it is, is noise. And these kids go mad over that stuff. My God, the haircuts. I swear, I don't envy them. I know I'm out of fashion now, but I'm glad I came along when I did, knowing what I know.

Q: Well, a contrast to your own experience, you mentioned briefly that you were involved in the youth club work. I'd appreciate it if you could cover that in some more detail, please.

Dr. Barnes: Well, in a town like Oberlin, it was a duty to help the younger ones. So I had a Boy Scout troop in the church. The younger kids you would teach in the Sunday school, and then you would take them on picnics and such and such a thing. So it really wasn't structured. It was the kind of thing that we did because we enjoyed working with these youngsters, you see.

And that was another reason why I think I got involved in youth work. When I was at Livingstone, Homer Tucker, the minister of our church in Oberlin was elected to be executive secretary at the Ninth Street branch YMCA in Cincinnati. He wrote and asked me to come there as a boys' work secretary. So that's when I left teaching and went into YMCA work.

It was because of what I had been doing in Oberlin that he remembered. He said, "You'd be the very person I'd like to head up as the boys' work secretary, because you were always involved in volunteer work in Oberlin with some of these smaller kids." So I always did that. I always enjoyed it. I really miss it now because I don't do it as I used to do it. I did it because I wanted to do it, and because I felt that I had to pay back some of what I had been given as I was coming through. I just felt an obligation to do it. And I enjoyed the kids.

I got a call recently from a kid who has been at Florida A&M for 30 years. When I went to teach in Salisbury, North Carolina, there was this little group of kids. Every time I turned around, they were either running around with a football or snatching something, taking off with it. So I called them one day and I said, "Hey, come over here." And they all came together. I said, "What are you all going to do tonight?"

They said, "Well, I don't know."

"I tell you what to do," I said, "Let's go over to Walt's house." And that's how I started a little club, which is known still in Salisbury as the Rookie Club. This man had been a Rookie, and he called up to tell me that he had sent me a jacket, because he's at Florida A&M. He sent me a jacket and he said he ran into Coleman, who's punting now for the Redskins, who was punting first for Minnesota.* Coleman was the guest speaker at their football banquet, and Coleman said, "I remember some person that you met that you took me to in Oberlin." And he said, "When I get back, I'm going to talk to him." He still calls me now, and others still call me. They're doctors or lawyers, whatever they are, but they still remember the Rookies. And the Rookie Club I had down there for five, six years.

Q: What kinds of things did the Rookie Club do?

Dr. Barnes: We'd get together; we'd go on hikes; we would play little games. We would meet and the mothers would fix a little something for us, and we would talk and would play ball, play games, play hide-and-seek. But we were always

---
*Monte Coleman, Washington Redskins.

S. E. Barnes #2 - 182

together, and we were always mentioning to them that, "You do this not because you want to, because of what effect it has on other people. You don't live in a world of your own." So you try to do it by example rather than by explanation. But I enjoyed that. I always was involved in that until I came to Washington. Then things in Washington were different. I was so involved at Howard that I didn't have a chance to do the volunteer work that I had done prior to coming to Washington. I did it in North Carolina, and I did it in Cincinnati until I came here in 1947.

Q: The fact that you became an athletic director suggests that you're an organizer. When did this trait manifest itself? Did that go all the way back to the youth club days?

Dr. Barnes: Well, it was one of those things that was always in the process, but I never really identified it as that particularly. It was just something that I enjoyed doing, and I liked working with the kids, and I liked taking them on hikes. And we used to go frog hunting in the frog ponds.

I said to these boys, "Now, there's going to be a time when you can't ask your mother and father for money." So what we started doing then was gathering dandelion greens. I don't know whether you heard of it or not, but they also made dandelion wine. So these kids, I'd say, "Well, look, here's what we'll do. We'll all get our baskets and we'll go out and we'll pick wild strawberries and wild raspberries, and we'll sell them. The money you get, you can keep. But I want everybody to come to me and show me what they have earned this week. Then you'll get a star or something emblematic of the fact that you are doing something other than just playing." So we made that then a sort of a competitive thing. I said, "We are going to see who makes more than the other person. You have to do it legitimately. You can't steal from one another and you can't pretend that you are when you haven't. You have to bring your money so I can see it and I know it's yours. And then we'll give you credit for it."

I did the same thing at the YMCA in Cincinnati when I was boys' work secretary. But I did it because I felt like it was an obligation to pass on to others what had been passed to me. And that's why I enjoyed it. They enjoyed it, too, because they still call me. They still talk about it in Salisbury even now. They remember the Rookie Club, because it was really pretty well known. We would march in the parades. We didn't have anything, but we marched with what we had on. But we were involved. So I really felt good about that, and I felt that I was making a contribution, which I felt all of us were obligated to do, in some place or some way.

Q: Well, there's the person who's known as the take-charge type, the shouter, and so forth. You certainly don't seem that type to me. Yours must have been a more quiet, persuasive ability.

Dr. Barnes: Well, first of all, I tried to conduct myself in such a way that there was no criticism of what I was doing. I mean, I didn't do the drinking, I didn't carouse, and I wasn't at the parties, and so forth and so on. That was because I just didn't want to be. That, I think, had a lot to do with having youngsters respect you and, in a sense, look up to you. You had then an obligation to maintain that image so that some of the things that others were doing, you wouldn't do because it would reflect on what you were trying to do with the youngsters. You can't tell them to do one thing when you're doing something else. You have to lead by example, and that's what I tried to do.

Q: Well, you were also providing them with the satisfaction that they were earning what they were getting rather than having it given to them.

Dr. Barnes: That's right. Well, I've always felt that an individual appreciates something more when he earns it than if it's given to him. I really do. Because I know the money I made, I was very proud of it, because I earned it, and my parents were proud of the fact that I had earned it. But sometimes a kid would come up to me and say, "Give me a quarter, a nickel, or whatever."

I said, "What do you mean, give you something?" I said, "Are you prepared to earn it?"

"What do you mean?"

I said, "I would rather you earn it than for me to give it to you, because then it would mean something, because it came through your own blood, sweat, and tears." For instance, I said, "Now, if you'd come in and say, 'I'll shine your shoes for a quarter,' you're more apt to get that than if you come in asking me to give you a quarter. So you have to earn whatever it is you want, and you have to do it, not in a sense that somebody owes you something. Nobody owes you anything, so you have to earn that just as you earn respect. You do it by what you do and the way you act than a demand that you make because you expect people to give you whatever you want. It's not going to be like that. So there's no point in you developing that at this level, because later on you're going to be in a position where it's going to be different. If you don't make it, you won't have it."

Q: What do you remember about the Boy Scout experience specifically? What sort of leadership roles did you have there?

Dr. Barnes: In the scouting, you always had these merit badges and, of course, you had the book and you were associated with the national chapter. So the kids had to meet certain requirements to get a certain emblem. Of course, the more of those emblems you got, the more status you had. But at the same time, it was a learning situation. It was never, "Give me." It was always, "You will be helped if you're willing to make the effort."

I miss that in athletics today too. I think that athletics has gotten to the point now where it's just ridiculous. The kinds of things that they offer these kids, and the kinds of things that these kids expect. I was looking the other day at a baseball player who's making $1,500,000 a year. He's going to arbitration because that wasn't enough money. He wants $2,500,000. I said, "Now that is unbelievable." I said, "A million dollars! The people who come to see you may not make that in a lifetime."

I think we've gotten to the point where we've given up service, and now we expect to be given to. Now we've got people getting paid a million dollars to play a game that we used to enjoy playing for nothing. They're getting money from an activity, which, in my judgment, is recreational. I don't think what it reflects is anything that we should be particularly proud of.

Q: Well, I don't have much problem with somebody who obviously works hard. But it's the mediocre player who gets the big salary just because everybody else is that I have more of a complaint about.

Dr. Barnes: I have a complaint about it, too, because everybody now is not thinking in terms of anything other than what's in it for me. I think that will eventually come back to haunt them. It haunts society, I know that. But people are willing to pay for it, so football players say, "Well, I have a maximum of four years in the NFL.* So I'm going to get all I can while I can." And sometimes their demands are out of line with their productivity.

I like the way Doug Williams has handled the situation in Washington because he had never demanded the high salary.** He said, "Well, if I'm worth it, I'll get it." And he got it. He got it.

Q: He earned it first.

Dr. Barnes: He earned it and he deserves it.

Michael Jordan is making a lot of money, but he is producing, he's producing.*** Magic Johnson is producing.

---
*NFL--National Football League.
**Doug Williams, quarterback for the Washington Redskins professional football team at the time of the interview.
***Michael Jordan, professional basketball player for the Chicago Bulls.

Bob Cousy once played with the Celtics.* You probably have heard of him. He said once that there's nobody worth a million dollars. I don't care how good he is. He said that years ago and I agree with him. A million dollars! It's unbelievable.

Q: Did your parents pass on to you the idea that you owe society something in return?

Dr. Barnes: Yes. They've always said to us, "You have an obligation to return some of what you got, and this is the way it should be. You've gotten it by virtue of somebody—nobody makes it alone. Nobody. I don't care how big you are or how smart you are. Whatever it is, somebody helped you because you couldn't have made it by yourself. And you owe then that obligation to pass on the same thing to someone else."

See, among the lessons that we were taught was that it was not only a family situation, it was community. There was that community closeness which we don't have anymore. And I think it takes something from what we can be and should be while we're doing what we want to do.

I'm very, very, very happy with the home training, community training, and church training that I got when I

---

*Earvin "Magic" Johnson, professional basketball player for the Los Angeles Lakers; Robert Cousy, a pro basketball player for the Boston Celtics in the 1950s and 1960s.

was growing up. It was just not me; this was generally the picture.

Q: Mr. Cooper described the setup when he was growing up in North Carolina where people would come around. If they didn't have the means to eat, his mother would feed them. Was there that kind of situation in Oberlin, also, during the Depression?

Dr. Barnes: Oh, yes, yes. I mean, no one was ever turned away. If they needed something and it could be provided, we'd provide it without any expectation of return for it. But the people never came unless they really and truly could not get it otherwise. We had tramps when we were growing up. We saw these people who rode the railroads, but they still had some pride. They would come to the house and if they needed something, they would ask, "What can I do to earn this?" Then you gave it because they returned by doing something in return for that. And I think it develops the individual.

As I said earlier, I told the kids, "You can't expect people to give you when you give nothing in return. That's the way life is."

But now you don't get that anymore. I agree with George. My father and mother never turned anyone away from our house if they were hungry. When they needed food, they got it. But in return, the persons never ate and left; they always did something in return for that.

Q: What subjects did you do best in when you were in school?

Dr. Barnes: Well, I liked history. Mathematics I wasn't too good at. Economics I didn't do as well as I should have done. But I guess I was more interested in the social sciences than I was towards a particular career in economics, or whatever. But I guess that's true of any person. Whatever it is you like, that's what you do. It's a God-given talent, much of it. The other is hard work, sweat, and blood, and tears.

I didn't have any particularly favorite subjects to tell you the truth, because the curriculum was there, and you took part in it. There were some subjects that I enjoyed more than I did others. But it wasn't because I felt that this was my life's work.

Q: How demanding were the teachers in terms of homework assignments, writing papers, and so forth?

Dr. Barnes: Everybody took assignments home. Oh, yes, you took your books home, and you studied. My parents had a study period. When we came in the house, before we could do anything else, Mom would ask, "Have you done your homework?" If you hadn't done your homework, there wasn't anything else. You went back to school and they always gave you homework. There was never an instance where you would see kids walking home with nothing in their hands. They had homework, and they went back, and they had to show what they had done. So that was emphasized. There was never any doubt about you having homework. Because you were given that to do and bring it back the next day. So that, I think, had an end product on me, too. But that was a period through which we came.

Q: Well, you've described the situation in which there seems to be one common denominator and that's discipline.

Dr. Barnes: Definitely. You're right. That's the word for it, was discipline, which we don't have now. There was discipline. And you were disciplined, not only at home, but in the community, in the school, in the club. Wherever you were, there was always that discipline. So you never got away with things that these youngsters get away with now.

Of course, I think there was a lot of concern. The persons who were teaching were teaching because they wanted to teach. They were dedicated, committed people. They really were.

Q: Discipline doesn't necessarily mean punishment, of course. It's an adherence to a standard.

Dr. Barnes: That's right; that's right. Standard, that's the word, because there was always that foremost in whatever was done.

There are certain standards which we set, standards which are to be maintained, we expect you to do both. And we never had any problem with our teachers. They were not demanding to the point where they intimidated us. It was done in an atmosphere of friendliness, cohesiveness, and a commitment and dedication to doing that which was expected of you and do it the very best you can. If you can't, we'll help you.

Discipline--that's a word. We don't have discipline. Disciplining now is very, very shaky. You have youngsters who tell you in a minute, "I'll sue you." You ever have your hands paddled in school?

Q: No, I managed to escape that.

Dr. Barnes: Well, I've had mine paddled. And the teachers would not hesitate to do that. If you needed it, you got it. And the parents agreed with it. So you were never out of the scrutiny of some adults at all times, 24 hours a day. In the morning you'd go to school. You'd come home from school, and there were certain chores that were expected of you. When you finished that, then you had your meal. Then you did your studying and went to bed. We could listen to the radio at certain times, but it was not something we turned on as soon as we hit the house. As I look back on it now, there was nothing that was demanded which we had to do it or somebody was pressing you that you did it. It was done in a very, very relaxed but a concerned atmosphere. It really was.

Q: It wasn't oppressive, because you just accepted that that's the way it was.

Dr. Barnes: Everybody else was doing it. And whenever you went to someone's house, then you respected that place. You didn't do anything there that you wouldn't do at home. They wouldn't have that.

You worked all day. We didn't have power mowers in those days, but I used to have a lawn mower that I would push around town and I would cut lawns. I have cut lawns that took me all day, for which I got $2.00. But I really appreciated the $2.00 because I earned it. Our parents never gave us allowances. You had to earn what you got.

They said, "Whatever you need, we'll see that you get. Whatever you want, you provide." So that's the way it was.

So if I wanted to go to the movies, then I earned the money to go to the movies. This was not something that had anything to do with my upbringing in terms of whether or not I got the correct amount of food and so forth and so on. They saw to that. We had shoes, we had clothes, and so forth, but if it was something I wanted, you earn it. And that's the way it was all over town. You know, as I said, we were disciplined anywhere we were found doing less than we should have been doing. And we knew that, and we respected that. But the things that these youngsters get away with now are just unbelievable. But I came along too early, I guess.

Q: Well, I think that's typical in every generation, that feeling that the younger people are really screwing it up.

Dr. Barnes: Doing differently from what we did. I guess that's the better way to say it. Well, times were different then--no doubt about that.

Q: I think it's typical that each generation takes the way it came up as the norm, and anything different from that is wrong.

Dr. Barnes: Is wrong, yes. But actually I think that we have lost rather than gained in many areas. It's beginning to show itself in the kinds of things that are happening worldwide. It's definitely happening at home. What we accept now would never have been accepted before, but it's a new generation. People don't do things now like they used to do. We can't do anything about it, and if you start talking about it, they look upon you as though you came along with the dinosaurs.

Q: Part of the reason that the Japanese are so successful is that they have the kind of work ethic that this country used to have more of.

Dr. Barnes: True. That's true. And I can see where this is just beginning to make inroads into our situation. America used to be the largest country in the world as a lender. Now we're the big debtors. The Japanese own a lot of the United States. Other countries own a lot of the United States. It's just unbelievable that we have gone down to the point where now we are accepting rather than giving. But what can you say?

We've got a debt that I don't think the United States will ever get out of.

Q: President Reagan certainly didn't help.*

---
*The national debt increased substantially during Ronald Reagan's term as President, from 1981 to 1989.

S. E. Barnes #2 - 196

Dr. Barnes: You know, they're in the trillions of dollars now. Used to be millions. Then it was billions; now it's trillions. And they're talking about the budget and those kinds of things. I just can't believe the way prices have gone up. We purchased this house in 1962. We couldn't afford it now. Things have just gone so high that it's just almost difficult to make a living.

Q: What were some of the extracurricular activities you were involved in while you were growing up and going to school?

Dr. Barnes: Well, as I said, you know, the choir, the town clubs. When it snowed, we had the sleigh rides; we would go skating on the ice; we would go sledding; we would take hikes, overnight hikes; we'd fish. These are the activities which were fun for us.

We used to play hide-and-go-seek and kick the can. We'd get together and have fun all day long playing kick the can. We'd set a can up in the middle of somewhere. There would be one person who was to guard this can, and then everybody else was sneaking around to try to catch him off guard. If you kicked over the can, then everybody who was caught could escape. Then you started the game over again.

Another one was king of the hill. You'd get up on top of this mound of dirt and try to protect that dirt when other kids were coming. You had to push them away, keep them off. But king of the hill was one of our big games. Oh, yes, indeed. If you could stay king of the hill, that meant you had a lot of stakes. But those were the kind of things we engaged in and we enjoyed it.

We'd come home tired because that's the way we'd sleep better. We were never in structured activities; they were just spontaneous. When we played hide-and-go-seek, we'd run and hide. Then if you could touch the goal before the man could, then you were home safe, and you just kept that up until everybody was either caught or everybody was free.

Q: Did you develop a love of the outdoors?

Dr. Barnes: Yes, because in a little town like Oberlin, there was nothing but outdoors. In the summers we would go and pick corn. I was part of an operation in which the farmers used to have what they called the threshing machine. We'd follow the threshing machine from farm to farm to farm to farm to farm to farm. I got involved in that because you could earn money. It was a very close relationship when you'd go from farm to farm to farm to farm. I enjoyed that.

So we did much to make our own entertainment. It

wasn't structured like it is now. Whatever you did, you really did yourself. The only structure was the movies. You'd go to the movies on Saturday for ten cents, and popcorn was a nickel. If we went to the movies on Saturday, we'd go and stay almost a half a day. We'd go in, see the movies, eat popcorn, come out, and go home. We really enjoyed that.

I don't know whether I answered your question or not, but it certainly was the way we came up.

Q: Knowing what you do about sports, how sophisticated would you say the coaching was in the time when you were in college and starting out as a coach yourself?

Dr. Barnes: Not as sophisticated as now. For instance, football at that time was very restricted. You never worried about multiple defenses or multiple offenses. Everybody ran the single wing, or everyone ran the Notre Dame T. We never had any of the sophisticated things they have now. So I know when I was playing in college, we always played a five-man line or a six-man line. And if you got on the goal post, then we went into a seven-man line. But now they got twos and threes--they've got so many sophisticated things that their play books are that thick. They have six or seven plays off of the same formation. The play looks the same, but it does something else. So our blocking was not difficult, because we knew where people were. I guess that's why they have so many coaches now. They have coaches for everything. When I was playing, there were three coaches: the head coach and two other coaches. Now they've got 12, 14 coaches for each team. And the game is very sophisticated.

Q: And much more specialized also.

Dr. Barnes: Oh, yes. Indeed it is. Basketball too. Everything has gotten to the point now where it's almost calculated. It's almost like it is computerized.

We didn't have any game films because nobody took movies. So the coach, I guess, would have to remember what the plays were and what you did, and so forth and so on. When we came back for practice next week, they worked on the mistakes, but that was it. I couldn't be playing now because these people are bigger, they're faster, they're stronger, and there's a difference. Of course, this steroid stuff that they're taking now that's making people bigger and stronger, they're just also cutting short their lives. No, it wasn't as sophisticated as it is now, but it was enjoyable. I think eventually that's what it amounts to, that you enjoy it.

Now sports are an end in themselves. At that time it was a means to the end. I mean, this was part of your development as you grew up. Sports were a good way to learn discipline. But now it's different, really different. I wouldn't coach now. Even if I could, I wouldn't, because I'm just too far antiquated in what I believe are basic and fundamental standards. You're going to be here for a few years and gone, and it's not the end. But that, I guess, is being kind of altruistic, I don't know.

Q: That's a dirty word today.

Dr. Barnes: Seems like it, and I'm not surprised at all. No, you don't talk about that now. No, indeed. The game is the thing.

Q: During a break here, we were talking about the decision by the Golden Thirteen--or however many there were--to work together as a group. I would appreciate if you could please go back over some of that.

Dr. Barnes: Well, once we found out why we were at Great Lakes and were told that we were going to officer training school, we had to go back to Camp Robert Smalls, where we would meet our commanding officer, our executive officer, and our teachers. We were isolated in a barracks by ourselves. So we came back to the main side, and we sat down to talk that night and we said, "Well, we are going to succeed, in spite of those who feel like it shouldn't be this way and they're looking for us to fail. We will not fail because we have an obligation, not only to those who came before us, but certainly those who follow us."

We never at any time felt that we were privileged. But we felt we were fortunate; therefore, we had a larger obligation. So we sat down, and we said, "Now, we are not interested in any one person emerging as the number one, or two, or three person in the class. This will be a unified effort, and what one of us knows, he will teach the others of us. We will study together, and we will succeed as a class, not as individuals."

So we were supposed to have lights out at 10:00 o'clock or 10:30. We would turn out the lights, but we'd go in the head. We'd take a blanket, we'd cover the windows, and we would cover under the door so they couldn't see anything from outside. Then we would study.

Arbor, who was a quartermaster, taught us the Morse code. He taught us the signal flags, and we would pop signals to one another. He would give us a sentence and say, "So-and-so." And we had to pop those flags or we'd hit the Morse code. That's how we learned. So we went to class the next day. There was very little that they could ask us which we hadn't already practiced. When we were learning airplane recognition, we didn't have any kind of

S. E. Barnes #2 - 202

movie projector, so we just imagined.

White was a lawyer, so he taught us Navy regulations. Cooper had been at service school. Well, it was fortunate every person had some skill which he could impart to the others, and that's what we did. We were unified when we started, we were unified all during our course, and we were unified when we were finally commissioned. But we always have been very close because of that experience. We said, "We're going to do this because there are those who expect us not to succeed. But we will succeed, not only for those who were before us, but for those who will follow after us."

That's one of the reasons why our class average, our class average was 3.7 or 3.8--the highest class average they'd had up to that time in any officer candidate school. But you don't see Cooper number one, or Baugh number two. No, our grades were the same, because we studied the same. We knew what we were doing. There was nothing that they could teach us.

The only thing we didn't have an opportunity to do in our barracks was marksmanship. They would take us out to the rifle range, and we'd have to fire. But that's the only thing that we didn't do in class. We did everything else. In the evening we would go over what was given us in class that day. So we reviewed what had happened, and then we thought what might be. What had been we knew, and what was to be, we would learn. And that's how we did it. We acted as one person.

Q: How did this idea come about? Was there somebody who emerged as a leader who suggested this is what you should do, or how did it come to be?

Dr. Barnes: I think it came about as a result of our not knowing why we were there. We said, "We are here not because it was designed that we should be here, because we know that they hadn't had any colored officers, and the reasons why, so now we are the guinea pigs. We are the ones they hope will not succeed. Then they can always say, 'Well, we gave you the chance and you didn't take advantage of it.'"

We said, "We'll take advantage of this." No one emerged as a leader. It was something that came about from our talking. The idea was promulgated that this was what we needed to do. So I don't think any one person stood up and said, "I think we should do this." No, that was never done. But we knew that there was something that had to be done, so there was open discussions, open forum. The idea came about because it was a good idea and we accepted it. It could have come from any source. I don't think any man who's living now can tell you how it started, but we knew it had to be. And that's the way we decided it would be.

Q: Was it your perception at that time that those running the school either wanted or expected you to fail?

Dr. Barnes: One person in particular. After he had taught us, he told us that it was not his choice to be sent to this school as an instructor. He was the person who had just finished the Naval Academy. He was a lieutenant, and he was one of our officers.*

Q: Do you remember his name?

Dr. Barnes: I have it somewhere.

When we finished school, he congratulated us and said, "I didn't come because I wanted to come. I was forced to come." And he said, "I deliberately made it difficult for you. When you finished the course, you had actually finished what was equivalent to a semester at the Naval Academy." They piled the work on us, and that's the reason why we were determined that we were not going to fail.

So we ate that alive and went back and waited for more. And he'd give it to us. If we didn't know it that day, we'd know it the next day. All of us would know it,

---

*This is probably a reference to Lieutenant (junior grade) Paul D. Richmond, USNR, who has done an oral history as part of the Naval Institute series. He confirmed in his interview that he was assigned to the program rather than choosing it. He does not agree with the contention that the black officer candidates were set up to fail.

not one or two; all of us would know it. So we never studied individually. We always studied together. And whatever one didn't know, we'd go around the group and somebody would have the answer to it. Then we'd discuss that and we'd have it. We would go on to something else and say, "Well, So-and-so asked us in class today such-and-such a thing." It might have been in Navy regulations. White, being up on that, would then become the instructor, and he would go over that, and we would go over that. We would ask one another questions, and we would come up with answers and so forth. Then we'd finally come up with what we felt was the most legitimate, and the most reasonable, and the best answer, and it usually was correct.

Q: Did you ever get the feeling from the instructors that they knew that you were doing this studying in the head?

Dr. Barnes: No, if they had known that, they would never permit it. But we never announced it.

Q: Why do you think it wouldn't have been permitted?

Dr. Barnes: Well, first of all, because we were supposed to be in the bed, lights out. And that was against regulations.

Q: Well, presumably, though, they permitted you a study period.

Dr. Barnes: That was after we came back from dinner. Then we had a study period. We'd go to dinner at 6:00 o'clock, chow at 6:00 o'clock, and we'd be back in the dorm by 7:30. So from 7:30 to 10:30 we were permitted lights on.

Q: And that was individual study during that period?

Dr. Barnes: During that period we studied individually. Then once we had a chance to go in the head we were able to exchange ideas. You know, you're reading a book and you get one thing out of it. But we then would go to the head, and we would ask one another, say, "Look, I read so-and-so. What do you think about that?" Then there would be a discussion period. It was an instructional period; it was an opportunity for all of us to make some contribution to the total situation.

Q: How long did that session last each night?

Dr. Barnes: Well, it would always last till after midnight. I can't recall it ever lasting any less time than that. We stayed in there as long as we felt it was necessary. When we went to bed, we all went to bed. The lights in the head could stay on, because you have to have lights to go to the head. So we all moved the blankets and so forth, and we went on over to where we were sleeping and went on to bed. We never turned the regular lights on to go to bed, because we knew if we turned those lights on, somebody would know what was going on.

Q: So what did you get, maybe five hours of sleep a night then?

Dr. Barnes: Well, we would average five or six hours, because we had to be up and at the chow hall by 7:00. We'd have to march to chow hall, and we'd have to march back from chow hall. We were in class from 8:00 until 12:00; then we'd go to chow. We were back at the dorm for our classes by 1:00 o'clock, and we went on till 5:00. Then we had chow, and then we'd have the evening to study. That's when we would study with lights on in the regular part of the barracks. After that we would go in the head, and that's when we would really put in some intensive time. So there was never any time when we'd say, "We're going to study till 1:00 o'clock," or whatever it is. We studied until we felt that we were prepared for the next day. So there may have been times when we didn't get that much sleep, but I don't know exactly.

Q: Did duty officers ever come around and check on you in the barracks?

Dr. Barnes: That was a privilege. Of course, we were under scrutiny at all times by whoever was in charge. If he didn't see any lights on, he didn't have any necessity to come in. That's the reason why we extinguished our lights as though we were going to bed. We didn't have a Morse code key, so we tapped out messages with pencils on a paper or with our fingers. One person would give us a clue, say, "Okay, ship approaching on a such-and-such-and-such side." We'd tap it out, "Ship so-and-so," and you had to answer. If you got it wrong, you got to go back and do it again. That's the way we tested one another and got to know the Morse code.

We'd pop flags and practice with flashing lights for the visual signaling. We took turns. Each person would do it till he got the hang of it. And we really and truly grilled one another very, very hard. We were really tougher on ourselves than we would have been had the instructor been present. It was a determination and a commitment, and it turned out to be exactly what was needed. It was great.

Q: The hard part of that is that so much of it is just

strictly memory work and in an unfamiliar discipline too. None of you had majored in Navy when you were going to school.

Dr. Barnes: That's right. One thing that we did say was that there's nothing that surpasses repetition. If you do it enough, it becomes an active part of you. So we wanted to be sure that we knew the Morse code; we wanted to be sure that we knew the flags and what certain things meant. So we drilled ourselves on those things. It wasn't that we were told that, "This is what you're going to have tomorrow." But we knew we had to go to the Navy regulations; we'd have to go to Navy recognition; we'd have to go to quartermaster. So we wanted to be sure we knew the code. And that's really what we impressed upon one another: know the Morse code, know the light flashes. So no matter what he gave us the next day, if we knew the alphabet, we could handle whatever it is he needed or wanted.

Q: It sounds as if your real test was at night in the head, and the easy part was taking the written test, maybe, in class.

Dr. Barnes: Well, I don't think the instructors could have been any tougher on us than we were on ourselves. And I think that was very important, in that we didn't become upset or flustered or anything if we were asked a question. Because we knew that we could do it because we knew the alphabet. An instructor would be in class, and he would say to one of us, "Okay, give him a message," and we would pop out something. And he would give the answer. We were watching, and we could tell that he was doing all right. If he didn't, then we went and worked with him that night. The next day we came back. He wouldn't make that mistake the next time. So I think we were harder on ourselves than our instructor was on us. We didn't know what he was going to ask. Whatever he asked, we wanted to be ready to respond correctly.

Q: How would you say that the pace compared in terms of difficulty with being an undergraduate in college?

Dr. Barnes: First of all, we were in wartime. It was intense. You had to learn quickly, because you never knew when you were going to find yourself in a situation where you had to use that information. Whereas in college it was more relaxed. The pressure wasn't on you like it was here. Therefore, in college you could move more leisurely, and you had more opportunities to ask questions. See, we were not relaxed in this training, because we never knew what was coming next. Like, for instance, you wouldn't have but so much time, to recognize a plane--whether it was an enemy plane or whether it was your own plane. If we were in school, you would have plenty of time. You might look the plane over, look out the window, and so forth. In wartime that plane could be devastating, so you better recognize it immediately. Give yourself time to make some kind of a move, either protect or destroy. So the pressure made it different.

Q: Another type of pressure is that in college your instructors are generally there to help you succeed.

Dr. Barnes: True. That's right, that's true. But they would give you work, which you would take out but which you had to do yourself. Maybe there were several other students with whom you would study, and you would grill one another, but this was much more intense. See, if you were in a college class, you could make a mistake when you went the next day. And then, of course, it would be discussed, or your instructor would tell you it's something else. But here you didn't have the luxury to make a mistake, because that mistake could be very costly. So there was that much more pressure, plus the pressure of the fact that we were the first. Therefore, we were in a school with which we were unfamiliar. This is nothing that any of us had ever expected. But here it is. So you respond. You must be ready. It's like the Boy Scouts: Be prepared." And that was in the Bible, I guess: "Be ye ever ready. You know not the hour or the day when He cometh." And that's true.

Q: How did you release the tension that built up in a situation like that? You couldn't be on guard 24 hours a day.

Dr. Barnes: We would relax while we were marching to chow, or the time between when we got back and when we had to study. We would have some recreational time, but it wasn't anything where we would give precedence to that. Oh, we had fun. We would kid one another and laugh. We used to always give Nelson hell. So we had this camaraderie, where we never lost sight of the purpose. We couldn't become so exalted in what we were doing that we would forget why we were there.

Q: What kinds of things would you kid Nelson about?

Dr. Barnes: Well, Nelson, as you know, was very pompous. He was a guy who had a great respect for himself. And he really and truly irritated us at times because he was that way. And we would have to, as we called it, put him in his place. Arbor too. Arbor used to talk a lot. We told

Arbor, "If you don't shut up, we're going to put you in the head and lock the door." Now, you wouldn't know Reagan was there unless you turned around. Sublett was very quiet; White was very quiet. Cooper was more aggressive, as was Baugh. They were the aggressive persons. And the others, even now, show the same kinds of characteristics they showed then. They really did.

Q: How about Phillip Barnes?

Dr. Barnes: Phil was quiet. I would say the take-charge guys are the guys who carried this over in civilian life were Cooper, and Baugh, and Reagan, probably. But Cooper and Baugh definitely, and Nelson. Reginald Goodwin was a take-charge guy. He was an attorney. Of course, I had met him in Cincinnati. But the quiet ones were White, Sublett, Reagan, Hair, Martin, and Lear. So you really had a double personality--the quiet ones and the more aggressive ones. But they're a very intelligent group of men, and I think have done very well and were doing well when they came into the service.

Q: Now, the ones you've called more aggressive, would you put the term "leaders" on those, more so than some of the others?

Dr. Barnes: We never had any leaders. That was a term we never really would permit in the conversation, because we didn't need leaders. What we needed was cooperation, because this was a corporate effort; it wasn't individual effort. It was not one guy trying to get ahead of somebody else because he was more aggressive, because he was smarter, or whatever. It never entered the picture--never. Individuals would sometimes accept a role of leadership, but that was given by the group. It was not something that the individual took upon himself to do. Because we were always reminding one another what our mission was, so there was nobody who stood out beyond everybody else or was the one who was questioned, or the one who was always asked, or the one who was given this kind of responsibility. No, we never permitted that. We said, "We are a class, not individuals."

Q: How was this aggressiveness demonstrated?

Dr. Barnes: Well, first of all, someone might be the first one to get ready for chow, or he might be the one who spoke out more often than others. Or they were the ones who might have made more suggestions than the others, which were accepted as a part of the growing process. But it wasn't that they were lifted and selected out as, "You be the leader, and we'll follow you." Unh-unh.

Now, Nelson was very loquacious and very ostentatious. But he was also sincere. We never permitted him to let this be the thing that gave him precedence over anybody else. It wasn't because we feared anyone, but because we felt we could not in any way abdicate the responsibility, which was all of ours. Because we said, "We're all going to be out there in separate places; we're not going to be together. So what we need to know is what we can do for others. Whatever skills we have, we're not imposing ourselves on anybody. We're not going to do that, we're going to be a part of the picture. But we'll always be ready, if called upon, to assume responsibility for it."

But, no, we never selected a leader. Leaders are people who will sometimes pugnaciously push themselves into these positions. They were not the kind of persons that we sometimes see--some leaders are people who stand back and see where others are going, then jump in front and lead them. No, we were all in the same boat; we all had the same paddles; it was up to us, everybody, to bend his hand to making the boat move. We didn't have a coxswain like Lear if we were in a shell. There wasn't anybody giving directions. We never had that.

Q: Sounds as if Nelson was more than willing to take on that role, though.

S. E. Barnes #2 - 216

Dr. Barnes: He would love it. If we'd have let him loose, he would have.

Q: So how did you hold him back?

Dr. Barnes: Because all of us told him, "If you don't shut your mouth, we're going to put you in the head." So we let it be known, "Wait just a minute now. Now wait a minute." We would have to caution one another. If one got a little more aggressive, "Wait just a minute now. We listen to what you have to say, but don't assume for one minute that we have to take any orders from you, or you're going to jump out in front and try to tell us what we should be doing. Nobody tells us what to do." He could suggest. If we want to, we would; if we don't, that's part of the picture. It's not anything that's personal; it's just that we want to keep our eye on the reasons why we're here and what we intend to do as a result of being here.

Q: Was it treated like a democracy, that you would vote on issues?

Dr. Barnes: Well, we never voted because we never felt it was necessary. In other words, if somebody came up, "Well, how many are in favor of this?" It was never that. We were all in favor of it, or we were all opposed to it. And we could always discuss it. If you had an idea that you would like to advance, we'd listen. But it was not in a way that you were putting yourself in a position to dictate to others, or to us. It was all done in what I would call a friendly and a contributory way.

Q: It sounds as if there was some kidding if one guy went too far.

Dr. Barnes: Yes, we did that while we were studying. If a guy went too far, we'd put him in his place. We would just let him know, "Wait a minute. You're still one of us."

Q: Apparently you would discuss an issue till you got to a consensus on it.

Dr. Barnes: That's right. We agreed to it. It wasn't that one person had to get a vote in order to say it, because all of us were pursuing the same pathway. We were all going to be judged on the basis of what we did as a class, not as individuals. They were not going to select one of us out here and make him an officer and send the rest of us go down the drain. We said, in effect, "We were started as a class, we'll stay as a class, we'll leave as a class."

Q: What might be examples of some of these types of issues that you would go back and forth on?

Dr. Barnes: Well, for instance, we might discuss Navy regulations or navigation. A problem would come up and, "So many degrees longitude, so many degrees latitude. The ship is moving at this number of knots going northeast, and you're in a ship here and you're such-and-such-and-such. What would you do?" There would be certain suggestions, so-and-so-and-so-on. But whatever we did agree to was a consensus.

We all agreed that this was the better approach to it. But we discussed it. We had discussions, lively discussions. But whatever we came up with, we came up as a group, not as one individual placing himself ahead of the rest. Maybe it was his idea to start with, but that was emasculated in what we were trying to do. We all wanted to understand it. We didn't want one person saying, "Well, I told you so." No. He didn't tell us so; he suggested and we accepted it. But nobody was designated as a leader. There might have been some who tried to assume the role, but it wasn't done aggressively because there was not a group leader. Nobody led us. We were a group and we were all striving for the same thing. We wanted all to get there the same time, the same way.

Q: Did you get discouraged at times going through this process?

Dr. Barnes: Well, we never knew what the end of this thing would be. I don't think we were discouraged as much as we were concerned, because we had made up our mind we were going to succeed. So nothing they could do or say was ever going to deviate our intentions. We would not be deviated from what our goal was. We had a goal; we intended to reach it.

There were never any arguments. There were sometimes some differences of opinion. And they certainly had the right to say how they felt about it, that's all right. But it wasn't done aggressively; it wasn't done in a way of trying to give an impression he was smarter than anybody else. It was just a contribution which he could make because he had had previous experience, or because he felt that, perhaps, we ought to look at both sides or some other side: "Have you discussed this?"

The same kind of thing came up when we were finally commissioned. We decided, "Well, one of the things we're going to be, we're going to be the best dressed officers in the Navy." So instead of going to ship's store to buy our uniforms with the money they gave us as an allowance, we went to a company in Chicago that Arbor knew of. We went there and had our uniforms tailored. It was a little bit more than we would have paid in ship's store, but we said, "We're going to be straight." We went in town, and we got uniforms that were first class. Nelson went even beyond that after he was sent to other places. Nelson had everything conceivable an officer should have, even a sword. He had the sword, he had the cape, he had the formal uniform, he had the informal uniforms. He had everything that he was supposed to have, and he was something. He was something else.

Q: Didn't the rest of you have swords?

Dr. Barnes: No. We were never in a position where we needed them, to tell you the truth. But whatever the occasion, Nelson was prepared. He had the sash and the whole nine yards. We used to laugh at him, because we would say, "Hell, Nelson, where you going to wear this?"

He'd say, "There'll be a time." And there were times when he would wear it. I never saw him dressed formally, but I understand he did dress formally.

We said, "Nelson, you're always on parade." He laughed, but it was true. Nelson was never without everything being as it should be: in place, orderly and ready to move.

Q: Mr. Martin used the word "peacock" to describe Nelson.

Dr. Barnes: That's the way he was. That was a very good description. So if you could picture a peacock, you'd have a picture of Nelson. He was very pompous, oh, very pompous, but always, always, in shape as he should be. He was well-groomed; he was clean; his shoes were shined. You never found Nelson in a situation where he was not ever ready, especially when we were still there after we had been commissioned. Before we were assigned different places, we still stayed in the barracks, but we had leave permission.

Wherever he appeared, you'd know he was there. And he was always spic and span. You know, some of the rest of us might be a little slouchy, but not Nelson. His tie was straight all the time, his uniform was pressed. Wherever he was going, he was very, very much in evidence. He was not the least bit ashamed; it didn't bother him. That was his way, and we accepted it because that was him.

Q: But I have a feeling, also that there would be times when you'd challenge him and say something like, "Aw, come on, Nelson, that's enough."

Dr. Barnes: Oh, we would, yes. We stayed on his case; we never let him rest and never agreed with him. But we always respected him and never were surprised at anything he did. Never.

Q: Now, a person that seems to me probably was at the opposite end of the spectrum was Phillip Barnes. Did you try to boost him up, maybe, give him a little more self-confidence?

Dr. Barnes: No, we never tried to influence anybody to be anything other than he was. But whatever he was, he had to be straight because we told him, "You don't reflect yourself, you reflect all of us. If they see one Negro officer out here tearing things up, then they'll think all Negro officers are that way. So don't do anything which would not in any way reflect positively on the group. You don't have that freedom to be what you want to be or do what you want to do. No, you have an obligation to everybody who's in this class and everybody who's coming along behind this class. So don't do anything which is going to cause anyone to reflect that this was a usual expectancy."

We were very, very careful, very, very conscious of what we did, what we said, where we were, and with whom we would associate, because we had that obligation. We didn't have that freedom just to be what we wanted to be, whenever we wanted to be. "No, because you're carrying all of us with you. So even though they wouldn't know who you are, they'd say, 'That's one of those colored officers.' That could be any one of us. So we all carry the stigma, even though you may not know what it is you did, so you be careful." We monitored one another, but we weren't antagonistic. As you suggested, we were very friendly about it, but we were very firm about it too. Whatever really and truly affected one of us affected all of us.

Q: Do you have examples of the way that worked? What might bring that sort of discussion about?

Dr. Barnes: Well, it might just come up in a conversation. Then we discussed it, and each of us expressed our feelings about it. I would say 99% of the time, we would end up agreeing. It wasn't that nine agreed, or five agreed and seven didn't, or eight didn't. No, it was 100% we agreed.

If I felt strongly about something and we got into a discussion, I didn't just arbitrarily maintain my position because it was my right. If there was a preponderance of evidence to the contrary, it was accepted. So there was always 100% vote, even though there may have been others or myself who might have disagreed with it initially. But we agreed that whatever we agreed to was the thing it should have been to start with.

Q: So it sounds as if there was policymaking going on from time to time.

Dr. Barnes: That's right. And the nice part about it is nobody was trying to be like a crab in a basket. As soon as one got up there, they all would pull him back down. No, if you got up there, fine. Now you owe us something. What do we have to do to do the same thing? How can you help us? Because this is the level we all have to be on--not just one of us on top with the rest of us in the hole. All of us would be on the deck the same time. That's the way we've been, and it proved out to be very beneficial.

This is why, as I said, we developed a relationship which, really, was almost like family--was family, was family. And we are now. I guess Hair told you when he came aboard the USS Kidd, we hadn't seen him in 38 years. And that was a reunion that was just free spirited. We just whooped and hollered and raised Cain just like children. We were just so happy to see him, because we thought he was dead. It was a genuine concern by everyone for him. It really was. It was very, very touching, and it was very sincere. That's the nice part about it. No one was trying to put on or play. If we might have felt that way in the beginning as we all grew closer and closer together, it was less and less and less of a me situation. It was always us, ours, we. Even though we're separated now, we still have that same attitude when we get together.

Q: Well, I think that's a kind of a natural tendency in

that situation, whether it's a sports team, or a platoon in military outfit. The shared experience brings you together.

Dr. Barnes: That's true. Well, and you might add that survival had something to do with it. The more we agreed, the more we were together, the greater was our possibility of survival. It really was. So it may have started off being a little selfish, but as we grew to know one another more, we would continuously remind ourselves of our mission. Then whatever antagonistic thought that you might have had, you knew it was not in the best interest of the group. And you didn't accept it reluctantly. I mean, you accepted it as, "Yes, as you talk about it, that makes sense." Then that question was over; we'd pass that one. "Oh, we won't discuss that anymore, because we already made a decision on this." And it was a decision with which all of us agreed.

Q: What was the group view about the men who didn't receive commissions?

Dr. Barnes: You know, it was something we never discussed. Even now, 44 years later, we still don't know. Because we ask one another whenever we meet, "Say, did you ever find out what happened to So-and-so, and So-and-so?" We didn't find out about Mummy until we were at Great Lakes when they dedicated that in-processing center and later on when we were together.* One person said that he had heard that it was because of the union activities. We never knew that before. In fact, I don't think any of us can recall the names of those other people who were there, outside of Alves. We remember Alves and we remember Mummy Williams and there were several others.

Q: A man named Pinkney.

Dr. Barnes: Pinkney, he was a yeoman. I don't know why they got Pinkney.

Q: I presume that those of you who made it felt bad for those who didn't.

Dr. Barnes: Oh, yes, but it came about so suddenly, it was like a mirage. You see it and then you look and it's gone. You don't know when it went; you don't know how it went; you don't know what made it go. But it's just not there. It was never discussed because none of us had any information. We couldn't ask our officers. Nobody told us so we didn't ask. But it was strange. It was really

---

*Lewis Reginald "Mummy" Williams was one of three men who went through the training program with the 13 but did not become an officer.

strange. You know, here's a guy with you all this time, and all at once you get, "Where is So-and-so?"

"I don't know. I haven't seen him. Have you?"

"No, I haven't seen him."

"When did you see him last?"

"He was with us yesterday." That was it. And nobody ever got any information on it.

Q: How well did John Dille do in keeping you informed on what was going on?

Dr. Barnes: Well, he never actually came from his position as an officer. It wasn't a palsy-walsy thing. But he was a person who gave the impression that, "Whatever I can do to help you, I will do. If you need something, I will help you." We never lost sight of the fact who he was and what his station was, but he never made us feel that he was superior to us. I think he was one person who recognized the limits to which we were going. He was very sympathetic and in ways that did not in any way detract from his position. He never brought himself to our level when he was talking by saying something like, "You fellows." No, it was never that way. But he always gave the impression that, "Whatever you need, if I can do something, I will." He was that way and he's always been that way to us.

Q: What kinds of things could he do to help you during that period?

Dr. Barnes: Well, for instance, if we had a problem which we felt we needed some information on, we would ask him. If he had it, he would help us. If he didn't know, he would try to lead us toward where we could find out. But he was more of a friend than he was an adviser. He was just a friend.

Q: What might be a kind of a problem he could help you with?

Dr. Barnes: Well, for instance, we had to take turns out training the companies of men in boot camp. We had to go work with the commanding officer of that company and all that sort of thing. This was new to us. And then we'd be officers of the day. If we didn't know something we needed about that duty, we'd say, "Well, let's ask Lieutenant Dille." One of us would ask, and Dille would give us the answer. But he was always in our corner. He was always available to help if he could. He was friendly enough to give the impression that, "If I can be of any assistance, I will be." So he adopted us. That's really what it was. He adopted us; he was sort of our surrogate father.

Q: Did he provide moral support?

Dr. Barnes: Oh, yes. And he provided it in such a way that it wasn't ostentatious. It wasn't something that you could put your finger on. He did it in a very quiet way, without being prominent, and we knew we could depend on him. He just left the impression that whenever any of us needed him, he would be available.

Q: I can envision a situation in which he might say, whether overtly or otherwise, "Guys, you can make it; you can do it."

Dr. Barnes: That's what it was. That's exactly what it was. He may not have expressed it in those terms, but he certainly led us to believe that, "You can do it, and you will do it."

So he was our moral support. In fact, he was the only one upon whom we could depend if we ran into a situation. He would do it but not in any kind of a way that would lend any credence to the fact that he was playing favorites because he didn't.

He's always supported us. Wherever we go now as a group, he will be there. And whenever he's there, we always recognize him. When they introduced us, we introduced Mr. Dille, because he is our plus one. We stay

S. E. Barnes #2 - 230

in touch with him and he with us. He was a great help to us then, and he's still a great help to us. We all admire, respect, and love him very much.

He's really been our harbor in a storm. It really meant he was present when we really needed that kind of support. But he couldn't show it in terms of being visible doing it, but he did it in a very quiet, and efficient, effective way, and without pushing his attention on us, or trying to get us to do anything. He was just very kind, very kind, and was one of the big reasons why we felt when we finished that he was actually instrumental in making it come about and helping us to make it come about.

Q: Was he the kind of person you could confide in?

Dr. Barnes: Yes. Most of our confiding was Navy. I mean, we never confided any personal things because any personal problems we had we always discussed among ourselves. We never really had that many personal problems. No, we didn't. If they did, they kept them to themselves.

Q: What might be an example of one of these few personal problems?

Dr. Barnes: Well, for instance, the guys felt that we were being hurried. We never had any leave the whole time we were in school. We never had leave. We could never leave the base. We always had to march to chow. We always had to sit in this isolated position. We always had to march back from chow. We were a little bit upset at first because it was so regulated. And we never had any contact with anybody else in the camp. We were just like an island. They kept us isolated over here like we had a scourge or something. We even had a private spot way over in chow hall away from everybody. When we came down the chow line, we came down on a different side. We got our food and went over there. We never came down the chow line with the others in the camp.

Q: Were you given any explanation for that?

Dr. Barnes: I think it was one of the things that we thought about later on. Maybe we were being indoctrinated into the fact that being an officer means that you cannot have association with persons of lesser rank. You just don't associate with enlisted personnel, because that's not the way it's supposed to be. So we were taught that in a very hard way. There was no interaction at any time between ourselves and the enlisted personnel, or the officers or anyone, other than our own group and our own officers. Everything was there for us: our own instructors, our own XO, our own CO, and we ate all at one

S. E. Barnes #2 - 232

spot by ourselves. We were isolated, we really were.

Q: Was this something that you resented?

Dr. Barnes: Not that we resented it, but we were concerned because we couldn't understand this. When we talked about it, we said, "Well, this is part of our indoctrination. This is the way they're showing us how things are done. There's no association on a fraternal or a social level with an enlisted person. You just don't do that.

Q: Well, another possible explanation I've heard might be the idea that the Navy didn't know if this was going to work or not, so they weren't going to give it a lot of buildup in advance.

Dr. Barnes: Well, that's a possibility. I don't recall it coming up, but it could well have been in the organizational structure of this thing. Then on the other end, I think it was deliberate--that we were pushed through tests and pressures deliberately, because they wanted to see under what circumstances we could be depended upon to react in an emergency, if necessary.

Q: What were some of these kinds of tests?

Dr. Barnes: Well, for instance, we would go on the rifle range. Regardless of what we were doing, we were never--he was never satisfied with what we were doing. That way he was always on our case, not screaming, because after all, we were officer candidates and we had to be treated a little differently than enlisted personnel. But he would let it be known that he was not happy.

Q: Who was this that you're referring to?

Dr. Barnes: Well, one of our instructors whose name I don't recall now. I wish we still had those names, because they did play a very important role. I think they deliberately did some of these things because they wanted to test us: "What would you do under fire? Could you be depended upon? Can you accept criticism? Can you react to criticism in a positive way? Or do you let your personal feelings take precedence over a judicious reaction? At all times you have to remember that your feelings are secondary to the feelings of the safety of all the others." This was being given to us, so the stress was there. And it was deliberately done. As Lieutenant Richmond told us, he deliberately put us through paces that at the Naval Academy they didn't have that much pressure. He said he gave us a semester's work in two and a half months.

S. E. Barnes #2 - 234

Q: Well, maybe not the concentrated pressure of the academic part of it, but stress has certainly been part of the Naval Academy routine all along. It's a kind of test to separate the men from the boys.

Dr. Barnes: Right. That's true, and I think at all times they were testing us individually and as a group as to how we reacted under pressure. Sometimes the pressure was deliberately there. Even though we might have answered a question correctly, it was not right. "How do you know that's true? Where'd you get the impression?" We knew that the answer was correct, but the instructor still wasn't satisfied. I think that was the time they would find out how we would react to criticism, how would we react to stressful situations. Would we let our personal feelings come out, or would we remain professional at all times? Because this is what you have to do as an officer.

Of course, when we saw other officers we found instances where this didn't apply. But that was not something which we could afford. We didn't have that luxury. There was always the pressure of knowing that they were focusing in on us. We were in the limelight. We were constantly under surveillance. We had to remember that, so there was no relaxation. There was no relaxing because we had to remember why we were here, what was expected of us, and what was hoped that we wouldn't do. So that was ever present. But because we were so close, we were able to help one another. As I say, we had jovial moments. We laughed. It wasn't always stressful. There was that time when we would let our hair down and have fun. We would play cards, but not for money, because we tried that one time, and we quickly shut that off. We said, "No, there will be no money."

Q: Was that another collective decision?

Dr. Barnes: That's right. Because there were several who wanted to play cards, poker or whatever the thing was. We said, "No. First of all, it's a bad way to be caught. Second, you don't have time to do that when there are other things that need more attention. We don't have that much freedom." We had enough freedom so we didn't feel constricted. But we recognized that ever forward was like the sun. You get up in the morning and there it is. That sun is still up there, so don't think you got darkness creeping in, because you don't. We recognized that in unity, we would survive. We were determined that we would survive.

When we finished school, we never had a graduation ceremony. We went to the other side, and we raised our hand. He inducted us in as officers and told us to go get our uniforms, and that was it. When they finished and we were officers, the executive officer said, "Now you are an officer and a gentleman."

I said, "Well, I wish, sir, to say one thing. I was a gentleman before I came. You can make me an officer, but my parents made me a gentleman. So I respect what the Navy's saying, but I just wanted you to realize that these values were taught to me prior to coming into the service. I want to give my parents credit for that."

I thought he was going to put me on court-martial. But I was not saying it in a manner which was repugnant, and I wasn't trying to lower his esteem of himself. But I just wanted to remind him that the Navy, as strong as it is, can't be everything. You came in as a gentleman, and the Navy made us officers. That's the way it was.

Q: Do you remember the name of that executive officer?

Dr. Barnes: When we were in Atlanta last year, the guys were trying to remember some of these things. Someone said, "Hell, this is getting damn near 50 years ago."

I told them, "Well, hell, I can't remember what happened last week; I can't remember what happened 45 years ago." But little things come back, and, as I said, if we had been in a group talking, you would have gotten a whole lot because what I forgot, somebody else knew and somebody else knew. We really refreshed ourselves, just like you were saying we do as we read these things.

Q: I talked to an individual named Van Ness.* Do you recall him?

Dr. Barnes: The name sounds familiar.

Q: Could he have been the executive officer?

Dr. Barnes: Could very well have been, Van Ness.

Q: He was a Naval Academy graduate who had a reserve commission, I think, because of his eyesight, and he worked with Commander Armstrong.

Dr. Barnes: He might have been the XO. I can recall the name, but I can't put any activity or anything to it. But the name sounds very familiar.

Q: What was your view of Commander Armstrong?

Dr. Barnes: He was very much like Nelson. He was a peacock. I mean, he stalked around very, very much in command. He really did. He let it be known that he was commanding officer. Nobody crossed him. Even though he

---

*Lieutenant Donald O. Van Ness, USNR.

was pompous, he was a stickler for detail. I don't know whether it was because of his background, his father and all, who was responsible for Hampton Institute, but he was never approachable.* He was strictly military, strictly military.

Q: Would you say that he was disliked by your group?

Dr. Barnes: No, he wasn't disliked, but he wasn't well liked. Well, if he was disliked, there was nobody who was going to say so, because he was still the CO of the whole camp. And he had a lot of influence.

Q: When you'd have your private discussions, did you talk about Armstrong?

Dr. Barnes: No, not in open discussion. We might say, "Well, Commander Armstrong said so-and-so. Did you know about it?"

"Yeah, I heard about it." But nobody was going to discuss the pros and cons of it. You see, we really were not on a ground which we felt was firm enough for us to make any kind of an observation, not at the CO, anyway.

---
*Daniel Armstrong (1893-1947) was the son of Samuel Chapman Armstrong, a Civil War general who in 1867 founded Hampton Institute, at Hampton, Virginia, as a trade school for black students. General Armstrong died the year his son Daniel was born.

Because we didn't even make it of our own officers. We might have disliked him; we might've expressed it, but we didn't pursue it. There was nothing to be gained from that, anyway. You had the right to dislike a person, but we never discussed why you disliked him. We knew that you did, but we didn't ask you often enough for you to express reasons why.

Q: Well, and it may have been so commonly understood that you didn't have to verbalize it.

Dr. Barnes: But he was disliked, I would say, by the majority of the enlisted men, because he was very pompous and he was very unbending. He was strictly military all the way down the line, and he didn't let you forget that. He was another person like Nelson who was immaculately groomed at all times. He had white hair, and he had a straight stature. He walked very briskly, shoulders back, everything in line. His hat was in perfect position. He was something. But we never came that close in contact with him, really, even when we were in boot camp. You would see him; he would review the troops and all that sort of thing, but he was never that close to anyone whom I knew.

Q: I've gotten the impression from Mr. Arbor that Armstrong projected the idea that he knew everything.

Dr. Barnes: He was proud; he was proud. But you accepted that because of his position. Nobody was going to question him. Someone might be interested in something, but he was not foolish enough to pursue it with Commander Armstrong. Nothing can be gained from that.

Q: Well, that's part of the Navy system, too, that the commanding officer is God.

Dr. Barnes: He is above reproach, above reproach. He could say or do whatever he wanted to say or do, and who was going to question him? Nobody. Nobody. He was respected, but I don't think he was that much liked, even by the commissioned officers.

Q: Was there an element of fear also?

Dr. Barnes: You might say there was that in the air, because they recognized that if they stepped out of line, they were going to be reproached and rebuked, and really given a hosing. So people were very, very careful around him. They would never be out of line. When we thought he was coming, everything was shipshape, because he would really rake you over the coals--had no compunction about it either. He was sort of what you might call a quiet person. You never saw him in terms of high attitude, or high fives, or whatever you want to call it. He was not that close to his officers.

Q: Was he harsh?

Dr. Barnes: No, but he was precise. He was precise. He wouldn't accept anything other than a top operation. Precision was one of the requirements, and he certainly kept Navy regs where they should be. You didn't deviate from Navy regulations. No.

Q: So it sounds as if he was rigid.

Dr. Barnes: He was. He was rigid, but I think he was fair. I don't think he took advantage of that, but he let you know that he could. Shape up or ship out was his way; that was his way.

Q: If somebody is rigid but fair, you can respect that person.

Dr. Barnes: That's right. They respected him. They might not have liked him, but to me that's incidental, anyway, because liking a person doesn't have that much longevity, anyway. But respect is something that you strive for, because they don't have to like a person to respect him.

I'd rather be respected than liked, anyway, because like is a fleeting emotion, anyway. You know, people can like you one minute, and they don't like you the next. They may not tell you why, but that's the way it is.

Q: Did he ever come around to your barracks?

Dr. Barnes: No, when we were in the officer candidate training he never came. We never saw him. We might see him if we were marching to the chow hall, or something like that. But he never, ever came in contact with us. The only ones we saw were our CO and XO and the petty officers, or the warrant officers who were involved with our class. I don't recall Armstrong ever coming to pay a visit. In fact, he wasn't that interested, anyway, because he was just a commanding officer of a base. He had nothing to do with our being there, so I guess he felt like there was no reason why he should go. He certainly wasn't going to lend any kind of support, because he wasn't going to let us get that close to him. No way.

Q: What other aspects of his personality do you remember besides the competitiveness?

Dr. Barnes: He was like Nelson. He was pompous as hell. I mean, he walked around straitlaced, and he was always in command. He was the kind of guy that you knew you couldn't joke with, because he just wouldn't stoop to that kind of frivolity. He was always in command of himself and of others, and he maintained that posture. He really and truly did. He was a nice-looking man. He walked straight and carried himself in an upright manner. He didn't slouch. His clothes--just like Nelson's--were always pressed. And he walked around the camp like a peacock over hens. You knew who he was.

Q: Was he a man of dignity?

Dr. Barnes: Yes, he was. I thought he was. He wasn't a person who would make you angry because of his attitude when he was ordering what he wanted done. I didn't get the impression that he was selfish to the point that he wanted to be idolized. But he certainly wanted to win, which, of course, is understandable. We all do. There's no point in losing if you can win. But it's how you win and how you lose which is important to me. Because nobody's perfect. You're going to lose some, but you have to accept that you can't win them all.

I kind of respected him, although I didn't want to emulate him, for I didn't feel like I particularly liked the manner in which he moved around. But he didn't in any way give the impression that he felt better than anybody else, although he maybe had a right to because of his father, who founded Hampton.

Q: So he was not condescending?

Dr. Barnes: No, no. He kept his posture. No, he would not stoop to that. That was beneath his dignity.

Q: Why do you say that you respected him?

Dr. Barnes: I respected him because, first of all, he was a person who knew what it was he expected, of not only himself but of others. He didn't deviate from that. I mean, you didn't see him one day jovial and laughing and patting everybody on the back, and the next day his face was all the way down on his chin. He was consistent in his performance. He was the same if you see now; he was the same if you see tomorrow. So I respected him for that, because I would not have cared as much for him if he was condescending, if he was overly condescending, or if he was overly pompous, or if he actually turned people off by virtue of the attitude that he exhibited.

He's not a person whom you could get friendly with, not--certainly not, I can understand, being an enlisted man at that time. Nor was he a person with whom you could feel a close relationship because there was that stateliness and because he came from a family of some influence. I guess that touched him too. You can't feel like a king if you've never been around kings. You can imagine what it's like, but it's not the same. It's a pompousness that you wouldn't have, because there's a difference between naturalness and artificiality.

Q: Did you have contact with him after you were commissioned?

Dr. Barnes: No. I never came in contact with him, but I would see him because he might come to the drill hall or something like that. But at that time, since I was in charge of the athletic intramural program, I would have one of the assistants take care of those kind of things. I would speak to him, salute him, and all that, but after we were commissioned, he would never ask me to play a game of badminton with him. I spoke to him, saluted, and recognized his presence. But that was it. There was never anything else.

Q: Was it your perception that he was acting in the best interests of the men of Robert Smalls?

Dr. Barnes: Yes, and I think it was because of the experience of having his father president of a black institution like Hampton. So he really had gotten his indoctrination. It wasn't like he hadn't known blacks, or hadn't been around them. I think one of the reasons why he was selected for that job was because of his previous contact with blacks.

Q: Did you experience any racism during the course of the training period?

Dr. Barnes: Not that I can recall. It wasn't overt. If it did exist, it was covert and very well disguised. I didn't sense any of that. We were so involved in what we were trying to do that we may not have recognized it if there had been racism.

Q: Did you feel that the instructors were condescending to you in any way?

Dr. Barnes: No, they were anything but condescending. They, too, were told that, "This is to be a tough course, and do whatever you do, be sure that they do it correctly." There was no giving. There was no giving. There were very military at all times. They never "broke bread with us." We were from a different situation altogether, and they kept that distance. We were never friendly with any of our officers or our teachers. They would speak and they would answer a question if you had one, but it was known that there is a line beyond which you didn't cross. That's the way the school was operated, and that's the way we operated.

They were not speaking to us as if they were on top of a mountain looking down on us. No, they didn't give the impression that, "You're lucky that we're here, and you ought to be glad that we take this time to help you." They were straightforward, and I certainly appreciated that. They did not in any way give the impression that they particularly looked forward to anything but a teacher relationship. That was was all right, because we were enlisted men and they were officers and you don't associate anyway. So we were never on close terms with anybody except Jack Dille and that was disguised.

Q: How do you mean disguised?

Dr. Barnes: Well, he couldn't and we couldn't show that we had a separate kind of an attitude toward him and he toward us. It was very businesslike. I mean, he wasn't hale and hearty and well met. He didn't do that. He kept his military posture, but in such a way that he gave us the impression that he was still sympathetic and understanding, and knew that we needed somebody upon whom we could depend. But it wasn't in a way that anyone else would have noticed.

S. E. Barnes #2 - 248

He was always there for us.

Q: Would it be fair to say that he was the only white officer who was friendly to you?

Dr. Barnes: You don't have to say white, the only officer because there weren't any but white officers. Yes, he was. He was the only one who really and truly showed some kind of compassion for us, and seemed to understand the pressure under which we were operating. It might be just a smile when he went by; it might be just a smile. But never anything that was ostentatious, and never anything that anyone could misconstrue. Not any time. He never crossed that line of officer and enlisted, no. But he did it in such a way that you could feel that he was understanding and sympathetic. That's one of the reasons why we felt as close to him as we did. We knew he could help us and would help us, but he could not let that be known. He couldn't disclose it but so much as far as we were concerned.

So it was a very, very understanding relationship, but it was kept at a level that no one could misconstrue what was involved. We never took advantage of the fact that we knew he was helping, in our corner, and would help whenever he could. We accepted it, but we didn't take advantage of it, because we felt that it was kind of him to do this when he didn't have to. He didn't know us from Adam's house cat. He might have been associated with, maybe, one or two fellows who might have been in his battalion during recruit training, but nobody who would disclose that, even in our group.

Q: There was a barrier in the Navy at that time between officer and enlisted that was certainly more pronounced than now. That might account for part of the relationship between you and the other officers.

Dr. Barnes: Well, he was an officer. And he never let us forget that he was an officer. And we never forgot that he was an officer. But, like I say, some of the time we had to report to companies to take over as a company commander under the watchful eye of a chief petty officer. He would turn the company over to us, and we were responsible for that company. We also had to have duty as the watch officer. They were putting us through our paces.

Q: I'd appreciate it if you could talk about both those in more detail, please, both the work with the recruits and as a watch officer.

Dr. Barnes: Well, what we would do, we would be assigned to a company in a certain battalion. So we were all out at the same time. There wasn't one gone and the others here.

S. E. Barnes #2 - 250

We were all assigned and we had this particular company to which we were to report at 0800. And we were responsible for that company that particular period of time.

Q: How long did you do this duty with the recruit companies?

Dr. Barnes: Well, it was usually just a day at a time. But it wasn't only one day. There were other times when you were assigned. Then you had to assume the duties of an officer. That meant that we had the duty inspection; we had to check the sailors' activities. Then we were graded. See, the chief petty officer or the officer of the battalion had to make an evaluation of us, and that evaluation was sent back to the barracks. You know, I never saw one of them but they were there, and we had to be mindful of that.

You know, they'd check our uniforms, check our appearance, check our activities, check how we handle them, and so forth and so on. It was like a checklist. I guess you got anywhere from one to ten, I don't know. But that's how some of us came in touch with Dille, because Dille was the battalion commander. So some of were actually working in his battalion with some of his companies. But that's the only way that we ever saw him, because he never came to the barracks. We never saw him over in our school.

S. E. Barnes #2 - 251

Q: So he was not one of your instructors.

Dr. Barnes: No, he never was.

Q: Did he give you tips and suggestions on how to go about leading these recruit companies?

Dr. Barnes: Well, he might make a suggestion, if it wasn't something he felt we knew or should have known. Sometimes he would suggest it through his chief petty officers. I guess he discussed us with our own CO, whether Barnes was making any progress, or what was the petty officer's impression during the day. So he had to be aware of us.

Q: How frequent was your contact with Lieutenant Dille?

Dr. Barnes: Well, there were times that we would go as inspecting officers or whatever our duties were in that battalion. Eventually, all of us were in that battalion some time or another in one of the companies because they rotated us. You never were back to the same company again; you were sent to another company. So you'd be evaluated by more than one person. So every one of us had this duty more than once. If he saw something, he would call it to our attention, or, as I said, send it through his chief petty officer. But that's the way we learned that he was a person upon whom we could depend because the way he would bring suggestions to us. He might suggest some way that, perhaps you could do better at what you're doing. Perhaps it was a case of forgetting a certain detail, which is important if you're going to be an inspecting officer.

So some of us knew him better than others of us. I mean, that's for sure. I didn't know him as well as Cooper, and I didn't know him as well as Mummy because Mummy was there among the first blacks who became petty officers at Camp Robert Smalls. He was a third class petty officer. Watching him was just like watching a commissioned officer. Lots of people had their eyes on him because almost everybody else was a seaman. You had some old chiefs who'd been in the Navy quite a while, and they were boatswain's mates, and they were quartermasters, and they were chiefs, but there weren't that many of them. But we certainly respected them because we never thought we'd ever get anything of that sort. No, we were proud to get a third class, because that really was like having a commission at that time. For the most part, we didn't see anything but seamen.

Q: How helpful were these chief petty officers in the recruit companies you went to?

Dr. Barnes: They were helpful, but did not really do much

other than to turn the company over to us. They were always present, but the conversations were very limited. I mean, if they had a suggestion to make, they would make it. But it was not a conversational thing at all. We were there to do a job, and the chief was there to see that we did it. Then he would evaluate us on what he thought we did. If we had a question, we might ask him, but we tried not to, because we didn't want to give the impression we didn't know what we were doing.

Of course, these recruits didn't know really who the hell we were, because there were no black petty officers who were company commanders. So here comes this guy in here and he's colored, black, whatever. What's he doing here? But you never talked to him; he never talked to you. When he gave an order, they did it. And that's the way it went. Then we'd complete it, and we'd go back over to our barracks. Maybe a couple days later, we were sent out to another company, or another battalion. But eventually, like I said, we all rotated through Jack Dille's battalion, and that's how we got to know him.

When we became officers, then we really got to know him because then we could just come right out and talk to him, or he would ask us, "How do you think I can help? What do you need?" and so forth. That's when we really became close to him and he with us. Because then it was no longer that demarcation between officers and enlisted personnel because we were officers too.* He helped us on how to wear the uniform, what some of our duties would be, how you must carry yourself, and he would drop little hints. So we did get a chance to talk to him after we were commissioned because we were sent back to the barracks because we had to stay there until we were assigned to wherever we were to go.

It ended up with White and Goodwin and Barnes and Nelson at Great Lakes. The rest of them went other places, as far as Guam. Hair was sent to New York with Reagan. They had a tugboat. So we were spread all over. And then I stayed at Great Lakes. Nelson was in charge of the school for . . .

Q: Remedial reading.

Dr. Barnes: Remedial reading. I told you that you know more about us than we do.

That's the way we were dispersed. I saw two of my classmates, like I say, out in San Francisco. I never saw any of the others. Goodwin I saw because Goodwin stayed at Great Lakes too. He eventually became the head of the interviewing office because he had worked in it as an enlisted man. This is where he and Mummy and I were

---

*In his oral history, John Dille recalled this differently. He said he was transferred away from Great Lakes shortly before the commissioning of the Golden Thirteen.

working when we were called to the main side to be told we had been picked for officer training.

Q: In what ways was it helpful in your preparation to be officers that you worked with the boots and stood the watches?

Dr. Barnes: What it did was to give us a taste of what would be expected if and when you became an officer. Because now instead of you being the one who's doing it, you would be sure there would be someone else doing it. You would now be the officer in charge, not just the company commander. You might be the battalion commander. But it was a touch-and-go situation because, first of all, I don't really think they really knew how to treat us. And we didn't know how one was to act. So we just had to learn it through trial and error. There were many trials, but you better have few errors. You know, you weren't offered that luxury.

Q: Did these experiences out of the barracks increase your confidence in leading men?

Dr. Barnes: Well, interestingly enough, all of us had been involved in leadership roles. See, I had coached at Livingstone. So I had some experience, and the others had

had experience too. They had been in roles whereby they were responsible for certain things. I would say that every one of them had had some kind of leadership experience in one level or another. So it was not difficult.

Q: Well, but it's in a different environment, it's in this Navy setting.

Dr. Barnes: And there's a difference, too, because you really don't have that feeling of absolute individualism that you might have as a teacher. Once you're in your classroom, that's your classroom. Nobody tells you what to do and stays in your classroom. In the Navy it's different; it's not yours. You're merely here temporarily to handle the situation, and then somebody else comes along and you move on. So you are part of the whole, never the whole.

Q: I'd be interested in more of your recollections on Goodwin's role as an emissary both to and from Armstrong.

Dr. Barnes: Well, you see, he got there earlier than the rest of us. Therefore, he was able to get some assignments which elevated him to the position in which he was. He and Mummy Williams and Bill Thomas were three who were there before us, and they were the three who were third class petty officers. They had inroads that we didn't have. They were very helpful because they would tell you, "No, you don't do that," or suggest you do so-and-so.

Q: In what ways? Like what might they tell you to do or not do?

Dr. Barnes: Well, one thing when you're on duty, be sure you're on duty. Be sure to keep your clothes straight; be sure that your ditty bag's always ready. When we were interviewing, he'd give me hints on how to interview, or what I might have missed and I should have taken. Since they were the first blacks to make third class, they had inroads to Armstrong that they had established before we ever got there. I was on the base a while before I ever knew where they were.

Goodwin, in fact, was responsible for my becoming an interviewer. Mummy I had known because he was in Chicago. My wife went to the University of Chicago, and that's where she met Mummy and also White. Goodwin was head of the boys' club in Cincinnati back when I was working at the YMCA in Cincinnati. So there would come times our activities coincided. So I knew him. So they were helpful in any ways they could be, within the limits of what they themselves were experiencing.

Q: Were they able to speak with more influence in the group because they did have this special connection?

Dr. Barnes: We respected the fact that they did have inroads which we didn't have, and which they very cheerfully shared with us. But it was not done in a way which would make you feel that they were superior because they had this input. They didn't use this as a sword of Damocles over our head. They never did that.

Q: So you didn't resent their role?

Dr. Barnes: No. In fact, we were very happy for them, because there were so few who had those roles. So you look up to someone who has where you would want to be, or hope to be, and long to be. Goodwin wasn't the kind of person who looked with disdain down upon his lesser brothers, but who really was in a position where he felt like, "It's there, I did it, you can do it," and so forth. It was not protective but a sort of a way of letting you know that you're not here by yourself. But the ostentatiousness was not a factor. There wasn't any of that at all.

Q: Well, I'd say that takes a skill of diplomacy, to have that special relationship but not take advantage of it.

Dr. Barnes: And he didn't, not in my knowledge. I don't recall him ever taking advantage of that position, no. In fact, when we were commissioned, Goodwin and I both moved out to Lake Forest, where we rented a room from a lady and her husband out there. So we were roommates. Even at that time, he never tried to impress you with the contacts he had or what he knew. But we respected the fact that he had the contacts and he knew some things that we didn't know, because he had this law background too. See, he had left Cincinnati and gone to Chicago law school, or in some way he was connected with a law firm; I remember that. He enlisted from Chicago.

But I thought it was a very interesting and a very memorable experience, because I don't at any time remember anyone who deliberately tried to denigrate you, no. Maybe I was insensitive and didn't realize when it was happening. But I don't recall any incident where I was made to feel insignificant. Even our commanding officers and all led us to believe that we were important, but we were not indispensable.

Q: Were you treated with respect by the instructors in your course?

Dr. Barnes: Yes. They never actually made us feel

inferior, but they let us know we were there for a purpose. And this purpose was going to be realized, with or without our cooperation, because they were in a position to flush us down the toilet. And no one would've have been any worse off for it. So they let us realize at all times that they were in command, but they didn't have to force that upon us.

Q: Did you have any mechanism, either through Goodwin or Lieutenant Dille, for expressing a grievance?

Dr. Barnes: Whatever we said, we were not going to have any grievances to express because we were on trial. It's like a prisoner coming into court and expressing the fact that he had no business there. No, we didn't have that privilege. And we didn't really need it, anyway, because none of us at that time felt comfortable enough to do other than what we were supposed to do and do that well.

Q: You sort of suggested before that you were uncomfortable with this idea of herding and being separated from other sailors. It sounds as if you just decided to accept that rather than complain about it.

Dr. Barnes: Because there was nothing we could do about it. As I said before, we were in no position at that time to rock the boat. We tried to make ourselves as inconspicuous as possible. We couldn't make any demands; we couldn't say, "I don't like this, I don't like that," because we were under a spotlight. Every move we made was being scrutinized, and we couldn't afford that luxury of saying, "Well, I don't like this," or "I don't like that. I think you're a little difficult here," and so forth. Oh, no. We were very, very inauspicious. But we were all aware of what was going on. That's the reason why many times we would sit and discuss this among ourselves. Whatever waters may have been rough before, when we came out, it was a realization what our mission is.

We needed the cooperation and we needed the support of everybody, and we always got it. When we came out it was a consensus. Overtly it was unanimous. Now covertly, I might not have liked it, but it wasn't important enough for me to disagree with it, because, really, it was for the benefit of all of us. So we never permitted personal feelings to take precedence over our mission. I can say that because it was a mission. That's exactly what it was, couldn't be anything else.

Q: Inevitably, in that kind of a confined situation, people are going to get on each other's nerves. How did you deal with that?

S. E. Barnes #2 - 262

Dr. Barnes: Well, we had some levity. As I said, we had Arbor who was always talking. And there was a genuine liking among that group. When we once established that relationship, it stayed. We respected one another, and we liked one another, and we worked with one another. So that whatever the tension was, we could always get support from the other guys. They'd say, "Well, you know, you can do it. We're here. We're going to get together. We're going to do it together." And then they'd make you feel better.

Whatever you felt was unfair, you accepted that and said, "Well, it could be worse." But we needed one another. We really needed one another and supported one another. As a result, it helped all of us not to run into times that were just overbearing. No, nothing was so bad that it couldn't be dealt with--maybe not as an individual but as a group. You know, we were really like brothers once we got to know one another.

Q: Did you develop a more positive feeling for the Navy as a result of this experience?

Dr. Barnes: Actually, I never really felt that way. I accepted the fact that I was a naval officer, and I had duties and responsibilities as a naval officer, because the Navy did not do this. This was done at the President of the United States level. If the Navy had their druthers, we'd still not be officers. So it wasn't a naval decision. It came down from Franklin Delano Roosevelt to Knox, who was Secretary of the Navy. He never accepted it and very soon thereafter he died. But he never really accepted us. It was not something that if he'd had anything to do with it, it would never happen. But he was overruled. But he was never pleased with that. Never. He didn't even send us congratulations--nothing. He signed our commissions, but I'm sure he did it reluctantly.

Q: Would you have a comment on the sense of patriotism in the group?

Dr. Barnes: There was never any lack of patriotism. Not anybody was up there waving the flag, but there was nobody up there who was stomping on it either. I think we had a very balanced attitude about the whole thing. We never permitted ourselves to become angry or depressed or even discouraged. Disgusted, but you didn't permit that to become a part of your everyday attitudes. You didn't do it. So there was no antagonism as far as the Navy was concerned, because now that we were officers, we turned to do the job that was expected of us as naval officers. So there was no time for personal attitudes or personal feelings, or personal vendettas. Once we were commissioned, we accepted our responsibilities and did what we could do, whenever we could, the best we could. We were determined we were never going to do anything which would detract from the Navy, or lead people to believe that it was a mistake to even think about commissioning us.

Q: We're right at the end of the tape, Dr. Barnes. I guess we can look forward to continuing this at some future date. I thank you.

Dr. Barnes: At your pleasure.

Q: Thank you very much.

Interview Number 3 with Dr. Samuel E. Barnes
Place: Dr. Barnes's home in Washington, D. C.
Date: Friday, 12 May 1989
Interviewer: Paul Stillwell

Q: Dr. Barnes, I enjoy the opportunity to talk with you again. This is the concluding interview, as it turns out, in the series on the Golden Thirteen. We've had a couple sessions before, and one thing that we didn't explore is how much awareness you had of the armed services in general and the Navy in particular during your growing-up years.

Dr. Barnes: Well, I'd have to admit that I had very little, because there was no particular reason why I would have any more contact. No one in my family had served in the services, so that it was just like not having anything other than hearsay information about it. Since I wasn't involved, I didn't pay that much attention to it.

Q: Moving on to your athletic career, you were an athlete, a coach, and athletic director. I wonder what you could say about the trend over the years on relative emphasis on winning. We know what the situation is now. Can you take it back several years?

Dr. Barnes: Well, as I look at the situation, I prefer the way it was when I was coming along, and when I was not only a player but also a coach. The emphasis was not there for you to win. If someone played well, which seemed to be the objective of athletics, then that was all you could expect of him. There was no pressure on the coaches to win or lose their jobs. There was no pressure from outside sources to have you endorse a particular product for money.

But now the coaches are so involved, not only in what's happening in coaching, but also the extra contracts with persons who want them to publicize their products. So what the coaches receive is not only what their salaries call for, but also the use of cars and the extra money which they get from speeches, clinics, sponsorships. I mean, they have a very lush situation now. And I think the pressure is beginning to tell. We wanted to win, but there was no pressure on us of having to win in order to maintain respectability and your job.

The responsibility of dealing with these young men is very important. Our first responsibility, we felt, was to help the individual in his total development. But, of course, they didn't have the professional teams, either, on the side beckoning. We didn't have the colleges offering all kinds of inducements for individuals to participate. So the pressure now, which has been developed, is about to engulf the whole area of athletics. We have now steroids, which is something we never heard of. The only thing we knew of at that time was that if you had a headache, you took an aspirin. But now these people, it's pathetic. It's really pathetic. I think the whole area of athletics is being adversely involved in something that I think has grown bigger than they can handle.

Q: You could use the term "perverted" to describe what has happened. It's a perversion of the original purpose, which is competition for the sake of competition.

Dr. Barnes: That's true. Well, that's what it was all about. It was an extracurricular activity. In order to fill out your development, you need the physical, as well as the mental, as well as the psychological, and the other kinds of experiences that you were gaining in higher education, as well as in the high schools. I really and truly am upset about what's happening. I read it in the papers and I hear it at meetings. And I don't see it getting any better; I don't see it getting any better. The competition has just made the coaches into persons who they would not be normally if the pressure is put on them by the alumni and by boosters, by the newspapers, by television, by radio. Place pressure on them that they have to either deliver or get out. Many coaches have been fired, or their reputations have suffered.

Q: Well, and the sanctions from the NCAA too.

Dr. Barnes: Oh, mercy, yes.

I won't go into that because I really don't intend to do anything other than to say athletics are moving in a very, very tragic manner towards, I think, a disastrous ending. I really do. I feel that people are losing their confidence, not only in high school athletics, but also in college athletics, and in the pros. I think the pro attitudes begin to seep down. The kids are taking steroids in high school, because they want to be big enough to play in college. Then they take them in college, because they want to be strong enough to make it in NFL. And in the NFL, they want to be so outstanding that they get more money. So the whole thing, I think, centers around money. I really do.

Q: Did you feel that pressure toward the end of your career when you were an athletic director?

Dr. Barnes: No, we never had it, fortunately. That's why I say very often that I'm glad I coached in that period, because I really wouldn't enjoy coaching under these circumstances. Because you feel that there's a certain obligation you have, not to the athletes, but to the institution and to the alumni, to the boosters, and to the townspeople. So your projection goes beyond what your job is to try to satisfy those people who buy the tickets. If they don't have tickets, you don't sell tickets, you don't get any money. If you don't get any money, you can't develop your program. If you don't develop your program, you can't get the athletes. If you don't get the athletes, then you don't win. If you don't win, you don't have a job. I mean, it's a vicious circle; it's a vicious circle. And I don't see it getting any better.

The NCAA has tried to do what they had intended to do, which was to keep athletics within an honest category. Sports should be a part of the institution, not apart from the institution. This is why the NCAA by-laws, the constitution, always emphasizes student-athlete, which meant that the athlete was primarily a student. But he had the opportunity to engage in some additional activities while in college.

People laugh at that now.

Q: Sometimes to me, at least, as an outsider, these NCAA regulations defy common sense. Bob Wade is in a lot of trouble with Maryland now for transporting a basketball player so he could make up some credits so he could be eligible.* Well, this was facilitating his education, but it's wrong.

Dr. Barnes: That's the way it happens, true. But, see, the constitution states that no incentives can be given to an athlete which is not also available to any other student in that institution. That has caused many problems. You can't even take a kid to the airport, because if you do, you got to take any other student who wants to go. So that's the part of it that causes many problems. So some of it's intentional, and some of it people have gotten into it innocently.

I know when I was on the council of the NCAA, the handbook was less than an eighth of an inch thick. Now it looks like a Bible. Every year they have to have by-laws to the by-laws. And they have to have additional interpretations to the interpretation of the interpretation. Every year it gets to be more and more. So that you really, truly have to be very careful, look at the language. The athletic director now must almost be a lawyer and be able to think legally like that, because it's very easy for an individual to fall prey to a violation which he either had forgotten, was not familiar with, or didn't know about.

---

*Robert Wade was head basketball coach at the University of Maryland at the time of the interview. He subsequently lost his job because of questions about his adherence to NCAA regulations.

Q: When you were a coach, was it a standard expectation that the athlete would graduate from the school?

Dr. Barnes: No question, no question. There was never any question about whether he would graduate. I mean, that wasn't even considered. Of course, you graduated; that's what you came here to do. But not now. And if you look at the statistics of the number of persons playing pro football who have graduated from college, it's astounding. Now you have J. R. Reid from North Carolina, who's not going to participate his senior year because he's coming out and going to be in the draft.* He's going to miss his fourth year of college. The idea is, "Well, I don't know when I might have an opportunity to get this kind of money again. I'd better take it while I can. I can always go back to school." Very few of them do, very few. But as I said before, the main ogre is money, money. Tragic, really tragic.

Q: Shifting subjects completely, we talked before about your marriage when you were an enlisted man. You were separated from your wife during your time in the Navy? What happened after that?

---

*In 1989, the year of the interview, J. R. Reid, a forward for the University of North Carolina, was drafted by the Charlotte Hornets of the National Basketball Association.

Dr. Barnes: Well, as I mentioned previously, when I met Olga she had a job as a librarian in Trenton, New Jersey. One of the stipulations was that she could not marry for two years and keep her job. So we postponed the marriage for two years. At the end of the two years, we were married in December 1943. Then she returned to work, but she was not able to get a leave of absence. But that made very little difference, because the two-year period had passed. Then after I got out of the Navy, I was teaching at Howard. The reason that she resigned was because she became pregnant in 1948 with our first child. Then she came here to Washington. I had thought of going there, but after I went up to New Jersey and had an interview with the people in athletics and physical education, I decided that I would prefer to teach in a college rather than a high school. So very briefly, maybe not too articulately, that's the answer to the question.

Q: To switch subjects again, to go back to the World War II environment, when you were at Camp Robert Smalls, obviously a segregated environment, how would you describe the sense of patriotism in that all-black camp?

Dr. Barnes: It was very high. In spite of the circumstances, there was a loyalty there. It was less of a feeling of being isolated than it was that, "Here we have a responsibility and duty to perform. It's not a matter of my wanting to do it or preferring to do it. It's a matter that we all have to do." So there was never any kind of rebellious attitude that I could sense at Robert Smalls, relative to the fact that, "We are segregated and yet we're asked to do the same job that other nationalities are to do, but we don't receive the same recognition." No, I thought there was very high morale, even though there were no opportunities in terms of promotions in grades or ranks, but there was a closeness that I think carried us through whatever this period was. I saw no evidences of rebellion in the troops at Robert Smalls, and I think that's exemplary because there could have been.

Q: It's a real irony that the nation was not giving you the full privilege of being a citizen but was expecting the full responsibility of being a citizen.

Dr. Barnes: That's right. That's exactly what happened, and I think it's well that we had made a decision--I say "we," I'm talking about the troops--that it was as much our responsibility as it was anyone else's to meet the crisis which had enveloped the world, and that we had a part to play in it. There might be a situation where we might disagree with one another, but at this point in time it wasn't expeditious for us to do so. But as soon as this particular situation had passed, then we could go back and hit at one another as much as we pleased. But the job in front of us was too important for either of us to disregard that for personal attitude or vendetta.

I feel that this was the thing that was quite apparent to me at Robert Smalls.

Q: The very fact that there was a Golden Thirteen demonstrates that some of the demands of the wartime environment helped foster positive changes.

Dr. Barnes: Yes, and I'm sure you've heard from Hair that Mary McLeod Bethune, who happened to be a very dear friend of Mrs. Roosevelt's, was able, through her contacts with her, to emphasize the feeling that blacks were being discriminated against in the service when, as you say, they were expected to perform the same service. Anyway, Mrs. Roosevelt understood, and she evoked her husband, who eventually made the decision that the Navy should open its opportunities in all branches, regardless of race, creed, or color.

Q: Going back before that to the time when you first enlisted, for some people, anyway, it's a great adjustment to go from the civilian environment to this demanding military regimen. What do you remember about that in your own case?

Dr. Barnes: Well, I think that it was a situation where, whether you wanted it, whether you believed in it, it was something you had to do. So it wasn't a matter now of kicking up a fuss, because it was not a time, nor would anybody have accepted. You're not feeling a loyalty to a nation which, at that time, needed all the loyalty they could get. But I never had a problem making the adjustment, because there was in our family a certain amount of discipline, which was expected, and a job was to be performed, regardless of how you personally felt about it. Therefore, you did it, not because you wanted to do it, but because you should do it, and do it as well as you can at all times. Strive for something higher than what you had.

Q: I wonder if you could cover, perhaps, some of the specifics of that regimen, whether it's getting up early and marching, cleaning the barracks, uniforms and what have you.

Dr. Barnes: Well, I would say that for some it was a quite different experience, the discipline, the regimentation, the fact that you didn't question an order; you fulfilled it. Someone above you had more authority than you had, so it was getting used to the fact that you had to accept orders whether you wanted to or not. And you could not decide what you would or would not do. Orders were given, and orders were carried out. But you have to have discipline, because it depends on that for the welfare of everyone else. So it's a hand-in-glove situation. You have to walk together or you will be devoured singly.

Q: I can imagine that it was less of an adjustment for you, because you had already known the discipline of the academic world and the sports world; whereas, we're talking about a wide range of backgrounds in that boot camp, all the way to people with little or no formal education.

Dr. Barnes: That's a very good observation. That's true. I found it less difficult because I had been in a disciplined environment. And the same kind of an environment existed in colleges, though perhaps to a less intense degree. But orders from above were received and followed through. That was the order of authority. And you didn't question the order of authority. The only thing you could say was, "One of these days I'm going to be up there, and then I'll be able to give some orders." But until that time you accepted what you were told to do, and you did it to the best of your ability.

So we didn't get too much, I don't think, of the attitudes expressed where people resented authority. They may have, but it wasn't done in an overt way. I think that as persons begin to see other individuals involved in the same thing, accepting the situation, though maybe they rebelled inwardly about it, they still did what they were supposed to do.

So that was what I found out, and I felt that, "What can I do about it? I'm here. It's necessary that I do a job, because every job is important in the total picture."

Q: Was there group support to help out some of these men with the less sophisticated backgrounds?

Dr. Barnes: No, when they came through the interviewing, we tried to get as much information about them as possible, because we wanted them to fit a place in the service which would be to the advantage of both the Navy and the individual. So they were interviewed, but at that time we had no standardized counseling service, because, actually, I didn't think there were that many who fell by the wayside. I think they handled the stress of the situation very well.

Q: I wondered if there was something, perhaps, comparable to what happened among the Golden Thirteen, where there was the group effort. Was there something like that in boot camp setting?

Dr. Barnes: Yes. Now, in spite of the fact that all of the chief petty officers and company commanders were white, all of their troops were black. Maybe inwardly there was a resentment. But, again, you recognize the fact that beefing and being unhappy is not going to alter the situation. And the loser will be yourself.

So what we tried to do in the various companies was to instill in everybody, "Let's be of one accord. That we will be, and we will do the very best that we can." So the competition between the companies, I think, had something to do with the solidification of attitudes, and a feeling of togetherness in the base. Sure, we pitted one company against the other, but it was clean competition.

Q: Well, and that probably fostered improved performance on the part of all as you tried to outdo these other companies.

Dr. Barnes: That's right. And it brought loyalty within the group, because we will do this together, and no one person can make a difference, when all of us have to play a part in it. Yes, I found that.

Actually, I don't recall any overt, intense kinds of

disciplinary circumstances which were large enough to even consider on a larger basis. If it happened, it was just like in a home. You fight at your house, but you never let it go outside the door. Maybe that happened, but in my company it didn't.

Q: Well, that's right. There may be some guy, for example, who has trouble getting his locker or his uniform, squared away and you try to help him rather than let the authorities do it.

Dr. Barnes: That was closeness. I think that camaraderie developed as one became more familiar with, and more knowledgeable of those who were his shipmates. So we do it together because, as a company, we will achieve. No one man is going to get the accolades that we can all get if we work together.

Q: That's the same phenomenon you've all seen dozens of times on sports teams.

Dr. Barnes: Right. I'm sure you've read about Notre Dame. Under Knute Rockne they had what they called "the four horsemen and the seven mules."* But you never heard

---
*In 1924 sports writer Grantland Rice described the backfield of Coach Knute Rockne's Notre Dame football team as "the four horsemen." In time, the linemen up front became known as "the seven mules."

anything about the mules. All you heard about was the four horsemen. So one day the mules got together and said, "Well, if they're that great, maybe they don't need us." So what they did, they would snap the ball, and all of them would sit down. Of course, the backs were clobbered, but the point was made: it's a total effort, and no one person can take responsibility for success. You contribute to it, but you are not the only one who's contributing.

So they learned a lesson. This was one of the things that I always stressed with my teams, and I told them that story. I said, "I don't care how great these backs are. Without blocking, they're nobody, so we give credit to everybody, because that is the way that one can succeed and feel a part of the total picture."

Q: Harry Stuhldreher, one of those four horsemen, was the head coach at Wisconsin when Frank Sublett was there.

Dr. Barnes: Yes, that's right. Until Red Grange came along, I guess they were the topic of everybody's conversation.* They were one of the highlights of the football situation. Then others, as you mentioned, came along, blossomed and like stars, they shined and then they go and another star rises. I found out that if you go back

---

*Harold "Red" Grange of the University of Illinois was one of the country's top college football heroes in the 1920s.

to your college after you'd been away for 10 or 15 years, people don't even know who you are. So don't get a big head because you did well. Others stars come along; other heroes come along. Although you did your part, you're no longer newsworthy.

Q: Well, you must be the exception to that, getting elected to the Hall of Fame.

Dr. Barnes: Yes, but those people on campus didn't know anything about me. It went back 50 years. None of the youngsters was born, and probably some of their parents weren't even born at that time either, so how are they going to remember about me? They've got new heroes. They've got new people that they worship. You're old stock now. Although they think well of you, they don't know you, and they've got other people that they'd rather talk about, people in their own generation. Sure, it's an honor. I appreciate it. But I know that if you would ask any of the kids beyond 1940, they probably may have heard of me and know me from Adam's house cat.

So if I go back to Oberlin expecting everybody to turn out a parade, I'll be disappointed. Other people are doing it better, and they're doing it now. So people can see them. They can't see what I did, because we didn't even have television in those days. In fact, we had no movie cameras, so there was no such thing as scouting another team except to send somebody there with a pencil and paper. But now they telegraph these things and they have sessions, and they can see it again as many times as they want to. So there is a difference. That's why, I guess, a lot of pressure is exerted. Because they have so many things now in there that help them that we didn't have.

Q: You mentioned these white chief petty officers in Camp Robert Smalls. Would you, as a generalization, say that they were sympathetic to the blacks, or hostile, or how would you characterize it?

Dr. Barnes: If they felt hostile, they didn't exhibit it, because that would have really set off a stampede. So they recognized their roles, and as I mentioned earlier, you take orders and you do what you're ordered to do. If they're ordered to be company commanders, then that's the job they have to do to the very best of their ability.

Evidently, it was believed that these persons were not fair and they didn't do what they were supposed to do. There were no racial riots, and there weren't any confrontations. But there were those who said, "I wonder why we got white officers." But it wasn't something that was articulated to such an extent that it became a problem. I think we accepted what we had, because it was all we could do to make the best of a bad situation.

Q: I think the answer to that concern was, just as you were saying, these black chiefs were so rare, that there couldn't have been enough to fill all the jobs.

Dr. Barnes: Well, at that time, they didn't put them in jobs of responsibility, because they felt that this was something that was reserved and you don't fall in that category. Although you're given certain responsibilities, never responsibility which would, in any way, influence anyone else. So you were sort of isolated in your role, and you did a job, but you never received all the credit that you should have gotten for doing the job.

Q: How would you assess the overall quality of the recruits that were in, say, your company at boot camp?

Dr. Barnes: Well, I think you touched on it very well when you said there was a diversification. They were quite a mix, and they came from all walks of life. They came from all home situations from all the states, so that you couldn't get a conglomeration of like personalities.

Perhaps that's one of the reasons why we probably were drawn close together, because, "Regardless of where you came from, you were still the same color, and what affects you will affect me, regardless of what our circumstances may have been prior to coming into the service. So we have to do this to protect one another." I never, never really felt that there was that much antagonism. There may have been, but it wasn't overt to the point where it made a scene.

Q: Are there any specific incidents that stand out in your mind from the boot camp experience?

Dr. Barnes: Well, I think you touched on it because the kinds of experiences we had were the same kind of experiences that were exhibited throughout the Navy. In other words, you knew that you had to wake up at a certain time; you knew that you had to clean your deck; you knew that the stations had to be manned; you had to go out for flag raising in the morning. You'd go to meals, come back, and you had duties assigned to you, which you did. You did this, and it became sort of routine. You really didn't have to worry about what time you were going to get up; you knew what time you were going to get up. You knew what time you were going to bed, you knew what time the meals were.

I think that the experience was overwhelming for some, because I'm sure some didn't know what three meals a day meant. They didn't know what it was like to have clothes enough. They didn't know what it meant to know that you must clean your clothes every day. You must make up your bed every day. You must appear at all times for inspection, recognizing that you're going to be given very close scrutiny. So you were forced to learn that circumstances will not change because of you. If you don't recognize this, you're going to be a square peg in a round hole and you're the one that's going to suffer. So you can either get in line, or you won't be in line for a period of time.

Q: The individual has to adapt to the organization instead of the other way around.

Dr. Barnes: That's exactly correct. Exactly. I thought at one time the adaptation was going to be intense because persons had been doing things for so long it was very difficult for them to change to a new environment, with which they weren't even familiar. But little by little, there was a great deal of patience shown. There was a great deal of camaraderie, because even though we came from different backgrounds, we were all in the same situation. Therefore, we would have to face it together, and it was easier together than it was separately. I think that had something to do with the acceptance of a situation which we didn't care for, but had little we could do about it.

Q: It would really be helpful if you could, perhaps, think of some of the examples of that patience you mentioned.

Dr. Barnes: Well, for instance, I think it grew out of what you'd said earlier: a closeness which developed as a result of seeing the same people every day, in all circumstances. Because we did things as a company. We marched as a company, we went to chow as a company, and we had our medical exams as a company. Everything we did was as a company, so guys got closer as a result of having been associated with one another so long. Therefore, as you become more adjusted to a person, you were more apt to disclose yourself to this person, or you learn more and more about a person with whom you are closely associated. It got to the point where it was almost a brotherly relationship. Because if you felt that, the guys would center around you, and they'd do all that they could do. If you had to go to the sick bay, they got you to the sick bay, and nobody stepped back and watched the others because they felt that they were better. So we're all in this. We were all being affected, so we'd better take care of one another.

I don't remember any overt instances where an individual was bodily taken out of camp, or bodily put in the brig. I'm sure it happened. I think it happened in the Navy, period, not just on the black side.

Q: Oh, sure.

Dr. Barnes: It was just something that people rebelling against, and the rebellion just reached proportions where it could no longer be tolerated. They had to take whatever action they felt necessary, so that they wouldn't contaminate the other people. See, a bad apple can spoil the barrel, and the bad apple has to be moved before the others become contaminated. And they, too, might feel the same result.

Q: There are some people that just don't have the aptitude to succeed, and some just don't have the attitude to succeed.

Dr. Barnes: I think that's well stated. This is true, this is true. But a person is not going to be unrecognized because his status is different. The one thing we tried to keep in mind is that regardless of what you think of a man, he's human, and he has a right to express whatever disturbs him. But we try to keep it within a context where what we could understand, we will try to help you, because I don't know but what you may have to do the same for me at another time. So that was done by, I guess, survival, because we could survive better as a group than we could as individuals. Since we're all here, whether we like it or not, let's make the best of the situation. We would prefer not to be in it, but since we are here, let's do what we can.

Q: My guess is that for you with a college background the academic portion of it was not very challenging.

Dr. Barnes: No, but I didn't parade that around because I didn't see that it meant that much anyway. The degree was all right from a theoretical point of view, but a degree doesn't make you a better person. A degree does not make you more than others are. In other words, a station in life is not dictated by what you've got but who you are and what you aspire to be. That's where, I think, it had helped me, because I never felt superior to anyone. My parents always told us, "You are not better than others, but you're just as good as others, so you don't have to go around parading what you are. Performance counts."

Anybody can speak, but it's performance that counts. This is what people were going to judge you by, not by what you say, but what you do. So I've never been a person who was particularly aggressive in terms of trying to take advantage of other people because I might have a smithering of something that you don't have. I mean, it doesn't make that much difference. You judge a person by what they do and not what they are, because what you are, you may not have had anything that you could do about it. For instance, you had nothing to do with who your parents are. So when you do have an opportunity, then your responsibility is that I will do the best I can with what I have.

If I had a chance to select my parents, perhaps it wouldn't be these again, knowing them as I do, well, I could have done worse, not necessarily better. But it's a dissatisfaction of things that I think are irrelevant that cause many problems. If you can do something about something, fine. Do what you can as long as you can, the best that you can. But if there's nothing that you see can happen, then don't become so distracted and so morose that it affects what you were able to do before.

Another thing that I think kept us very close was the idea that one spends too much time concerned with what he doesn't have, instead of being happy with what he does have. See, it's just like the Aesop's Fables. You remember those stories where the dog came and looked in the water and he saw a dog in there with a bigger bone than he had. In reaching for the bone that was there, he lost the bone that he had. So he neither gained more, but he lost more. I've seen that happen--and I'm sure you have too--where people who are aspiring lose track of what they have while they're grasping for something which they don't have.

Now, don't get the impression that I'm a person who becomes satisfied that easily or that I accept things without conquest. That's not true, not true. I still believe that persons have to show some signs of aggressiveness, and maybe some arrogance, in order to keep their own spirits going. But you shouldn't get to the point where you begin to let it affect other people. Now, when you ask us about our impressions of one another and I was saying some were gregarious, some were very aggressive, some were tempestuous.

Q: Well, you can certainly can look at the Golden Thirteen and say, "These men didn't all come out of the same cookie cutter."

Dr. Barnes: That's for sure. There was a great diversity among that group. You better believe it. But I think as we endured together, it drew us closer together. And that's been going on now for years. Even though our ranks are decreasing, the feeling of brotherhood is still there as strong as ever.

Q: Did you get picked positions of leadership during the boot camp period?

Dr. Barnes: Yes. Again, I don't know why, just like I

can't answer the question, "Why were you selected for officer candidate school?" I don't know. I certainly and truly didn't campaign for it. But I was selected the company clerk. You know, you have your boot camp master-at-arms. And you'd have the hierarchy, but I was selected as company clerk. It may well have been because I was a college graduate. I had taught, and perhaps the company commander felt that I could handle the details of the company clerk's duties, perhaps, a little better than anyone else. Well, the company clerk then was in charge of all records, which he had to keep, even the medical records, short-arm inspections. Everything that affected the company I had to record. I certainly wasn't elected to that job, so I knew I had to be selected by the company commander. Because we didn't have any votes on who would be the master-at-arms, who would be this or that. You were told what you'd be.

Q: The military is neither a democracy nor a popularity contest.

Dr. Barnes: No, it isn't. You'd better believe it, that's true. I agree with that.

Q: What recollections do you have of the period between the end of boot camp and before you were selected for officer training?

Dr. Barnes: Well, we always had graduating companies all going out simultaneously. And an honor man was selected from each graduating company. The honor man was called up to the stage, and he was given a certificate and all. But the other thing was that the honor man also had the option of selecting the school which he would like to attend. I was surprised to find that I had been selected as the honor man of the company. Being very protective of myself, I said, "Well, I will go to aviation mechanic school," because I knew where it was, and I liked to deal in those kinds of things, so that was my choice.

Then I went on leave and came back. And when I got back, I was approached about remaining in ship's company as the assistant in recreation and athletics and intramurals. I gave it deep thought because I said, "Well, at least this is something with which I'm familiar." Whereas, motor mech, I knew I wouldn't be as happy in that as I might in ship's company. So I accepted the duty in ship's company. I stayed in ship's company for one year, and then I was asked about, I think, Goodwin and Mummy Williams, and Bill Thomas, who were already in the interviewing office, and whom I knew. There was an opening and they said, "Well, why don't you come over and see about interviewing?"

I accepted, because it did mean a raise in grade.

See, before that, I was a seaman first class. As I moved over there and did well, then I had a chance of becoming petty officer third class. So I went to the interviewing office and stayed there until I was summoned to the main side as part of the group that had been selected to attend an officers' indoctrination school. That was the sequence of how this thing evolved.

Q: I think it's a fair guess that just the fact that you were in that office gave you the visibility that got you selected for officer training.

Dr. Barnes: Well, it might have, but I don't think it did because it wasn't that much of one standing out above others.

Q: Yes, but you were there.

Dr. Barnes: That's true. I was in the office.

Q: People like Armstrong had a chance to observe you. Had you been off repairing airplanes somewhere, it's anybody's guess what would have happened.

Dr. Barnes: Well, you have a point there, being in the right place at the right time. That's what it all amounts to, and perhaps that's true. I hadn't thought of it that way, but visibility cannot be ignored. The more you're seen, the more you're remembered. So, as you say, maybe Armstrong did see me when I wasn't paying any attention or had no idea that he was looking.

The only contact that I had with Commander Armstrong was that he was an athletically inclined person. And I think I've told you this, so I don't want to repeat it.

Q: You did tell me about your badminton game.

Dr. Barnes: That's what it was, and that's the way that I was able to meet him. But once the game was over, he stalked off. He laid the racquet down, the birds down, and he was gone, expecting me to clean up just like he expected it to be ready when he walked in. But that's the only experience that I had with him.

Q: What led you to be chosen as honor man? Can you speculate on that?

Dr. Barnes: I've never seen the criteria. I don't even know what they were, and I feel just the same way I do about why was I selected to go to officer candidate school. I don't know. But I did tell my son, "Do your best at all times, because you never know who's watching you." You don't do it for accolades, you do it because you want to be the best that you can be at all times. You don't make up your bed for somebody to see it; you make it up because it's the thing to do. And you never know how you're going to come back home, anyway.

I've heard people say that mothers always said to their young ladies, "Now you be sure that you wear good underwear, because you never know if you might be hit by a car." You see what it would mean to you? So always have clean underwear on, and always have underwear that is not tattered or torn. Well, you remembered that, say, "Well, that's true. There's no way of knowing what might happen." It would be very, very paralyzing to be hit by a car and then go to the hospital and find out that you have on tattered underwear or none at all. So you check those two things before you--you do that even before you think about eating. That is a routine that you follow daily.

Q: How large was the company from which you were chosen as honor man?

Dr. Barnes: There were always about 100 to 120 men in each company. And that's the reason why as the number of blacks increased, they had to expand to the next camp, which was Camp Lawrence, because Smalls had just gotten too limited. As blacks continued to come into the service, they expanded beyond Lawrence and went to Camp Moffett. So we then were housed in three different camps, in three different locations.

Q: Then it was indeed an honor then to be chosen out of more than 100.

Dr. Barnes: Well, you know, luck sometimes falls in your favor. It's like the lottery; some hit it and some don't.

Q: I have a feeling there was more to do with it than just luck.

Dr. Barnes: Well, as I've said before, it's doing the job the best you can at all times regardless of whether you get recognition or not because of self-satisfaction, then that may have been the reason. I don't know. If anything, it drove me to do better, even more. Some of it was in frustration, and some of it was in anger, because it was a frustrating situation. Because the company commander, I'm sure, had no more education than I had, and probably didn't have as much. And he was certainly near the same age as I was.

Q: But he had a lot more Navy experience, and that was the important differential there.

Dr. Barnes: Of course. Yes, that's true. You can't ignore that. You cannot, and I certainly concede that. I really do.

Q: What recollections do you have of that period as an interviewer?

Dr. Barnes: Well, it was very interesting because we had been given courses in how to interview, what to expect from an interview, and what can you do or say which would permit the information you wanted to be given. So it was a one-on-one situation, and you tried your very best, as you explained, that what we're interested in finding out is, "What experiences did you have before you came in? What job did you perform before you came in? What were your educational levels, and how do you feel you can contribute to the Navy?" We had to take all this down, and while we were interviewing we were also doing a little counseling too.

Those persons whom we felt qualified for service schools, we made that recommendation, and those who didn't qualify for service school were sent in OGU, the outgoing unit. When they were sent to the outgoing unit, you didn't know where they were going to end up or what they were going to be doing. So we tried to get them to find

S. E. Barnes #3 - 298

something with which they were familiar, and which they could do, to let us know so that we could direct them into the best direction.

Some of these people were actually artists. They had different kinds of experience. You would never know by seeing them, but after you talked to them, you were surprised at the qualifications that some of these kids had. Also, it was depressing to find out that some of them had such bizarre and barren existences. For some of them, as I mentioned earlier, three meals a day was something unheard of. Never got it at home. But that was part of the system and that, I think, had a lot to do with their acceptance of the circumstances.

Q: Then your job was to match up the needs of the Navy with the desires and skills of the individuals.

Dr. Barnes: That's exactly right, so that both would profit. I think that some who went to service school, which they might not have been qualified to do, received certain advancements because they were in situations with which they were familiar.

Q: The fact that the system picked you out for aviation machinist's mate suggests that's more on the basis of your native ability than any aviation background.

Dr. Barnes: Didn't have any. But I felt like it was an area which might be of some value to me later on. I didn't know anything about it, but I said, "Well, here's a chance to learn something else." I felt that that was a better opportunity than anything else I saw. I didn't want to be a quartermaster, and I certainly didn't want to be a boatswain's mate, or whatever other ranks they had because it just didn't impress me. But I felt this was something that had great possibilities, and it would be something I didn't know. So it doesn't hurt to gain some more experience, as well as some more information and knowledge.

Q: That has been one of the great things that the Navy has done for society over the years, is train people in a lot of different specialties.

Dr. Barnes: And you're paying for it now, too, because these people are coming back and taking from the service these well-trained people, and offering them some kinds of inducements, which are very difficult to ignore. So they're getting the benefit of services of people who have been trained to do the job and do them well. For instance, we're losing the aviators in the Navy because the commercial airlines are snapping them up. They say they're going to need maybe 40,000 more in the next ten years. So the Air Force, and the Navy, and the Army, and Marines are suffering in that respect.

It goes back to what you were saying about putting these people into situations with which they were already familiar because they can make a much more significant contribution than they would if they got into something new and had to learn. It would take time to learn. In the meantime the Navy can't wait for you to learn when they need the service now. Because all kinds of exigencies occur that you can't anticipate, not in the service.

Q: What do you remember about Goodwin and Williams from working with them in that period?

Dr. Barnes: Well, I had the highest respect for them. I liked them very much. I had known Goodwin, because both of us worked in Cincinnati. I was the boys' work secretary at the YMCA, and Goodwin was the head of the boys' club just a block away from where I worked. So we often crossed paths, because we had programs which coincided with one another. He went to the service first, and I think it was almost a year later before I was inducted.

When I got to Great Lakes, Goodwin had made such a good impression that he was a third class petty officer, and so was Mummy. Both of them got there early, and as well as Bill Thomas. They were on the ground floor, they made a good impression, and so when they select somebody, they've got ready-made people. Nobody was angry at the selection, because everybody respected them. And they carried themselves in such a way that you had to believe that they were the persons for that job.

So I guess you'd say that was the "in" that I had when I went to the Lakes. I went through boot training without ever being in touch with them. It was only when I came back to ship's company in athletics that I was able to see them more often because I had more freedom than I did as a boot.

Q: What qualities do you remember about the two of them?

Dr. Barnes: Well, Goodwin was a very astute person. He was sort of a lonely person because he was not what you might call a mixer, as Nelson was. He was not as ostentatious as Nelson was. But he was a person who was very steady, and who was very, very astute in what he did and what he had to do. He carried himself in such a way that you had to respect him.

Q: Sound judgment?

Dr. Barnes: Oh, yes. He wasn't flighty in any of the judgments he gave. He was a very steady person. And he didn't display this in an ostentatious manner. But he gained respect by virtue of what he did and how he did it.

Now, on the other hand, Mummy was quiet; you wouldn't know Mummy was around unless you turned around and found him there. He probably didn't have the same image that Goodwin had, because he was a different kind of person. Goodwin was a very, very fine-looking person. Because of his being a very handsome person, he would draw more attention than one who was not as handsome. He had a car, he had the clothes, he had the appearance, and he was just a person that you had to look to because of the way he carried himself. Goodwin would always draw the attention. He was that kind of a person. As soon as he came in the room, you would notice him. Mummy could come in a room and he might get around to you later, but he wasn't a person who came in and dominated a room. Goodwin did. Yet I thought both of them were very astute persons, and their judgments were quite well taken.

Q: But Goodwin was not one who got attention through a loud personality, was he?

Dr. Barnes: No, he was very, very quiet. Outside of Goodwin, I think probably the next quietest person was Phil Barnes, then Frank Sublett and Johnny Reagan. None of them are loquacious, and none of them are ostentatious. But they were very steady people, dependable people, people that you could place your faith in and know it was not going to be misplaced. Now, we had some others who were more loquacious; they were more ostentatious; they were more argumentative; they were more sophisticated. But each of us, as you said, had a particular quality which set him aside from the others. And that one quality made the difference. Otherwise, we were all about the same.

Q: I would guess that Williams was a highly motivated individual, judging by the fact that he had been involved in that union organizing activity for the redcaps before the war.

Dr. Barnes: He was, and he diligently applied what he believed. He wasn't afraid to involve himself in things that he felt were needed, or should have been addressed. But as I said, he would not dominate a group if he came in a room, and there are others who walk in as soon as they hit the door just like a light comes in, you would see people swarming toward him. That doesn't mean that they thought more of him, but they certainly felt more inclined to be associated with him because of his illumination than a person who was over in a corner very quietly, who might have known much more and been better than the person whom you were drawn to.

Q: I think it's human nature to see superficial things and respond to those.

Dr. Barnes: True. Well, the glitter certainly. It's like a diamond ring; you can put on a ring and the other person puts on a diamond ring. One shines and the other doesn't. Which one are you going to be attracted to? The one that shines, naturally. Not that it's more expensive because you're not looking at expense, you're just looking at the glitter and you're impressed with the glitter. After a while, if you look, you'll find out that it didn't make that much difference. But at the moment, it certainly impressed you. That's the way I look at people. There are those who glitter and are glamorous, and those who are steady and less glamorous, but more dependable.

I think along with this glamorizing is sometimes a self-serving background. These people like the limelight, and they're going to do whatever is necessary to stay in the limelight. Whether it's true or not, many people are not going to stop to analyze your intentions. But what do you say? You follow the crowd, you follow the leader. And you can see it in the world today. These leaders out there, they're certainly not people whom you admire, but somehow or another, they attract people's attention and people's loyalties.

Q: Speaking of a glitter person, that was Dennis Nelson. Anything else you recall about him?

Dr. Barnes: Whew, the only way you could describe him was there was no other like Nelson. Very pompous, very, very articulate, and very, very visible. I mean, he was just different, and yet he had a heart of gold. But he was a character. He liked the limelight and he did what was necessary to maintain it.

Q: Did any of the rest of the group resent that?

Dr. Barnes: No, it wasn't resentment. I think it was much more laughable than it was serious, because he didn't change. And he made no excuse for what he did.

But he was an enjoyable fellow. He was. I really enjoyed Nelson. I didn't resent him, because the only way we could describe was, "that's Nelson." That took into account everything, "That's Nelson." That's the way Nelson performed. So you're saying, in effect, well, "You'd better take him like he is because if you don't, you won't get him at all."

Q: It wasn't an act.

Dr. Barnes: No, but he could have been an actor, because

he performed his role well. He really did. He had a little car, for instance, that he used to turn the top back on. After we were commissioned and he was in charge of remedial school, when he left the base, his top was down. He was sitting there in his paraphernalia, and he actually looked for attention. When he went out of the base, he was sharp as a tack at all times. You never caught him with wrinkled clothes, or unshined shoes, or inappropriate uniform. No, sir. Nelson was the epitome of perfection. He really was, and sometimes you'd want to be piqued at that, but then you'd say, "Well, this is Nelson." And then you'd laugh because that's him; he's not going to change.

Q: Even though the Navy system may not look for somebody that ostentatious, it does seek individuals who have that kind of precision and concern about appearances.

Dr. Barnes: I think, though, actually, in some instances, Nelson's personality mitigated against him. Being one of the first black commissioned officers, Nelson should have been the first black admiral because he had a running start on the others. But because of the same qualities about which we're talking, there were those who resented him because they resented his presence, the way he acted himself. So coming out as a lieutenant commander, after staying in long enough to retire, seemed like he was shortchanged. But I think it was because of his attitude and appearance. I think they resented it and there were some of them were jealous of it. Like I've always felt, and you've heard, it's not what you know but who you know. And there's a lot of truth to that, not only in civilian life, but also in the services.

Q: One way to put it is that there are a lot of doors that Sam Gravely was able to go through because Dennis Nelson had kicked them open.*

Dr. Barnes: That's right.

Q: But the system does not usually reward door-kickers.

Dr. Barnes: No, indeed. I think they actually many times reward those who present less of a challenge.

Q: And less of a threat.

Dr. Barnes: Or of a threat. It's true. The person who is quiet and you don't hear much or see much of, the next thing you look, the person is in a very, very influential position. You wonder, well, why would he be there and

---
*Samuel L. Gravely, who was commissioned through the V-12 officer training program in 1944, eventually retired as a vice admiral. He was the U.S. Navy's first black officer in the ranks from commander through vice admiral.

here's a guy over here who's always in there punching? Somebody resents him; somebody's jealous of him; somebody doesn't like him. So regardless of whether you like it or not, as we said before, there's no way of disregarding what I call a mentor. Many times, as you well know, promotions are based on a political relationship rather than a relationship which emphasizes performance and qualifications. I guess because Navy's no different. It's a microcosm of life. Same thing happens out here. And I think some of it happens in the armed services.

Q: Did you have the chance to observe Williams's reaction when he found out he wasn't going to be commissioned?

Dr. Barnes: I think all of us have said from time to time that the disappearance of these persons was never explained to us. One day they were there, the next day we didn't see them anymore. We couldn't think of anything that would cause them to disqualify Mummy because he was in the class almost to the end. Mummy was involved very much in the union situation, which was not at that time very popular. I don't know what he was doing that caused them to disqualify him, but he disappeared.

Q: Williams told me that Dille said to him at the time that the reason he wasn't commissioned was because of this union activity.* I have some question about that, because that is something that would have turned up in the investigation, so the Navy would have known that even before putting him in the class. If that was a disqualifying factor, why didn't it disqualify him earlier? And I don't have an answer to that.

Dr. Barnes: That's a very good question, and I don't know who has the answer to that. But if it was a situation where there was to be only a certain number, I don't know why they picked the number 13. It could have at least have been less superstitious, or more superstitious and gone to 14 instead of 13.

Q: I think the original number was 12, but because of Lear's educational background, they saw a chance to make him a warrant officer, and add that to the 12 commissioned officers.

Dr. Barnes: The story hasn't been all told then, has it?

Q: No, I'm fairly sure it hasn't.

---

*This was in the course of a 1988 interview in Chicago with Lewis Reginald Williams, one of the original 16 who went through training. Dille was questioned on the point and said it is unlikely that he had such a conversation with Williams because he, Dille, had already been transferred away from Great Lakes at the time of the commissioning.

Dr. Barnes: By bits and pieces like this the story is coming out. I do say this unequivocally, that you have unearthed certain things about ourselves that we didn't even know existed. We have a different concept of one another as a result of your work. As I have said to other people, Paul Stillwell knows us better than we know ourselves. And you do.

Q: That's interesting.

Dr. Barnes: It is true. For instance, you mentioned today that Johnny Reagan and Frank Sublett were born on the same date, and they were each married to three different people. I never heard this before. It never came up. That's what I'm saying. And it still wouldn't have come up if you hadn't been in the role that you are.

Q: On this FBI thing, what was your reaction when you found out that you had been investigated?

Dr. Barnes: I was completely flabbergasted and surprised. We were married in North Carolina, and we went to Oberlin so my parents could have a reception for us there. That's when I was asked, "Well, who are these people who are asking these questions about you?"

I said, "What do you mean?"

"There have been people in the town talking to everybody, with whom they could get any kind of conversation, about you."

I said, "I don't know why I'm being investigated. I don't understand the investigation. I've never heard of it. I don't know what it is. Maybe it was something I've done that I didn't realize I'd done, and this is why they're trying to track it down." But I did find out that they did a thorough, exhaustive investigation. They touched base with everybody that they could touch: my high school teachers, my college teachers, the ministers, the people in the streets who knew me, people I grew up with, pals, friends, everybody. I never did know that until later in our training. Because the thing came up, "Well, why were these people selected?

"I don't know." But they did an exhaustive, thorough study.

Q: Did you find out what kinds of questions the FBI was asking?

Dr. Barnes: What they were trying to find out is the very same thing that you mentioned, were there any covert activities? Was this individual associated at any time, in any way, with an organization or persons who were suspects, or who might have in some way or another, have had information which, if disclosed, could be dangerous for all of us?

So I guess they were trying to find out whether I was a militant, whether I was a activist, and which organizations I was associated with. And they might say, "Well, if this is true, this is not one of the persons with whom we would like to place confidence or put them in a position where they could injure us." That's the only answer I have, and I've never really gotten the full story. But I was told that there was an exhaustive investigation made in Oberlin.

In Oberlin there were only 5,000 people, but they said they touched base with everybody who would spend time talking to them. The questions they were asking were pertinent to what kind of a person I had been. They asked what I did while I was growing up. I guess they asked, "Was he ever arrested? Did he ever get caught for stealing? Was he ever caught for whatever reason which might be detrimental or be a black mark on the service if this man was selected, and it was found out that he had been a part of a very nebulous situation." That's the only way, Paul, I can answer it. I don't know.

Q: In addition to being surprised, did it bother you?

Dr. Barnes: No, it didn't bother me because I feel the same way about that as people feel about taking AIDS tests.* I didn't worry about it because I knew I had done nothing which I had to be ashamed of or which I had to cover up. So my feeling was that if you know you are not involved, then why be worried about being examined? You can examine me any time you want. Wake me up in the middle of the night, because I know what I have been doing and I know that I am not afflicted with AIDS unless you can get it in your food. That and if I had a drink or two, then I'm serious; it could be.

But some of these people say, "Where's there's some smoke there's some fire." You know, there's a lot of truth to that. If you're not guilty or don't feel guilty, then why would you be resentful of asking to be tested? Steroids, AIDS, venereal diseases, all these kind of things. Sure test me. I don't mind. I have nothing to cover.

Q: Another view is that of George Cooper, who said that it bothered him that he had been checked when, presumably, the white officer candidates were not to that degree.

---
*AIDS--Acquired immune deficiency syndrome.

S. E. Barnes #3 - 314

Dr. Barnes: Well, he didn't really know that. I really don't know how Cooper could have come across that kind of information because all that we knew about was what affected us. We didn't know what criteria were used to select white officers. We know that there was similarity in the training program. We did know that we were separated; we did know that we had been ignored, but I don't know what the criteria were for them. I don't know what the program is, but there were only certain things all of us had to learn. I don't care whether you're black, white, green, yellow, or gray. You certainly had to know navigation; you certainly had to know communications, and so on and so forth. I don't see how anybody could have missed those, because they were essentials as far as being officers, or commanding officers was concerned. So maybe Cooper has some information that I don't have. I don't speak about the rest.

Q: I think probably it was more presumption than actual information.

Dr. Barnes: I've never heard that before. This has never come up in our conversations. I don't think that if one were to try to research it, that they would come up with any answers. If you can document this, then I'll believe it, but you've got to bring me proof, not just speculation or how you feel, or what you believe--proof. In other words, you're innocent until proved guilty.

But I don't know where George got that. Could be that he has some private information not privy to the rest of us.

Q: I would guess that one of the things the FBI was looking into is whether there any associations with the Communists because blacks were a recruiting target during that period.

Dr. Barnes: They were recruitable because of the circumstances under which they were enduring in the society as a whole. And these were war times. You could not afford to have someone in a position to cause injury. If he was associated with Communists, then they could use that connection to find out some other things which might ultimately affect all of us, so I guess they should be careful.

I have no knowledge of what was done in the case of white officers. I just don't know. They probably had a less stringent kind of qualifications than we did, because it had been a routine that had been going on with them for years, so it was almost second nature. You know what to look for and when. And there was a larger pool because there were those who were already in. We had nobody to whom we could look, or anybody with whom we could communicate. We started from point zero. So we would have to go through a much more intense kind of examination than white officers.

Q: Had the Communists made any attempt to recruit you specifically?

Dr. Barnes: Never. I guess I was just a poor prospect, or they didn't find me particularly interesting. But I never had been approached at any time. I guess the opportunity was there, but it just never impressed me. I've never been involved with violence. I just don't identify with that. I don't think that that's any way to prove a point unless you feel that you are incapable, head to head, of handling a situation.

Q: What individuals do you recall as instructors from that period of officer training?

Dr. Barnes: That's a good question. You know, I try to remember. I'd have to go back into the records, because this is 50 years ago and I don't remember exactly.

But I guess if I sat down and went back through the records and all, I could find the names of persons, but I just don't remember them now.

Q: One name that I have heard mentioned is a black man Noble Payton. What do you recall of him?

Dr. Barnes: Well, he was a chief, and he taught us mathematics, because we had to deal with mathematics in order to determine direction and speed of a ship, and so forth and so on. So we had to do some calculating, because at that time there were no computers like they have now. We had to figure that thing out manually. Noble, I understand, lives out here in Maryland. He's blind now, incidentally. But he had told me very bitterly that he had been advised that he would be selected. And he felt he should have been selected. It's embarrassing sometimes when I've talked with him, because I think he feels, "I don't see why you got it and I didn't get it."

Q: He thought he should have been one of the Golden Thirteen.

Dr. Barnes: He was told that he would be selected for officer candidate school if and when such a situation came about. Then it was difficult for him to be selected to come there to teach the same people that he had been told he would be one of. Now, he didn't openly show resentment, but I've caught that in his voice while he was telling me of this. We had taught together at Livingstone College in 1938. He taught physics and chemistry for a couple of years, and then he left and went to a larger situation.

Q: His reaction was perfectly understandable.

Dr. Barnes: I should think so. I would agree. It's hard to actually react to that when he felt he should have been a part of it. And I guess he has justification for it. But I couldn't answer it myself, because I don't know the circumstances. Certainly he was qualified. As I said any time anybody asked me about why I was selected, "There were 100,000 blacks. Why I was selected, I do not know, because I'm sure there were men better qualified, there were men as qualified. I cannot answer it at all. Sorry."

And it's true. I don't know. I really don't.

Q: Are there any of the other instructors you remember?

Dr. Barnes: I can recall their faces and I could identify them by face, but I just don't remember many of their names. Paul Richmond was our navigation officer. Later, as we finished, he told us that he resented being sent there. He did whatever he could to not only discourage us, but to disgust us, hoping that we would resent it and, of course, give him reason to dismiss us. Then he congratulated us because of our perseverance and our determination. He said, "You have been given deliberately a semester's course in the weeks that you've been here." He said, "We deliberately piled them like that." All we did was study and go to school. That's all we did. We never had any recreation. We didn't get any liberty, couldn't go to movies, didn't go to the library, didn't go out on an athletic field. We stayed in the barracks in classes. If we weren't in class, we were studying or eating. Nothing else.

Q: That's a tough routine for a married man.

Dr. Barnes: You better believe it. But you were so busy, you never even thought of that. You really didn't. I mean, if you had time to stop and think, you might have been affected. But I don't remember anybody even mentioning the fact that they needed female companionship. They might have said it. I never heard it.

Q: Maybe you heard it and just don't remember it.

Dr. Barnes: That could very well be. That could very well be. I think it was deliberate because our course was compressed into a short period of time. So there was no time that we could actually spend in any activity except that which pertained to the school.

Q: You talked about Richmond's attitude. I wonder if that was typical. Do you have a perception of how the white instructors, for the most part, viewed the group?

Dr. Barnes: I think they really and truly never accepted us per se. But because they were assigned, they tolerated us, and they were smart enough to disguise whatever their true feelings were. Though we never stopped to analyze or scrutinize their intentions, or whatnot, as long as they were teaching the course, we knew we were there to learn, so we had to accept whatever. But personality never came out. He was smart enough that he didn't in any way show what his true attitude might have been. So he always taught the class very precisely, never associated with us. You know, teacher-student relation, no. He taught the class, answered any questions, and left. We could ask him questions which, if he could, he'd answer. But he never dwelled on the subject in such a way as to give the impression that he really and truly felt any great degree of fondness for us. No.

Q: How did John Dille stand out from the rest of that group?

Dr. Barnes: Well, from the very beginning, John showed interest in us that had not been shown by anyone else. In other words, he did things that he didn't have to do to give us confidence and keep our spirits up. But he did it in such a way that he did not do this all the time. It wasn't a constant, but if he saw you, he would have a good word to say. Or if you asked him a question, happened to meet him in the drill hall--and we had to drill sometimes--or we met him in the chow hall, but he made it his business to help wherever he could. And yet he didn't do it ostentatiously. He was sincere in what he did, and that's what captivated us. That he was doing what he didn't have to do, was not expected to do, and perhaps shouldn't be doing. But he felt strongly enough about it that he sort of adopted us.

Q: Do you have examples of the sorts of things he did for you?

Dr. Barnes: Well, we knew he was available because some of us in boot training had known him when he was a battalion commander. So those persons were more familiar with him than some of us, because I never knew him while I was in boot camp. But I had seen him because he was a very striking person. He always had time to stop and spend some time with you, and it wasn't in a condescending manner.

You could tell that he was concerned in a very, very sincere manner.

Jack is the kind of a person that even now you would never know of his resources. We had a meeting in Atlanta last year. He tried to always attend the meetings, our yearly meetings. He has his own plane. He flew down there with his own pilot. He came over to the meeting, then he had to get back. He carried back with him one of the persons who was there who had to get back to Washington. But he never paraded this fact. He never boasted about his own airplane. Jack was an affluent person, but he never displayed this. He never did that. He was just "one of the fellows." He just kept that position. He never stood above us, but he always stood with us.

Q: I wonder how much of a sense of pressure the Golden Thirteen felt during that period of officer training.

Dr. Barnes: A lot of pressure, but it was pressure that we placed on ourselves because we recognized the roles that we were placed in. As we said, we felt that we were an experimentation. It was hoped by some that we would fail so there'd be an excuse to just discontinue any ideas of commissioning black officers because they were just not competent, they were not intelligent enough. Of course, that's like we were saying before, that's unprovable. But it was a good excuse. So that gave us a greater determination to succeed.

So we were not under any real constraints except that which we placed on ourselves. And we did it deliberately, because that way we would always have to remain alive and sharp. We couldn't afford not to be. In fact, I think we welcomed the pressure because, like pain, it kept you aware of the situation. See, if I have pain and the pain goes away, then I forget about it. But if I keep being probed, I'm conscious of that and I am motivated by that, and kept alive by that. That's the thing that kept us going. I think the tension was good. It kept us alive.

Q: Did you at the time put this in a larger context--that you're either succeeding or failing on behalf of a lot more people than yourselves?

Dr. Barnes: We felt that our selection was a foot in the door. It was up to us to keep the foot in the door, and eventually hope to open the door so that then those who came behind would have an entrance without difficulty. So there was a lot of burden on us, and I think that's what kept us going. I'm really glad there was pressure because if we felt there was no pressure, then we probably wouldn't have been as motivated as we were. And we actually stayed that way. It was a revelation.

I don't know whether that answers your question, Paul, but that's the way I perceived it.

Q: Others in the group have, apparently, felt there was more of a sense of stress than you do. Some, at least, felt uncomfortable with that amount of pressure.

Dr. Barnes: Well, you see, I can't really go along with that because we knew when we went into the situation what to expect. It was not going to be a gravy train. There was nobody out there going to be throwing posies in our paths. There was not going to be a parade for us. It was going to be a grubby, bone-rattling job. Like it or not, that's the way it was; that's what we had to deal with. Now, none of them showed any signs of despair or felt like quitting. None of them, so I don't understand this attitude where they felt the stress.

If it was stress, it was stress which was self-imposed, because we never were in contact with anybody else. All we had were our barracks, and all we did was go to class and study, and go to chow hall. So whatever stress was imposed by the individual, maybe they were thinking about things they would prefer to be doing, which was less tension and less stress, maybe more enjoyable. But any other reason, I can't conceive of it. I really cannot conceive of it.

Q: But I gather from what you say that the instructors did not make you feel uncomfortable.

Dr. Barnes: You see, Paul, I feel that any stress that is imposed upon me is magnified by my acceptance or rejection of it. I cannot say it doesn't exist, because it does, but I can say I will not permit it to affect me but so much, because it also tends then to intrude upon some other things, which makes the situation worse than it was. This idea of stress is something I never heard before in our meetings. Maybe, for whatever reason, it was never brought out.

Q: Well, it's not something you'd really have a reason to talk about.

Dr. Barnes: No, we really never went back into what we did when we were in school and this sort of thing. Because I thought it was very apparent that all of us recognized what the situation was. We had no alternative. Nobody said, "Well, I can't take it," and walked away. So whatever stress or strain there was we actually accepted, because they wanted that recognition. So you can't have it both ways. Can't have it both ways.

Q: There's no way to really determine whether the sense of motivation that made you do so well came from within yourselves or whether it was from the situation. And maybe it was a combination of both.

Dr. Barnes: It was, it was. And I said that earlier, because we recognized when we went into the situation what we would probably face. I mean, we didn't go in blindly, and we didn't go in without knowledge of what the possibilities were, yes. So that's why I say that we knew this; therefore, the extended pressure and tension was that which was imposed by the individual because we certainly didn't do it as a group. We certainly didn't. I thought the camaraderie of the group was excellent. I mean, there was a one-for-all and all-for-one. That permeated the whole time we were together.

So let's stay together, stick together, and work together. And whatever happens, good or bad, it will happen to all of us together. I guess there was frustration, but the frustration was not to the degree that anybody recognized it as being a problem, because I must say that I don't remember that. It could have happened, and maybe because I was a non-discerning person that I didn't recognize it when it came along. I didn't see anybody running around tapping on the walls, or speaking to themselves, or doing any little tribal dances.

Nobody showed any behavior which was different from anybody else's behavior. Just like, for instance, you say, "Well, you know, you're married, you've been gone." Well, I certainly didn't show it to the rest of the them how I felt. Sure, I guess there were times when I felt that I would rather be with my wife. But I couldn't be, so there's no point in making the situation worse by dwelling on it. That didn't help me at all.

Q: It's intriguing how these memories differ. Some of the group have said that there was this tension, and that someone like Jesse Arbor was useful in relieving the tension, because he would come up with a quip or so, and so forth.

Dr. Barnes: Well, you know, I guess, Paul, the truth of the matter is you'd have to get them all together in one room because the memories do need refreshing. My question to them then is, "When did this happen? I don't recall; maybe you can refresh my memory." I'm not being facetious, but I actually can't recall it. Of course, it's been a lot of years ago and my memory fades a little bit. But it was not such that it was something that would be stamped forever in my consciousness. If it had been that bad, or if it had been somebody who was a little off, I would have remembered that. I can remember that better than I would the positive things, because the positive things were much more concerted than the other things, which would have stuck out because it was so incongruous with whatever else was going on. Well, I'm not going to dispute them because I have no right to.

Q: Well, it's just that you have a different recollection.

Dr. Barnes: I would say that my recollection is different, but it doesn't mean it didn't happen. It could very well have happened.

Q: It's also possible that you perceived it differently at the time.

Dr. Barnes: Well, that's true too. But usually tension draws your attention because the behavior is so different from the behavior that would be congruous with the situation.

If I went out the door and I found my car had been tampered with, you can very bet your life that I'm not going to be passive. I'm going to raise some hell and let people know that I don't like what happened and I want to find out who the hell did it. No, I never found that. It was never expressed, to my recollection, that anybody ever said, "This pressure is too much." No, I think we tried to relieve pressure, as they said, by Jesse being as jovial as he is, but sometimes Jesse got unbearable.

Somebody else was talking all the time. George Cooper did a lot of talking, and George is an interesting person. He's very, very much on the ball. The one thing I remember about him, he was one of the first chiefs. The first thing he wanted was for us to walk behind him when we went to the chow hall because he outranked us.

I remember that scene: "Hell, don't let them stripes go to your head. I ain't walking behind you. You're one of us. Take that coat off, you look just like us." But he really and truly felt that that should be accorded him. He really did. But we never paid any attention to him. We laughed about it. Nobody ever made a big deal out of it because it didn't make that much difference. That was the impression that I had of the whole time we were together, that we relieved one another through being jovial and laughing at Arbor's jokes. But if it got too unbearable, we'd tell him. So, you know, "Shut up, you talk too damn much."

Q: Was Nelson a guy you had to quiet down once in a while?"

Dr. Barnes: Oh, Nelson always had something to say. We told him that if he kept talking, we would put him in the toilet. But that didn't faze him, because if he wanted to say something, he'd say it anyway. But at least it was under a controlled situation, because more of us were opposed to it than accepted it, so the majority ruled. But there was nobody who was accepted as the leader. We didn't have a president, a vice president, a secretary, a treasurer. We didn't have any line of command. Everybody was on the same level.

Q: There was one person, though, who did have a different role and that was Goodwin, who served as a go-between to Armstrong. How did the rest of the group perceive that?

Dr. Barnes: He never pushed that. It was a position which I think was more or less thrust upon him. He did not, in my judgment, ever actively give the impression that he was being the one to communicate with Commander Armstrong. He didn't do it overtly. Now, he may have done it covertly, but I don't remember him having stressed it to the degree that it stood out like a sore thumb.

Q: Was that a useful role that he played for the group?

Dr. Barnes: Yes, because we needed the contact with any persons or anything we could get. Goodwin had this rapport with Armstrong; he must have had to have been elevated as he was and be given the positions he was given. So he knew somebody and somebody knew him. I don't recall him ever leaving the barracks to go to Armstrong's office, but he could have. None of these things were overt enough that you would think about it more. It wasn't that important, you see. It just wasn't. But if the person said it, as I said before, I concede that they must have known more about it than I did, and I certainly respect their opinions.

Q: The fact that he was able to operate in that role without arousing resentment suggests that he was a pretty smooth individual.

Dr. Barnes: But I don't know when he got out to do it because we were always together. We always had to move wherever we went together. We had to go to chow together; we had to come back from chow together; we had to study together. I don't recall anybody leaving the barracks to do something other than what all of us were doing.

Now, there would have been a time when this was possible. We were assigned to different companies so that we would get the responsibility of carrying on the duties of an officer, so we would know the routine, and so forth and so on. That was a time when he could very well have done that.

S. E. Barnes #3 - 332

Q: Was that work with the recruit companies a useful part of your training?

Dr. Barnes: Yes, because it gave us insight. Now the one, perhaps, who understood it most was Lear. He really had more experience and more knowledge of a company commander's duties than any of the rest of us because he had actually done that himself. So I recall that's a possibility, because I think I overstretched it when I said there were never times when we got out of the barracks, because we did go when we were assigned to these recruit companies and our activities and our whatever was evaluated by the chief and sent back to the commanding officer.

And the other time we had artillery practice. We did that a couple of times.

Q: Where was that done?

Dr. Barnes: There was a rifle range we went to. There was one time that I recall we were on some beach, because at that time we were flying an image of a kite or something up there, which was to simulate a target, which we were supposed to cut down. So we got practice in how you lead your rifle and so forth.

Q: Did you fire antiaircraft guns?

Dr. Barnes: I don't recall that, because I would have remembered the chatter. Could very well have. As I said before, the better way to do this would be to have all these guys together at one time so they would refresh one another's memories.

Q: But maybe you couldn't agree on anything then.

Dr. Barnes: Oh, I think we'd do the same thing that we did when we were in training, "Shut your mouth. You talk too damn much. You don't know what the hell you're talking about." In a friendly manner, but we'd have to let him know, "Wait a minute. You ain't talking to a fool."

"I may be dumb, but I ain't stupid." That's the way we acted.

"What the hell are you trying to do?"

"Shut up. We'll put you in the head."

Q: Did you have any opportunities at all for relaxation during that training period?

Dr. Barnes: There was very little, but we just didn't press all the time. There were moments we would sit around and chat, but there were not moments that extended into long conversations because we recognized that we could not afford to waste any time. We did have moments of laughter and all. We just couldn't be the same all the time. But the joking was not a planned thing. It just happened spontaneously, and you laughed and relieved whatever tensions there were, I guess, and went on about our business. Because we knew what the most important thing was. We were not there to play, and whatever time we had, we should use it wisely because we didn't have that much time.

Q: Did friendships grow up in the group, people who were closer to some than others?

Dr. Barnes: I'm sure there was some of that, but I don't recall that it was obvious. There were preferences, but it wasn't anything so discernible that you could pick it out and say, "Oh, yeah, Nelson prefers Goodwin."

Now, later on, I think in the case of George Cooper and Dalton Baugh, I think that they had much in common. I think that they sort of gravitated toward one another much more than they did towards others. I'm trying to think now, Sublett never showed a preference. Reagan, I don't recall, showed a preference. I think the only ones were Baugh and George who showed preferences for one another, which was all right, because by that time we'd been commissioned and out of the service. During the service, I didn't notice, but both of them were involved in the same kinds of activities, community activity, and they had a lot in common. So I guess that was the thing that drew them together more than admiration for one another. I think the commonality of their endeavors sort of pulled them together. They had more in common with one another than perhaps they did with the others.

Q: You were commissioned in 1944, and got a picture in *Life* magazine and a number of newspapers.* Did you have a sense then of what a history-making step it was?

Dr. Barnes: Although we knew that we were going to face certain obstacles, it was a relief to get that over with. It really was a relief. There was some feeling later about our not having been sworn in with more dignity than we were. That was, we felt, sort of a slap in the face. But you can't wallow in pain or indecisiveness without it becoming a part of you. So there's no point in dwelling on it. You can't do anything about it. It's over and done with, and therefore we just have to live with it.

---

*The picture of the group appeared in the 24 April 1944 issue of *Life*. The picture and the accompanying caption are reprinted in *The Golden Thirteen: Recollections of the First Black Naval Officers* (Annapolis: Naval Institute Press, 1993).

S. E. Barnes #3 - 336

Q: Did you feel a sense of disappointment or frustration that you did not get into the active seagoing fleet?

Dr. Barnes: No, I really didn't, because you were so involved in what you were doing that you really could not give thought to where you would prefer to be. Besides, there was no person or persons to whom I could go and suggest that I would like to be at sea. Evidently, if they found qualifications which were suited to whatever it is they needed, I'm sure they would.

Q: The Navy had run you through all this training in seamanship, communication, navigation, aircraft recognition, and all that, and then you had no chance to use it.

Dr. Barnes: Well, now you take, for instance, Arbor. Arbor was a quartermaster and was involved in quartermaster duties. Reagan was an electrician's mate. So they had experience. I didn't have any of that experience, never went aboard a ship.

Q: Yes, but a lot of white officers didn't have any previous seagoing background either.

Dr. Barnes: No, but they were not thrust into a situation

as obvious and as illuminating as we would have been if we'd have been put in that situation. Expectations would have been higher or lower, but they wouldn't have been the same. We would go aboard expecting us to do more, or expecting us to do less. So the expectations varied, but you can believe that it was not going to be just the same as everybody else.

Q: Did you feel that your talents were effectively utilized as an officer?

Dr. Barnes: Well, yes. See, I wasn't trained for anything but educational pursuits. Therefore, my interests and my backgrounds were of that nature. Now, to match that up with something in the Navy would have been very difficult. The only real matchup was when I was in the interviewing office, and I could use some of the skills that I'd learned in psychology. But if they'd have asked me when we first met to indicate a knowledge of Morse code, I would have asked them, "What's a Morse code?" The rest of them, Arbor and Hair and some of the rest of them, boy, they were right with it. The flag popping thing--they had all that. They'd done it before, so they were way ahead of me. But, as I said before, that's probably one of the reasons why they were more knowledgeable and why, if we'd have gone aboard ship, they would have been in a better position than

I would have been. I would have had to learn by trial and error, but they already knew it.

Q: Yes, but the kinds of things you did on Okinawa, for example, were not really in your background either.

Dr. Barnes: Well, a lot of it was because it was dealing with people rather than with things. I say that advisedly.

I was better prepared for that than I was to go out like a carpenter's mate and build a house or some other things. I did not know how to use my hands. I never had had to do it. And that was, I think, a mistake, because I should have taken manual arts when I was coming through high school, but I didn't because we had two tracks, one going to college and the other going to work.

Q: Did you give any thought at all to staying in the Navy after the war ended?

Dr. Barnes: Not for long, because at that time there still weren't that many black officers. And it didn't look as though there was going to be any great influx of officers. I'd had a job when I went into the service. I had my collegiate degree, so I didn't say to myself, "Well, why should I stay in the Navy when I'm not certain of the future? I can go back to the job which I had before I came in." Actually, it wasn't the same because I was in YMCA work when I went in. But, anyway, I didn't really consider staying.

Q: You had come into the Navy because there was a war and now there wasn't a war, so you were leaving the Navy.

Dr. Barnes: Exactly. That's right. And I came in the Navy because I wasn't going to be drafted in the Army.

Q: After you got out of the Navy and got established in your civilian profession, did you get involved in the civil rights movement?

Dr. Barnes: Not to the degree that others did. I mean, I marched, but I was never out in front; I was just part of the crowd. I lent my support, but I wasn't one of those persons who was fanatical about it, no. I did certainly empathize with them, and I certainly did whatever I could. But I wasn't obsessed by it.

Q: Did you go to the Martin Luther King speech in 1963?*

---

*In the summer of 1963 Dr. Martin Luther King, Jr., made his famous "I have a dream" speech in front of the Lincoln Memorial in Washington, D.C.

Dr. Barnes: No, but I heard him at Howard, because he came up there several times. I was there when President Johnson addressed commencement, but I was not actively active--I guess you can use that term. But I did play a part, I did take part wherever and if ever. But as for being fanatical, no, I've never been.

Q: What sorts of things did you take part in?

Dr. Barnes: Well, rallies, raising money, carrying posters, and the kinds of things that I was involved in, but was not in front of. I wasn't marching along beside Martin Luther King as the mayor of Atlanta, Andy Young, did, or as Marion Barry said he did, and Jesse Jackson. I wasn't that visible. No, I wasn't one who were closely around him, but I was of the group that supported him.

Q: Do you have some observations on the current racial climate in our country?

Dr. Barnes: Well, unfortunately, I think it has deteriorated somewhat. I can sense it in the activities that are resurfacing that we assumed had long since been resolved. A case in point is these skinheads, a resurgence of the KKK.* The animosity that exists didn't exist. I

---
*KKK--Ku Klux Klan, a white supremacist organization.

mean, you may not like a person, but it wasn't something that you had to exhibit. But now the things are becoming even more noticeable. I think race relations certainly are not what they were many years ago. I think we're back to where we were in the Fifties, where we got some civil rights movement and the civil rights judgment, things looked like they were beginning to improve and we got more respect. Right now I don't sense that, and it's really perturbing.

Q: Do you have an explanation for that?

Dr. Barnes: Well, I won't place the blame anywhere. I have a suspicion, but, of course, I don't have any way of justifying it. It's just a personal reaction. But I think it came from the head down. That's where it started. I don't think that, perhaps, Reagan was as interested in doing as were some of the other Presidents before him. I think he went along with whatever the sentiment was. I think it deteriorated not because of him, but in spite of him. When I say that, I mean that he didn't appear to obviously make a stand. He sort of indicated and then he had the ball carried by somebody else. That's my impression of him, that he was in the backfield handling the ball. But he was the quarterback in what we would call at that time, a single wing, and he would hand off to somebody else to carry the ball. But everybody knew that he was still the quarterback, and, therefore, they respected the position he held. But he never really asserted; he was sort of sitting on the fence.

Q: Certainly it wasn't one of his priorities.

Dr. Barnes: No, it wasn't. And, of course, now we're reaping the whirlwind. And it's going to have to be a rebuilt respect, which will have to be renewed, because it's really taking a downward trend.

I don't know, there are so many unfortunate things that are happening that might actually contribute to this lack of respect for one another. But what it is, I don't think anyone can put a finger on it. It's just that a person reacts to the what he feels. They don't like it, so they have to react to it. But they just cannot quietly take an attitude and because of how they feel, they're going to try to impose the same attitude on other people. But it is happening; it is happening. And something's going to have to be done; otherwise, we're going to have a disastrous conclusion.

Q: I think part of it is that a negative attitude or a negative type of behavior is no longer as unacceptable by society as it was.

Dr. Barnes: That may be well true. I can't really say either one way or the other about it, but I sense there is a current, a group, that could swell into something very ugly. Or it could subside, depending upon the support and the attention that's given to it. I don't know. I really don't know. But it's disturbing.

Q: What is your philosophical outlook on affirmative action as a method?

Dr. Barnes: Well, you see, that's one of those situations where it's damned if you do and damned if you don't. If you say blacks have been disregarded, disrespected, and not given the opportunities, therefore, we're going to give them an edge. Then the whites, on the other hand, say, "Well, you're discriminating against us because, after all, we have as much as they have. And you're making it easier for them, which makes it more difficult for us." So what is the answer? I don't know, because, if you say blacks need more recognition, whites say we're getting recognition, which takes it from us, which we should have, then you get into this thing about the Privacy Act. I find the greater the deficit, the more tense are the reactions. In other words, they've taken our jobs, jobs that we should have, and, therefore, you're giving them more than they deserve to have. You remember this young man who sued because one black was accepted into medical school because of a quota system, and the white student couldn't get in. He sued the government because he said this was blatant discrimination--discrimination in reverse.* Therefore, he was very, very upset about it. So you're in the middle. Any way you go is wrong.

Q: Presumably, the ideal situation would be true equal opportunity.

Dr. Barnes: If it were, if it were.

But I don't agree with giving because your conscience is hurting, and you say, "Well, I should have." If it warrants it, then there should be no question about it.

I think women have the same problem that blacks have. They're being denied positions for which they're qualified, and they claim that it's a man-dominated, powered world. Sometimes it looks that way.

Sometimes I have redressed people by saying, "Well, you are expecting more than, actually, you deserve to have by virtue of your contribution to the situation. If you're standing out there with your hand out without putting forth

---

*Allan P. Bakke sued the University of California because he was denied admission to medical school. The university reserved 16 of the 100 places in each new class for black students. Bakke contended that he was being dscriminated against on the basis of race. The U.S. Supreme Court ruled in his favor in 1978 and he later became a doctor.

any effort, then I can't respect you for that, and I certainly am not going to support you. But if you're out there doing the very best you can, then I'm going to feel that you need support because you're trying. You just haven't hit the button that will open the way for you. But I can't stand inertia and screaming. I cannot stand a person who's always saying, 'You just don't do this because I'm black.' Well, look at yourself. Maybe they're not doing it because you are not qualified. And you're just asking for this because it's a cop-out. I don't appreciate it, and I'd be one of the first ones to disown you. But if you're trying, I'm going to help you."

I don't hold that blacks are right all the time, and some of the things that happened to them are not deserved. But I also recognize some of the things in the opposite corner are not given when deserved. So we have to balance those very, very gingerly. Because in either instance personal feelings begin to tip the scale one way or the other. But if I'm doing my job, I'm not causing you any problem, I'm on time, I stay after, and so forth, I don't want to hear about not being promoted on the basis of preparation or on the basis of performance just because my skin color's different. I'm bothered if you give it to somebody over here that I know has not topped, or even challenged the position I have. Then I think that you should forget what I look like and give me that job based on performance, which is what you want, which is what you say. But when it comes down to practice it, you come up short. But I'm just as hard on one as I am on the other. Don't preach to me. I'd rather see a sermon any day than hear one. So if you believe what you say, show me.

Q: One thing that has happened since our first interview is that the in-processing center at Great Lakes was named in honor of the Golden Thirteen.* What do you remember of that event?

Dr. Barnes: Oh, that was stupendous. It was really one of the highest points in my lifetime. This is a building through which all recruits who enter Great Lakes have to be processed. This was a building that was dedicated to us; it was overwhelming. The way it was done--the day of celebration, the activities and all--made you feel like whatever you've been through was worth it. If this is a result of that, then whatever blood, sweat, and tears we had was worth it. You've never seen the building.

Q: No, not yet.

---

*The dedication of this building took place in June 1987. For pictures see The Golden Thirteen (Naval Institute, 1993), pages 260-262.

Dr. Barnes: It's beautiful. The swimming pool is there. They get their outfitting there; they get their medical exams there, everything. When they walk out of there, they're ready to go to their companies. Everything is done there.

Q: What are your memories of that dedication day?

Dr. Barnes: Very pleasant, because, first thing, every one of us was taken care of as we came in. The people at Great Lakes knew when we were to arrive, what airline, and so forth. There was a car there to meet you--not a bus--a car. Each of us was assigned a commissioned officer and an enlisted man. And they took care of us in every way. They met us at the airport, picked up the bags, took us out to the Lakes, took us over to our barracks, helped us get situated and said, "We'll be back, and if you need us this is the number you call."

I said, "I can see how people enjoy being rich because they get this every day. You know, I get it once every lifetime."

Q: That makes it all the more special.

Dr. Barnes: Oh, it was special, I mean the food and everywhere we went, we were recognized. We were given seats in very conspicuous places; we were given the respect that was just something unbelievable. And the whole time we were there, we were treated royally. When we had completed the stay there, they drove us back to Chicago. Took us back to the airport; they knew what airline it was; they knew what time the flight was. Our bags were there, and they helped us out with them. They put us practically on the plane. So we were under their care the whole time we were there, and there was never anything that they thought we wanted or needed that they didn't anticipate and get. And the ceremony in the building was just outstanding.

Q: What do you remember about the ceremony?

Dr. Barnes: Well, first of all, they had white chairs for us to sit in up on the stage. Admiral Hazard, a woman, was commander of the base.* Sam Gravely was there. He was the officer of the day because they also had graduation exercises. They had a banquet for us; they had several lunches for us; they had receptions. Every one of us had single quarters, you know, because the officers did stay there, I guess. But there was nothing left unturned. Everything that you could imagine was done, and some things that you couldn't imagine were done.

---

*Rear Admiral Roberta L. Hazard, USN, Commander Great Lakes Naval Training Center, July 1985-July 1987.

Q: Such as?

Dr. Barnes: For instance, having somebody pick you up, and somebody coming by waking you up, or somebody wanting to know what do you need: "Just mention it, and we'll see that you have it." It was just something I had never experienced, to have this kind of attention given without asking for something in return. Everything was done to make us feel honored. We were the first to leave. At the dinner, we all sat at the head table. At the luncheons there was a special place for us. And sometimes it was so overwhelming that it was kind of embarrassing. Because every time you looked up, you were being introduced, or you were out in front of something, and the reception you received was really awe-inspiring, really. It was awe-inspiring.

Q: What do you remember about the speeches that were made?

Dr. Barnes: Well, at one luncheon White was the speaker because he was considered to be citizen-of-the-day. At first, we wondered why, but it occurred to us because he lives in Chicago. His position is quite identifiable, and he was a Golden Thirteener too. So that's the reason. He gave a very good speech.

I'm trying to remember whether Cooper spoke or not. I know Gravely did. Gravely spoke at the ceremony in the in-processing center, when they dedicated it. They had a ribbon. Each one of us was given a pair of gold scissors, and then this ribbon was stretched out in front of everybody, and we all had to move up to the ribbon. On signal, all of us cut, and all of us got a piece of it. They had caps for us which said "Golden Thirteen."

In the processing center, they carried us through every stage of what the recruit would do. In the entrance way, they had pictures of the Golden Thirteen. All of the paraphernalia associated with us is there, still on prominent display.

Q: What sort of paraphernalia do you mean?

Dr. Barnes: Well, anything that any one had of his uniform left or any part of his uniform. Or if he had a picture, or something that could be identified as being part of the Golden Thirteen, they want it in their museum. So each of us has sent whatever he had to contribute. I haven't been back since we were there. Frank Sublett, who lives outside of Chicago, in Glencoe, goes there as our representative. And, of course, Arbor goes. White, not as often. The most active persons are Arbor, then Frank to a degree, and Syl

S. E. Barnes #3 - 351

to a degree. But Arbor stands head and shoulders above either of them. But Frank is closest, so he is the one who goes out and checks to see what's missing, or what needs to be sent, or whatever. So he's our key man out there.

Q: You said that people were doing nice things for you and not expecting something in return. I think it's just the other way around. They were returning the kindness for something you had already done.

Dr. Barnes: Well, that's very nice of you to say that, but I really and truly can't remember what it could have been.

Q: It was going through this training in 1944.

Dr. Barnes: Well, yes, it probably could be, but, you know, it's interesting now that you brought that up. Because now you've made me stop and think when, or if, this happened. We felt that the red carpet was spread unselfishly. I think sometimes they went beyond what was expected of them and actually enlarged upon whatever it was they were doing. You know, they had graduation exercises, great big drill hall, and all of these troops were gathered. And yet they showcased us.

S. E. Barnes #3 - 352

Q: You said earlier that the Navy had not given you any sort of a graduation ceremony in 1944. It could be that this ceremony in 1987 was making up for that.

Dr. Barnes: That's a nice way to look at it. I certainly appreciate that observation, but I don't know whether that was actually true or not. It's nice to believe that, anyway. We'll accept that.

Q: Another thing that has happened since we first talked was your trip to Scotland.* What are your recollections of that?

Dr. Barnes: Oh, Paul, the job those kids did over there was miraculous. The only thing is that it's a place that there's not much going on. It's a very desolate spot. During the time we were there, it was cold. I mean, it was cold. My wife said when we came back after ten days that this was the first time that she walked in the house that she was warm since we left here.

But I was very impressed with the activities, the reception they were giving in dining rooms and other places. These kids had been working on this project for one year. They had raised all of the money for our passage

---

*In February 1989 the surviving members of the Golden Thirteen visited the submarine tender Simon Lake (AS-33) at Holy Loch, Scotland. They were guests of the crew, which had raised funds to pay for the trip.

over there. Now, we paid for our wives. We traveled in a 12-passenger wagon bus from London to Holy Loch, 100 miles. We were cramped up, but it was their intentions that really touched us. We had a chance to meet with them individually, to talk with them, and they sought us out and asked questions.

We went to the chief petty officers' ball, which is a big affair for them every year. We were invited to that. There were cars or vans that picked us up every day. They took us on tours. We went to Edinburgh; we went to Dunoon, we went to Glasgow. They showed us where the plane went down, flight 103, at Lockerbie. We passed the place, but we didn't stop. They pointed it out to us: "This is where the tragedy had taken place."*

But they really bent over backwards, they really did, to make our stay pleasant. The officers were pleasant. We were invited to change of commands, put in prominent places up in the front, introduced, sort of made over, which was sometimes rather embarrassing, because, you know, it got to the point where you said, "Well, I appreciate what's being done, but does all of this have to be done?"

But it was the sightseeing and the contact and the getting together and the activities, and so forth. Because

---

*On 21 December 1988, a few months before the Golden Thirteen visited Scotland, a Pan American Boeing 747 en route from London to New York exploded as the result of a terrorist's bomb. All 269 people on board were killed. The wreckage fell on the village of Lockerbie.

some of us lived with the officers who were already there. So they put us in various homes. Then six of us stayed in chalets: Arbor and his wife, my wife and myself, and Frank Sublett and his wife. They would come every morning, pick us up, take us where we were supposed to be, come back maybe if we had to go someplace else, change clothes and they'd take us wherever we needed to go. There was always somebody available. They paid everything.

Q: What do you remember about your interactions with the members of the crew?

Dr. Barnes: Absolutely fantastic. We had no restrictions. They were glad to show us anything that they thought we wanted to see. We were up on the bridge. We had to be ferried out to the ship, which was in the Holy Loch. They had one of the submarines alongside. We didn't get a chance to get on a submarine, because that particular day the water was very, very hazardous, but we had dinner aboard the Simon Lake. They gave us ball caps, and everything that they could imagine to do, they did.

It really was one of the most pleasant experiences that I can recall. And we congratulated the youngsters because they did a fantastic job. Frank Sublett spoke at the black history dinner sponsored by the crew, and the officers were there, including the outgoing commanding officer. Pictures were taken, as expected. Of course, the kids wanted their pictures taken; they wanted autographs and we really enjoyed doing it, because they had done so much. I said, "You all paid a whole lot for so little."

And they laughed and said, "What do you mean?"

I said, "Well, I don't know whether we're worth all this or not."

They said, "Oh, yes, you're worth every penny."

But it was really a most memorable occasion, it really was.

Q: In contrast to that, interestingly, you told me before the tape started today that the Navy itself has decided not to fund your reunion this year.

Dr. Barnes: That's right. That's what I understood in a meeting last week--that they would not fund it because they didn't have the money. So we won't having a reunion this year. We really stopped calling it a reunion, because that really wasn't the purpose of it. We wanted to get together to compare notes and to hear what was going on, and ask the same question, "What can we do to assist you in the recruiting process?"*

---

*In fact, the Navy did eventually agree to pay for the Golden Thirteen reunion in 1989 and has done so each year after that.

Q: It's interesting that the Navy can't afford it, and a bunch of sailors over in Scotland can.

Dr. Barnes: They really did, and they did it on their own. That trip cost the Navy nothing, and they got a great deal of publicity. Some of the fellows were a little skeptical about the Navy not having enough money, and George Cooper was a little upset. I said, "Well, George, I feel that you have a point. But I can't tell them, 'You're lying, you got money, you just don't want to give it to us.'"

I want to feel that their reasons are sincere and that they can't afford to do it because of the money that's spent on other things. But I would not question if they said that they couldn't. I wouldn't ask them, "Why can't you do it? Why can't you spend this kind of money?" Because we don't want to give the impression that we expect to be subsidized every year. But, by the same token, if we are making a contribution and you say that we are, then the meetings are not in vain, and make a contribution if you think it does, then it's worth paying.

I've noticed this though, Paul, that the Army still has TV time; the Navy doesn't. I've noticed that there has been a cutting off of that. I think they're paring down to those things that they really must have and do, and try to say, "We will try to do more, but it doesn't look as though we'll be able to do unless circumstances change very drastically. Because I do know that the Navy's budget was cut drastically. It's below that which the Army has at its disposal, but the Army's a larger organization.

I'm certainly disappointed because we enjoy getting together and exchanging ideas, meeting the people, talking to people, and this would be the first cessation. I hope that it's not something that's going to be permanent. I don't know.

Q: You told me another thing before the tape started today, and that is that the challenge for Navy recruiting in the black community is, perhaps, greater now than it has been.

Dr. Barnes: Than ever before. Than ever before.

Q: What are the reasons for that?

Dr. Barnes: Well, as I say, one of the reasons that our kids--and when I say "our," I mean black kids--are seemingly more involved by virtue of homicides and disturbances. Money seems to be the thing that's causing the problems with us, because the kids say they've been denied opportunities, and this, that, and the other. They claim this is their way of getting what they deserve to have to begin with. So the competition has increased.

The other thing which has increased has been the lack of promotions in the officers' ranks. Now our percentage in the officers' ranks is supposed to be about 6.2. It's never been above 3.3.* There are officers who are coming out of the service because they are disappointed that their promotions are limited. Now, the demographics show that have over 2,000 black officers in the Navy, but the percentage is not what it should be, and it's not getting better.**

There are those who are sort of stagnant at a particular level. Up to the lieutenant level, they're fine. It gets a little worse as lieutenant commanders, commanders, and so forth. I think we have four admirals now, but we'll have three because one is retiring.*** Four blacks were being considered for admiral rank, and none of them were approved. But in other instances, we see where other groups this doesn't apply to. Percentage-wise, by virtue of population, there should be more black admirals than Hispanic admirals, but it's not true. They're the same; they both have four. This is not something that shows rank discrimination, but you wonder how can the percentages be so lopsided.

---

*As of 30 June 1992, some years after this interview, 4.3 percent of the Navy's officers were black.
**As of 30 June 1992, there were 3,135 black naval officers.
***The Navy had three black admirals as of 30 June 1992.

Now, there's a possibility because they will be reintroducing those individuals who are qualified for admiral rank, and one may get it, but that's because one is leaving. And because the Hispanics now have four, the same as black. In order show some discretion, I think, they're going to have to elevate a black. Who it is, I don't know. That's to balance it off at four and four. It should be different from that, but that's the way it happened. I don't know the reasons for it.

But I do know what the trends are showing, and they're not very promising. We're losing officers who have been in a long time and have not gotten promotions and, therefore, are coming out. And they're coming out because there are opportunities that are available to them, which makes it so attractive that they're willing to pay that price and come out. And this is a time when I think we need experience; we really need more experience than we have. The 600-ship fleet, which they had talked about some time ago is a thing of the past. It really is.

Now, our enlistments are up--about 15% to 17%. But these people never get beyond a certain level, and I guess after a while they get so discouraged and disgusted that they just don't care. And that's unfortunate, very unfortunate. The competitiveness of it seems to been blunted for some reason or another, and the disappointments are increasing. Well, that's the reason why this year I thought it was very important that we get together, perhaps more important than other years, because we really--now the task force by Admiral Trost came out and indicated that the very things we're talking about were very evident.*

The information's there. Now what are you going to do about it? What do we need to do? You find the same problem in NRD Washington. There's a sloughing off there of interest, enthusiasm, and you can sense it. It's not there. We used to have a family-like situation. And although the NRD Washington is still number one in recruiting in area four, it's only because the others are worse. I was surprised to hear that at the RDAC meeting, that we're not what we were, but we're still better than the others and it's only because they're doing less.

Something needs to be addressed, and I don't know what it is, but I know something needs to be done. I feel we might have made some impact. We would have liked to have made an impact, but we won't know, because it's very difficult to disseminate information to five different people when you're right in the room and listening to everybody and putting it all together and coming up with a plan that would be instrumental in helping the situation. I don't know.

So you asked earlier what are the reasons, and I can't give them. I don't know what they are, but I do recognize

---
*Admiral Carlisle A. H. Trost, USN, was the Chief of Naval Operations at the time of this interview.

that there are differences. And it's discouraging, because now we need more than ever a concerted drive, whatever program, to reinterest especially black officers in the service. And I know that sometimes that people expect more than they certainly are qualified to get. Well, I can deal with that, and when I talk to them, I ask the first question, "Well, what are you doing? What are your evals?"* I've often said that an eval of very good is not good. The only way you're going to get a promotion, evals have to be excellent, excellent, excellent for not one year, but for several years. Well, we still have black COs in certain areas who indicate that there have been some positions of authority given, not based on a percentage in the population as depicted in the percentage in the armed forces.

Q: Well, let us hope that the dissemination of the story of the achievements of the Golden Thirteen can help, perhaps, in some small way to turn that around, to provide a useful example for others. To that end, I'm certainly grateful to you and your colleagues for the generous donation of your recollections you've made through the oral history program.

---

*"Evals" is short for the periodic evaluations that officers and enlisted personnel receive on their performance.

Dr. Barnes: Well, you know, really, we're the privileged ones because you have brought out certain things about us to us that are really very important.

Q: Thank you.

Index to

Reminiscences of

Dr. Samuel E. Barnes

Member of the Golden Thirteen

Alves, A.
Black Navy enlisted man who went through training with the Golden Thirteen in 1944 but was not commissioned as an officer, 65-67

Arbor, Jesse W.
Golden Thirteen member noted for being talkative and humorous, 56-57, 144, 212-213, 262; taught quartermaster skills to the rest of the group, 201

Armstrong, Commander Daniel W., USNR (USNA, 1915)
As officer in charge at Camp Robert Smalls, Great Lakes, Illinois, during World War II he liked to play badminton, and he liked to win, 40-54; had a pompous, overbearing personality, 237-246

Army, U.S.
Margaret Barnes, the sister of Samuel Barnes, was one of the first black women to be an officer in the Army in World War II, 77-78

Athletics
Benefits to be gained from participation, 15, 24-25, 199-200; coaches as role models and advisers, 18-19, 30-31, 108-109, 151-152; results of Barnes's postgraduate studies in the field of collegiate athletics, 96-99; today's college sports place too much emphasis on winning and have gotten away from traditional values, 98-101, 265-269; the role of a collegiate athletic director compared with the coaches of individual sports, 106-113; professional athletes now command high salaries, 186-188, 271

<u>See also</u> Badminton, Basketball, Boxing, Football, Track and Field

Badminton
The officer in charge at Camp Robert Smalls, Great Lakes, Illinois, during World War II liked to play badminton, and he liked to win, 40-54

Barnes, Alexa
Daughter of Samuel Barnes, she is a successful artist and architect, 120-122

Barnes, James, Sr.
Father of Samuel Barnes, he worked as a chef at Oberlin College, 1, 3-6, 10-11, 148, 153, 172-173; stressed importance of education to his children, 3, 146-148, 168-169; advice to his son on job choice, 18-19; values

on racial matters, 151-153, 162-163; discipline of children, 170-171, 191-195

Barnes, James, Jr.
Brother of Samuel Barnes, he was a graduate of Oberlin College and a top-flight athlete, 1-2, 12-13, 17, 20; served as a hero for his younger brother, 133-134, 175

Barnes, Margaret
Mother of Samuel Barnes, she did laundry to help support her family and was active in Ohio state politics in the 1930s, 1-6, 10-11, 148, 173-175; stressed importance of education to her children, 3, 146-148, 168-169, 190-191; values imparted to family, 7-8, 151-153, 162-163; discipline of children, 170-172, 191-195; provided food for homeless people during the Depression, 189-190

Barnes, Margaret
Sister of Samuel Barnes, she was one of the first black women to be an officer in the U.S. Army in World War II, 77-78

Barnes, Michael
Son of Samuel Barnes, he has served in the Coast Guard and Navy, 119-120, 122-123

Barnes, Michelle
Daughter of Samuel Barnes, she is a successful university professor, 120

Barnes, Olga Lash
Wife of Samuel E. Barnes, tried to discourage him from joining the Navy in 1942, 32-33; courtship and marriage to Samuel Barnes in 1943, 39-42; post-World War II reunion after being separated by the Navy and jobs, 272

Barnes, Phillip G.
Member of the Golden Thirteen who was quiet and dependable during the group's training at Great Lakes, Illinois, in early 1944, 59-60, 222

Barnes, Dr. Samuel E.
Parents of, 1-8, 10-11, 18-19, 146-148, 93, 151-153, 162-163, 168-175, 189-191; siblings of, 1-3, 12-13, 17, 20 77-78, 93, 147; boyhood in Oberlin, Ohio, 1-10, 157, 163-168, 190-198; as a student at Oberlin College, 1932-36, 11-19; leadership positions, 12-13; achievements as athlete, 13-17; worked as teacher and athletic coach at Livingstone College in North Carolina in the late 1930s, 19-25, 148-149; elected to Oberlin College athletic hall of fame in 1986, 25-26, 281-282;

worked in youth program at YMCA at Cincinnati, 1941-42, 31-32, 180; enlisted in the Navy in 1942, 32-33; wife of, 32-33, 39-42, 272; recruit training at Camp Robert Smalls in 1942, 33-35, 274-291, 294-297; officer training at Camp Robert Smalls in 1944, 36-39, 43-49, 54-70, 200-264, 316-335; courtship and marriage to Olga Lash in 1943, 39-42; experiences as a commissioned naval officer in 1944-46, 70-90, 336-339; postgraduate education in the 1940s and 1950s, 91-93, 96-99; work as a teacher, coach, and athletic director at Howard University from 1947 to 1971, 101-102, 106-115; worked at the District of Columbia Teachers College in the early 1970s, 103-104; served from 1971 to 1973 as a member of the council of the NCAA, 104; various honors awarded to Barnes, 104-105; children of, 119-123, 151; recruiting efforts on behalf of the Navy, 136-143; reading habits as a youngster, 175-177, involvement in the 1930s and 1940s working with young people, 179-186; service as a petty officer at Great Lakes before undergoing officer training, 292-294, 297-304; the Federal Bureau of Investigation conducted background checks on Barnes and other black enlisted men in late 1943 to see if they would be suitable as officer candidates, 310-315

Basketball
Barnes encountered name-calling in various Ohio towns when he was on high school and college teams in the 1930s, 10; at Livingstone College in the late 1930s, 21-22

Baugh, Dalton L.
Member of the Golden Thirteen who made up special stationery to honor the group, 48-49; mechanical ability, 57; developed a friendship with George Cooper, another member of the Golden Thirteen, 334-335

Belichick, Lieutenant (junior grade) Stephen N., USNR
Was the sole white officer to remain in an officers' club on Okinawa when Barnes entered it one day in 1945, 82-85

Bethune, Mary McLeod
Educator who had a role in the decision to provide expanded opportunities for blacks in World War II, 38-39, 274

Boxing
Barnes learned boxing from a book and trained a fighter who won a medal at the Olympic Games in 1952, 101-102

Byers, Walter
    Effectiveness of his work as director of the NCAA from 1952 to 1987, 110

Camp Robert Smalls
    Site of recruit training at Great Lakes, Illinois, for black enlistees in the Navy in World War II, 33-35, 274-291, 294-297; the Golden Thirteen received officer training at Camp Robert Smalls in 1944, 36-39, 43-49, 54-70, 200-264, 316-335; sense of patriotism among the black sailors trained there in World War II, 272-274

Cincinnati, Ohio
    City in which racial segregation was pronounced in 1941-42, 165-166

Civil Rights Movement
    Barnes's views on various matters involving the racial climate in the United States, 339-346

Columbia University, New York, New York
    The head of the physical education department in the 1950s declared no black student would get a doctorate from his department, 92

Communications
    Members of the Golden Thirteen learned Morse code and visual signaling while undergoing officer training in early 1944, 201, 208-210

Communist Party
    Attempted to recruit black Americans prior to World War II, 315-316

Cooper, George C.
    Member of the Golden Thirteen who was sedate and mature during the training period at Great Lakes, Illinois, in early 1944, 56-57, 61, 329; developed a friendship with Dalton Baugh, another member of the Golden Thirteen, 334-335

Depression
    Individuals in Oberlin, Ohio, provided private charity to jobless people during the Depression in the 1930s, 189-190

Dille, Lieutenant (junior grade) John F., Jr., USNR
    Reserve officer who provided valuable moral support when the members of the Golden Thirteen were undergoing officer training at Great Lakes, Illinois, in early 1944, 48-49, 227-231, 247-254, 320-322; role in the

1980s in trying to get a building named for the Golden Thirteen, 106

Discipline
Imposed by Barnes's parents on the family in Oberlin, Ohio, in the 1920s and 1930s, 170-173, 191-195

Education
Barnes's parents placed a high value on education for their children, 3, 146-148; race was not an issue in schools in Oberlin, Ohio, in the 1920s and 1930s, 166; quality of the faculty at Livingstone college in the late 1930s, 167

Eniwetok, Marshall Islands
Appeared barren when Barnes made a brief stop there in 1945, 82

Federal Bureau of Investigation
Conducted background checks on black enlisted men in late 1943 to see if they would be suitable as officer candidates, 310-315

Food
Cost and availability of food for the Barnes family in Oberlin, Ohio, in the 1930s, 5-6; Barnes's mother provided food for homeless people during the Depression, 189-190

Football
Barnes encountered racial name-calling in various Ohio towns when he was on high school and college teams in the 1930s, 8-10, 157-158; description of the teams at Livingstone College in the late 1930s, 21, 23-24, 27-29; Barnes's skills as a player at Oberlin College in the 1930s, 26-27; Coach Jake Gaither did better recruiting players in Florida prior to racial integration, 116-117; the Washington Redskins professional football team aided Navy recruiting efforts in the 1980s by sponsoring special recruit companies, 139-143; in the 1930s the sport was much less specialized and sophisticated than now, 198-199

Gaither, Alonzo S. "Jake"
Football coach who did better recruiting players in Florida prior to racial integration than afterward, 116-117

Golden Thirteen
Enlisted men who were trained at Great Lakes, Illinois, in early 1944 to become the Navy's first black officers,

36-39, 43-49, 54-70, 200-264, 316-335; Dalton Baugh made up special stationery to honor the group, 48-49; screening process as men were being chosen for the group, 39, 42, 72-73; efforts to name a ship or a building after the group, 105-106; the group has held a series of reunions in the 1970s and 1980s, 123-125, 128-132; as role models for others, 134-136; role of the group in recruiting minorities into the Navy, 136-143, 355-361; the Federal Bureau of Investigation conducted background checks on black enlisted men in late 1943 to see if they would be suitable as officer candidates, 310-315; dedication of an in-processing facility at Great Lakes in 1987 to honor the group, 346-352; reunion on board the submarine tender Simon Lake (AS-33) in Holy Loch, Scotland, in February 1989, 352-355

Goodwin, Reginald E.
Member of the Golden Thirteen who was mature and businesslike during the training period at Great Lakes, Illinois, in early 1944, 58-59; served in a liaison role between the black officer candidates and the white hierarchy at Great Lakes, 256-259, 330-331; description of personality, 300-302

Great Lakes, Illinois
See Naval Training Center, Great Lakes, Illinois; Naval Training Station, Great Lakes Illinois

Hair, James E.
Member of the Golden Thirteen who was dramatically reunited with his classmates on board the destroyer Kidd (DDG-993) in 1982, 130-132, 224

Howard University, Washington, D.C.
The sports program at the university included many aspects from the 1940s to the 1960s, 101-102, 106-115

Inspections
Strictness of barracks and personnel inspections at recruit training at Great Lakes, Illinois, in World War II, 34-35; "short-arm" inspections of men's penises at Great Lakes in World War II, 35-36; value of daily inspections in enforcing standards, 94-95

Kidd, USS (DDG-993)
Guided missile destroyer that served as the site of a Golden Thirteen reunion in April 1982, 128-132

Knox, Frank
As Secretary of the Navy during the early part of World War II, he opposed opening opportunities for blacks,

then died in 1944, shortly after the commissioning of the Golden Thirteen, 77, 263

Lear, Charles B.
Member of the Golden Thirteen who was quiet and effective while the group was undergoing training at Great Lakes, Illinois, in early 1944; death by apparent suicide shortly after the end of World War II, 126-128

Livingstone College, Salisbury, North Carolina
Description of the academic and athletic programs in the late 1930s at this church-affiliated small school for black students, 21-25, 27-29; quality of the faculty in the late 1930s, 167; Barnes worked with the young people in the community, 180-182

Logistics
Work of a logistic support company of black sailors on Okinawa in 1945, 64-65, 85-87; training of such men at Williamsburg, Virginia, 81

Martin, Graham E.
Member of the Golden Thirteen who was quiet and knowledgeable during the training period at Great Lakes, Illinois, in early 1944, 61; positive influence in his role as a high school teacher and coach, 105

Mitchell, Robert
Former professional football player who had an instrumental role in facilitating Navy recruiting efforts through the Washington Redskins in the 1980s, 139-142

Musick, Lieutenant L.W., USNR
Congenial, unprejudiced Naval Reserve officer who commanded a logistic support company on Okinawa in 1945, 85-86

National Collegiate Athletic Association
Barnes served from 1971 to 1973 as the first black member of the NCAA council, 104; role in policing college sports, 110-112, 269-270

Naval Training Center, Great Lakes Illinois
Dedication of an in-processing facility at in 1987 to honor the Golden Thirteen, 346-352

Naval Training Station, Great Lakes Illinois
Site of recruit training for new enlistees in the Navy in World War II, 33-35, 274-291, 294-297; the Golden Thirteen received officer training at Camp Robert Smalls

in 1944, 36-39, 43-49, 54-70, 200-264, 316-335; after the members of the Golden Thirteen were commissioned in 1944, they weren't permitted to use the officers' club at Great Lakes, and there was a delay in the opportunity to serve as full-fledged officers of the day, 70-71; Barnes ran recreation programs for blacks after being commissioned in 1944, 79-80

Nelson, Dennis D.
Member of the Golden Thirteen who was aggressive, gregarious, and pompous while undergoing training at Great Lakes, Illinois, in early 1944, 56, 58, 212, 215-216, 220-222, 305-307, 329-330; after commissioning he provided training in remedial reading; was very meticulous about cleanliness, 61-62; was instrumental in reuniting the surviving members of the Golden Thirteen in 1977, 123-124

Oberlin College, Oberlin, Ohio
Provided employment for Barnes's parents while he was growing up in the 1920s and 1930s, 4; Barnes's track and field achievements in the 1930s, 13-14; Barnes had little social life there as a student in the 1930s, 20; Barnes was elected to the college's athletic hall of fame in 1986, 25-26, 281-282; Barnes' work on a master's degree following his release from naval service in 1946, 91; philosophy of a former Oberlin college president, Dr. Frederick Starr, concerning the role of collegiate sports, 99; availability of the college library for the community, 175-176

Oberlin, Ohio
Barnes's parents chose to settle in Oberlin and raise their children there in the early part of the 20th century because of the town's hospitable racial climate, 1-9, 157, 163-168; Barnes's work with young people in the community, 179-180, 182-183; individuals in the town provided private charity to jobless people during the Depression in the 1930s, 189-190

Ohio State University, Columbus, Ohio
Provided segregated living accommodations for the athletes who participated in the state high school track and field championships in the early 1930s, 30, 165-166; Barnes's work on a doctorate in the 1950s, 92-93

Okinawa
Work of a logistic support company of black sailors on Okinawa in 1945, 64-65, 85-87; while serving on Okinawa, an enlisted sentry failed to show Barnes the respect due an officer, 74-76; white officers got up and left the

officers' club when Barnes entered, 82-85, 117-118; two devastating typhoons hit the island in late 1945, shortly after the end of World War II, 87-89; procedure for burying Okinawans in crypts, then in caves, 89

Owens, Jesse
Top-flight black sprinter who raced against Barnes in the early 1930s, 14-15, 17; characteristics, 15

Payton, Noble
Black chief petty officer who was involved in training the Golden Thirteen in 1944 but was not able to become an officer himself, 46, 317-318

Pinkney, J. B.
Black Navy enlisted man who went through training with the Golden Thirteen in 1944 but was not commissioned as an officer, 66

Racial Awareness
Organizations that existed in the early years of the 20th century to advance the cause of blacks, 155-157

Racial Prejudice
Barnes encountered name-calling in various Ohio towns when he was on high school and college sports teams in the 1930s, 8-10, 157-158; after the members of the Golden Thirteen were commissioned in 1944, they weren't permitted to use the officers' club at Great Lakes, and there was a delay in the opportunity to serve as full-fledged officers of the day, 70-71; while serving on Okinawa, an enlisted sentry failed to show Barnes the respect due an officer, 74-76; one day in 1945 white officers got up and left an officers' club on Okinawa when Barnes entered, 82-85, 117-118; Barnes avoided using his full name in North Carolina in the late 1940s because he didn't want to be addressed in a demeaning manner, 148-149; Barnes's parents provided guidance on dealing with the racial situation as he was growing up, 151-152; in the 1920s and 1930s, blacks were often portrayed in demeaning fashion in entertainment, 159-160; racist attitudes in the 1980s, 162-162

Racial Segregation
In North Carolina in the late 1930s, 28-29; in Columbus, Ohio, in the early 1930s, 30; in Washington, D.C., in the 1940s and 1950s, 102-103; football coach Jake Gaither did better at recruiting players in Florida prior to integration, 116-117; Barnes had to ride in segregated railroad cars when going from Ohio to North Carolina in the late 1930s, 150, segregation was pronounced in Cincinnati, Ohio 1941-42, 165-166

Reagan, John W.
　　Member of the Golden Thirteen who was quiet but made valuable contributions during the training period at Great Lakes, Illinois, in early 1944, 63

Recruiting
　　Role of the Golden Thirteen in bringing minorities into the Navy in the 1970s and 1980s, 136-143, 355-361

Religion
　　The Barnes family spent a considerable amount of time in the local Baptist church in Oberlin, Ohio, in the 1920s and 1930s, 7, 153-154, 171-173

Richmond, Lieutenant (junior grade) Paul D., USNR (USNA, 1942)
　　Reserve officer who supervised the curriculum for the training of the Golden Thirteen at Great Lakes, Illinois, in early 1944, 46, 204, 233, 318-319

Scotland
　　The Golden Thirteen were honored by the crew of the submarine tender Simon Lake (AS-33) at Holy Loch in February 1989, 352-355

Simon Lake, USS (AS-33)
　　Submarine tender whose crew honored the Golden Thirteen during a reunion on board the ship in February 1989, 352-355

Starr, Dr. Frederick
　　Philosophy of former Oberlin college president concerning the role of collegiate sports, 99

Sublett, Frank E., Jr.
　　Member of the Golden Thirteen who was quiet but made valuable contributions during the training period at Great Lakes, Illinois, in early 1944, 63-64

Track and Field
　　Barnes's achievements on behalf of Oberlin College in the 1930s, 13-14; Barnes sprinted against Jesse Owens in the early 1930s, 14-15, 17; results of Barnes's master's study in the late 1940s on times for running a mile race, 96-98

Training
　　Recruit training for blacks at Camp Robert Smalls, Great Lakes, Illinois, in World War II, 33-35, 274-291, 294-297; the Golden Thirteen received officer training at Camp Robert Smalls in 1944, 36-39, 43-49, 54-70, 200-264

Typhoons
Two devastating typhoons hit the island of Okinawa in late 1945, shortly after the end of World War II, 87-89

Uniforms--Naval
The members of the Golden Thirteen got tailored uniforms when they were commissioned in 1944 because they wanted to look particularly sharp, 47, 219-220; Golden Thirteen member Dennis Nelson had a vast array of uniforms, 62, 220-221

Venereal Disease
"Short-arm" inspections of men's penises were done at Great Lakes, Illinois, in World War II in an effort to detect VD, 35-36

Washington, D.C.
Racial segregation practices in the city in the 1940s and 1950s, 101-102; intercollegiate sports involving various area schools in the 1960s, 114-115; Barnes's role in bringing minorities in the Washington area into the Navy, 136-143

Washington Redskins
Professional football team that aided Navy recruiting efforts in the 1980s by sponsoring special recruit companies, 139-143

Weather
Two devastating typhoons hit the island of Okinawa in late 1945, shortly after the end of World War II, 87-89

White, William Sylvester
Member of the Golden Thirteen who was intellectual and analytical while the group was undergoing training at Great Lakes, Illinois, in early 1944, 57, 60-61

Williams, Lewis R.
Black Navy enlisted man who went through training with the Golden Thirteen in 1944 but was not commissioned as an officer, 66, 68, 225-226, 252, 302-303, 308-309

Williamsburg, Virginia
Site of training for members of black logistic support companies going overseas late in World War II, 81